A Prayerbook
of
Favorite Litanies

A Prayerbook

of

Favorite Litanies

116 Catholic Litanies
and Responsory Prayers

Compiled by
Father Albert J. Hebert, S.M.

*"And leaving them, he went again: and
he prayed the third time, saying the
selfsame word."*

—Matthew *26:44*

TAN BOOKS AND PUBLISHERS, INC.
Rockford, Illinois 61105

Nihil Obstat:	George Meiluta, S.M. Censor Deputatus
Imprimi Potest:	Donald A. Romito, S.M., Ph.D. Provincialis
Nihil Obstat:	Emanuel Camilleri, O.P., S.T.D. Censor Deputatus
Imprimatur:	✝ Joseph V. Sullivan, S.T.D. Bishop of Baton Rouge

Copyright © 1985 by Rev. Albert J. Hebert, S.M.

Library of Congress Catalog Card No.: 84-51858

ISBN: 0-89555-252-3

TAN BOOKS AND PUBLISHERS, INC.
P.O. Box 424
Rockford, Illinois 61105
1985

BLESS THE LORD

All ye works of the Lord, bless the Lord: praise and exalt him above all for ever.

O ye angels of the Lord, bless the Lord: praise and exalt him above all for ever.

O ye heavens, bless the Lord: praise and exalt him above all for ever . . . .

O ye sons of men, bless the Lord: praise and exalt him above all for ever.

O let Israel bless the Lord: let them praise and exalt him above all for ever.

O ye priests of the Lord, bless the Lord: praise and exalt him above all for ever.

O ye servants of the Lord, bless the Lord: praise and exalt him above all for ever.

O ye spirits and souls of the just, bless the Lord: praise and exalt him above all for ever.

O ye holy and humble of heart, bless the Lord: praise and exalt him above all for ever . . . .

O give thanks to the Lord, because he is good: because his mercy endureth for ever and ever.

O all ye religious, bless the Lord the God of gods: praise him and give him thanks, because his mercy endureth for ever and ever.

—Song of the Three Young Men
in the Fiery Furnace
(*Daniel* 3:57-90)

CONTENTS

vii

LITANIES OF THE HOLY SPIRIT

LITANIES OF
THE BLESSED VIRGIN MARY

LITANIES OF THE
ANGELS AND ARCHANGELS

LITANY OF THE SAINTS AND
LITANIES OF VARIOUS SAINTS

LITANIES FOR PARTICULAR
NEEDS AND INTENTIONS

OTHER RESPONSORY PRAYERS—
PETITIONS, PRAISES, PRAYERS, PROMISES

PUBLISHER'S PREFACE

This book was conceived to be a prayerbook, rather than a book for scholarly purposes. Therefore, to serve as such, it must be used again and again so that one gains familiarity with the litanies and prayers it contains.

Litanies, as prayers, possess two peculiar aspects. First, a person must be familiar with the litany being prayed in order for it to be profoundly and powerfully recited. It must—as with any well-said vocal prayer—be completely known to its user and contain no surprises, for surprises distract a person from attention to his prayer. Therefore, one must recite a litany again and again for it to acquire this power within his prayer life.

And second, a litany, by the very variety of its expression, remains ever new. Whereas at first thought, one might judge the recitation of a litany to become quickly boring and flat, just the opposite is true. A litany ever reveals to the reciter new insights and new channels of devotion. Much like a many-faceted gem, a litany reflects its light—first from one angle, then from another—with an almost supernatural charm and freshness.

From these observations it is obvious that with time one should adopt favorite litanies, which he will then incorporate into his daily prayer. Litanies said as prayer bring a wonderful variety to one's daily prayer routine and beautifully complement meditation, the Rosary and other vocal prayers.

Finally, the litanies in this book have been arranged for recitation by two or more persons, with the responses being in italics. It is strongly urged that this book be employed for group prayer, in addition to personal use. There is a litany here for just about every conceivable need or purpose.

May this beautiful book of litanies become a priceless source of inspiration, instruction and grace to those who possess it, and may it be spread far and wide throughout the Catholic world, to the greater honor and glory of Almighty God and of His Blessed Mother Mary, His angels and His saints.

Thomas A. Nelson
November 28, 1984

INTRODUCTION

Litanies have long been in use in the Church. The word "litany" comes from the Latin *"litania," "letania."* It stood for a form of responsory prayer which involved a number of invocations or petitions grouped around one main subject or sacred theme.

Litanies have long been employed both in public liturgical devotions of the Church and in private devotions. Only a limited number of litanies are authorized by the Church for use in public devotions and at public services. Other litanies may be used for private recitation by an individual or a group. An example of a litany officially approved for public use is the *Litany of the Saints,* the oldest litany in the Church and the model for all others.

Litanies vary in form and makeup: Some are longer, some shorter, and some vary in format—in invocations, acclamations, petitions and types of responses. Some are directed to Persons of the Blessed Trinity, some to the Blessed Virgin Mary, others to the angels or saints; still others are arranged around a theme, as is the *Litany for a Happy Death* or the *Litany of Humility.* Litanies are rich in theological and Scriptural content and should have a wide use in prayer and meditation.

The key element in the litany form of prayer is its series of varied invocations, followed by the same repetitive response. A priest or other leader reads the invocations, and the people answer with the responses (printed in italics in this book).

Usually, at the beginning of a litany, the Blessed Trinity is invoked, and at the end, the Lamb of God.

The Church must approve any additions to the officially approved litanies. Thus, in the *Litany of the Blessed Virgin Mary (Litany of Loreto),* the popes in recent years have added the invocations, "Queen assumed into Heaven," "Queen of Peace," and "Mother of the Church."

Where God is addressed, the response is "Have mercy on us." The answer to invocations or petitions to Mary, the saints and angels is "Pray for us." In some litanies there are other apt responses, such as, "We beseech Thee, hear us," and "Deliver us, O Lord." Often there will be a versicle and a response, indicated by "V." and "R." The litanies all close with a suitable short prayer introduced by the words, "Let us pray."

In the Old Testament period we find, in certain of the Psalms, prayer or song forms somewhat similar to our modern litanies. In *Psalm 135 (136)* we find repeated use of the identical phrase, "for His mercy endures forever," which is now used at the end of the sacramental rite of Penance or Reconciliation. In our modern, revised *Liturgy of the Word* at Mass, we have the Prayer of the Faithful with one or another repetitive response. So too, the old and the new usages are linked together when the lector reads the verses of a Psalm and the congregation answers with a repeated response.

Another ancient short form of litany appears in the old chants of *"Kyrie eleison, Christe eleison, Kyrie eleison,"* now one form or option of the penitential part of the beginning of Mass. Similar forms were found in the old Greek liturgy of the Mass and in the Milanese (Ambrosian) Rite and in the Stowe Missal. Also they are found in the old Breviary or official Office of the Church, and even in the new revised Breviary, where there are places for short responses.

The *Litany of the Saints* has been mentioned as the oldest. It goes back—though it has existed in many varied forms (content)—to the times of Saint Basil the

Great (d. 379) and Saint Gregory Thaumaturgus (The Wonder-Worker) who died about 270 A.D. The cult of the saints, especially of the martyrs, began early in the life of the Church, and litanies in their honor varied from one area to another. Older Catholics will remember the beautiful, if at times seemingly long, singing of the *Litany of the Saints,* with the Latin response of *"Ora pro nobis."* We also hear it in modern form, at the closing of Forty Hours services, with a group of the area clergy chanting it.

It has also been officially included in many ecclesiastical services or events, such as processions, the conferring of major orders and the exorcism of devils. We know it in the modified form, as used in the Easter Vigil service. Pope Pius V (1566-72) gave instructions for a uniform *Litany of the Saints* to be included in the liturgical books.

We have mentioned processions. Certain early processions in the Church were called "litanies." When the great persecutions of the Church in the first three centuries were over, public processions were organized. They were frequently planned for those days on which pagan festivals were held so as to offset and replace them with Christian devotions. In these processions, religious pictures and emblems were carried.

In Rome each day, but especially during Lent, the pope himself would go to a different church to celebrate Holy Mass. This is how the Roman "stations" came about, they being "stops" at the place where the procession began, along the way as the procession would move, and at its destination. The procession held on April 25 was called the *Litania Major,* or *Litania Romana,* because it was held to offset the pagan processional celebration of *Robigalia* held on that day.

In 590, when Gregory the Great had just become pope, there was a disastrous flood from an overflow of the Tiber, and its aftermath was a deadly pestilence raging in Rome. The holy pontiff organized a great "Litany" or procession in which, it is believed, an image of the Blessed Virgin Mary painted by Saint Luke was carried. As they came to the bridge where the great tomb of the Emperor Hadrian rose to the sky, the song of angels was heard, and Pope Gregory saw Michael the Archangel sheathing his sword above the tomb. This was taken as a sign that the pestilence was over, due to the procession and prayers, and in fact the pestilence did then cease. The tomb became known thereafter as the Castle Saint Angelo, and today a great golden-like figure of the Archangel can be seen shining high above this shrine. It is one of the most famous sights in Rome.

As these Mass procession-litanies became more and more popular in Christendom, especially in the Middle Ages, a great variety of litany prayer arrangements came into use. In 1601 the historian Baronius claimed there were about eighty forms in use. These included such litanies as those to the Holy Spirit, the Precious Blood, Mary, the Saints, the Poor Souls, etc.

To prevent abuse, Pope Clement VIII decreed on September 6, 1601, through the Holy Office of the Inquisition, that litanies could not be published, except those of the saints as found in official liturgical books and that of the Blessed Virgin Mary of Loreto.

Today, again, while many litanies exist for private devotion, the official litanies approved for public recitation are limited to only six: The *Litany of the Holy Name of Jesus,* the *Litany of the Sacred Heart of Jesus,* the *Litany of the Precious Blood of Jesus,* the *Litany of the Blessed Virgin Mary (Litany of Loreto),* the *Litany of Saint Joseph* and the *Litany of the Saints.*

Concerning the *Litany of the Saints,* the very earliest litany and the one having many variations, we mentioned Pope Pius V having established it in a uniform style. The *Litany of the Holy Name of Jesus* also has a long history. Saint Bernardine of Siena (1380-1444) and Saint John Capistrano (1386-1456) were great preachers of devotion to the Holy Name of Jesus. This litany was approved by Pope Sixtus V on July 11, 1587. Pius IX indulgenced it in 1862 for a certain diocese or dioceses. And Leo XIII, in 1886, extended this privilege to the whole world.

The *Litany of the Sacred Heart of Jesus* was approved for solemn and public use by Pope Leo XIII in 1899. Many of its invocations go back to Father J. Croiset (1656-1738). Of course, Saint Margaret Mary Alacoque had much influence on the spread of devotion to the Sacred Heart of Jesus because of Our Lord's revelations to her.

The *Litany of Saint Joseph* was approved by Pope Saint Pius X in 1909. The *Litany of the Precious Blood* was approved by Pope John XXIII in 1960.

The *Litany of Loreto* was approved by Pope Sixtus V in 1587. A little more should be said about this famous *Litany of the Blessed Virgin Mary,* the one many Catholics have known very well from their youth and from the May devotions to Mary.

There are many origins claimed for *The Litany of Loreto,* some writers tracing it back to Apostolic times. Others refer back to Pope Sergius I (687) or to a Gaelic litany of the eighth century, or to Pope Saint Gregory the Great (590-604). The name of the litany in honor of Mary comes from its association with the holy shrine of Our Lady of Loreto, Italy and the miraculous translation by angels of the Holy House of Nazareth to that place in 1294. At any rate, the Litany was well-known there when Saint Peter Canisius had it printed and published at Dilligen, Germany in 1558 under the title, *"Letania Loretana."* This is the oldest known printed copy, and it gives the Litany substantially the same as what we have today.

After Pope Saint Pius V's instructions in a *motu proprio* of March 20, 1571, there was a new version for a time which took invocations more directly from Scripture and the liturgy, but Pope Sixtus V approved the old form used at Loreto, and that is the one that has been handed down to us. Pope Pius VII, after returning to Rome from the Napoleonic captivity, added the invocation "Queen of All Saints." The titles "Queen of the Most Holy Rosary," "Queen conceived without original sin," and "Mother of Good Counsel" were added by Pope Leo XIII. During World War I, Pope Benedict XV added "Queen of Peace." When the dogma of the Assumption of Mary was defined in 1950, Pope Pius XII added the title "Queen assumed into Heaven." Pope John Paul II has added "Mother of the Church."

We have indicated which are the litanies officially approved for public use. All others are for private use and may be used in private devotions only. The official litanies, of course, should have preference over the private ones, even for private use. Of the many others, this or that one may suit the particular devotion of an individual better than others, or certain parts or invocations may be of help to different people in their private prayer. Litanies, of course, should never be rattled off in rote-like manner without attention of the mind and heart.

At times during one's prayer, a person may be more inclined to praise than to petitioning; at another time, to making reparation, or to pleading for succor for the great needs of the Church, the Holy Father, etc. If a person in private prayer finds a particularly striking invocation or petition, one that stirs his soul, inspiring or spiritually enriching him, then it is suggested that he pause there to gain benefit and spiritual fruit from it. One might even gather his favorite invocations or phrases from various litanies and make his own strictly private litany for private prayer and meditation purposes.

There are, to be sure, some litanies that are omitted from this volume for one reason or another, as for example, failure to find a copy. Moreover, besides the litanies, we have added a number of prayers similar in some respects to litanies, such as "Invocations to the

Heart of Jesus," "The Divine Praises," "Our Lady of Lourdes Invocations," and the *"Anima Christi"* or "Soul of Christ" prayer paraphrased by Saint Elizabeth Seton. We believe that in this grouping the reader will find some very beautiful prayers.

As there have been many variations in the long history of the approved litanies until they became standardized, so today one may come across different versions of the litanies for private recital. The variations are usually very minor.

In times of great need in the Church and in the world, and when great calamities threaten—such as war, hurricane or famine—litanies should be prayed publicly and privately for the common good. Along with them, processions should be held. Also, they should be prayed for the Holy Father. Finally, it is also good to remember that many of the litanies and litany processions traditionally led up to the celebration of Holy Mass or to the conclusion of the Forty Hours, with the *Pange Lingua* procession and Benediction of the Most Blessed Sacrament. This illustrates the fact that all our devotions are ultimately for the worship of God, the Source of all good.

To Christ and to the Father and the Holy Spirit be the honor, the glory, and the power!

ACKNOWLEDGMENTS

It is obvious that a book of litanies is not an original composition or contribution. Litanies come from elsewhere than one author's mind, and many have been around for centuries. Quite a few, too, have seen many variations. For instance, we have included two fairly different versions of the "Litany of Saint Michael"—for one reason, because we believe devotion to the great Archangel is urgently needed and should be encouraged in every possible way in our day.

Certain litanies in this book have come from old prayerbooks, which contain a rich legacy of them, and from various other sources, such as religious booklets and prayer leaflets from friends. The litanies officially approved are generally available in various devotional books. I might mention that TAN Books and Publishers publishes the "Litany of the Blessed Virgin Mary" in attractive prayer card form.

The first "Litany of the Holy Spirit" can be found on a leaflet of the Sacred Heart Archdiocesan Center, 110 W. Madison St., Chicago, Illinois with the Imprimatur of Cardinal Stritch. For the second "Litany of the Holy Spirit" I am indebted to the truly inspiring book entitled *About the Holy Spirit,* by the mystic Francisca Javiera del Valle, published by *Lumen Christi Press,* Houston, Texas. The "Litany of the Infant Jesus," the "Litany of the Miraculous Infant of Prague," and the "Litany of the Holy Childhood of Jesus" can be found in the paperback, *The Infant Jesus of Prague,* by the Rev. Ludvik Nemec, Catholic Book Publishing Co., New York. Published by the

same company is the *Priest's Daily Manual* by Rev.
Joseph B. Collins and Msgr. Raphael J. Collins. This
is a book I have treasured as a gift from an old friend,
Bishop Caillouet, retired auxiliary bishop of New
Orleans, and have also valued for its "Litany of the
Love of God," "Litany of Saint Pius X," and "Litany
of Saint Therese of the Child Jesus" (Litany Two).

For the "Prayer to the Holy Face" I am thankful to
the composer, Rev. Emery Pethro of Detroit; this
prayer was printed in the *Priestly Heart Newsletter,*
Issue 29, 317 Leroy Ave., Buffalo, New York 14214.
For "Promises of Consolation to Christ" (my own title) acknowledgement must be made to the booklet,
Holy Hour with Mary, published by the Montfort
Fathers, 40 S. Saxon Ave., Bay Shore, New York
11706.

The "Litany of the Mercy of God," which is associ-
ated with Sister Faustina of the Mercy of God devotion, is from Franciscan Publications, Pulaski,
Wisconsin. The "Litany of Reparation to Our Lord in
the Blessed Eucharist" is from *My Daily Visit* of the
Benedictine Convent, Clyde, Missouri. The "Invocations to the Heart of Jesus with an Act of Oblation" is
from *My Hour with Jesus,* a booklet of the National
Center of the Enthronement, Washington, D.C.

The "Litany of the Immaculate Heart of Mary" can
be found on a leaflet of the Abbey Press, St. Meinrad,
Indiana 47577. Also, in their pamphlet, *The Apparitions of Our Lady at Banneux,* one can find the "Invocations to the Blessed Virgin of the Poor." The "Invocations to Our Lady of Lourdes" are contained in
the leaflet, *Novena Devotions in Honor of Our Lady of
Lourdes,* Lourdes Center, Marist Fathers, 698
Beacon St., Boston, Massachusetts 02215.

The "Salutation to Mary," written by Saint John
Eudes in the seventeenth century, was found in a
leaflet of the Crusaders of Our Lady of Fatima. This
beautiful salutation of Mary was propagated by the
saintly Father Paul de Moll, O.S.B. (1824-1896); the

version which Father Paul promoted, "Affectionate Salutations to Mary," can be found in the book entitled *Father Paul of Moll,* by Edward van Speybrouck, published by TAN Books and Publishers.

Quite a few of the litanies given herein—especially those to Almighty God and many of those to the saints—were found in a book of litanies entitled *Kyrie Eleison: Two Hundred Litanies,* compiled by Benjamin Francis Musser, and published in 1944 by The Newman Bookshop. Mr. Musser had collected these from various sources—in many cases from old prayer books and booklets from the 19th and early 20th centuries—especially from *The Golden Manual, Compiled From Aproved Sources,* published by D. & H. Sadlier & Co. in 1851, and from *St. Benedict's Manual,* published in 1875 by Frederick Pustet. Most of these litanies, however, actually trace their origins back much further—some have come down to us, in much the same form, from medieval times. Among the litanies taken from this book I particularly mention the "Litany of St. Ignatius Loyola"; this was composed by Rev. Leo M. Weber, S.J. Also, the third "Litany to the Holy Spirit" was composed by Rev. Gerald M. C. Fitzgerald, C.S.C., the "Short Litany for the Souls in Purgatory" was composed by Benjamin Francis Musser, and the "Litany for Christ the King" was composed by Benjamin Francis Musser using elements of the Proper of the Mass for the Kingship of Christ.

"The Crown of Twelve Stars," sometimes attributed to Saint Joseph Calasanctius, can be found in the old *Raccolta* or *Book of Prayers and Devotions,* a book which is a treasure house of beautiful prayers enriched with indulgences from the old days; we have used a slightly different version as found in *Kyrie Eleison.* The old "Gaelic Litany to Mary," translated by Eugene O'Curry, comes from that beautiful anthology, *The World's Great Catholic Poetry,* by

Thomas Walsh, Ph.D. Published by the MacMillan Co., New York, in 1942, this is an anthology of a type we do not see anymore, due to the great decline in Christian culture.

For the third "Litany of the Holy Guardian Angel" I am indebted to Father Robert J. Fox's book entitled *The Work of the Holy Angels (Opus Sanctorum Angelorum)*, published by the Blue Army. For the "Litany of Our Lady of Fatima," I am indebted to a leaflet of the Dominican Fathers at the Shrine of the Infant of Prague, New Haven, Connecticut, and for the Memorial Prayer for the Suffering Souls in Purgatory, to the Divine Word Seminary, Techny, Illinois.

The "Litany of Saint Anne" can be found in a novena leaflet published by the old Archconfraternity of Saint Anne at the National Shrine on Ursuline Ave. in New Orleans. The litany of my patron saint, Albert the Great, is from a pamphlet, *Saint Albert the Great,* published by the Paulist Press years ago. The first "Litany of Saint Anthony" is from the booklet, *Dedicating the Week to Saint Anthony of Padua,* by Fr. Bernard, O.F.M., Box 598, Mt. Vernon, New York 10551. The second litany of Saint Anthony of Padua is from the Franciscan Friars of Marytown, Libertyville, Illinois. The first "Litany of Saint Rita of Cascia" is from the Saint Rita novena booklet published by St. Mary's Church, Rockford, Illinois.

The "Litany of Saint Philomena" and the first "Litany of Saint Jude" are from pamphlets of the Benedictine Convent of Perpetual Adoration Press at Clyde, Missouri. For the paraphrase of the *"Anima Christi"* prayer of Saint Ignatius Loyola by the American saint, Mother Elizabeth Seton, I am grateful to Msgr. M. J. Doyle, 1933 Spielbusch Ave., Toledo, Ohio 43624, from whom copies are available free of charge.

The "Litany for the Church in Our Time" may have an invocation or two which are puzzling to some. The phrases are not to be taken as any affront to Church authority. Many people merely wish to express their desire for an authorization of the former Latin Mass along with the present Eucharistic Prayers. The litany also demonstrates the stress present in our times and the need for charity and prayer for all. It is from a leaflet of the Christopher House, 2386 Pontiac, Columbus, Ohio 43211.

I wish finally to express my deep gratitude to the late holy Cardinal Merry del Val for his own "Litany of Humility," which I believe has helped my own spiritual life over the years. This humble cardinal might himself have been a great pope, but humbly served others, especially the humble and saintly Pope Saint Pius X.

For further background on litanies and their history I recommend articles in the *Catholic Encyclopedia* and in the *New Catholic Encyclopedia,* especially the article on the "Litany of Loreto," by Angelo de Santi, in the *Catholic Encyclopedia.*

I wish to express particular thanks to Miss Hermine Zotter for typing a number of these litanies for the manuscript, and also to Miss Jeanie Stein for her help in checking and proofreading, as well as to any other person or source that has inadvertently been over-looked. May God reward you all.

—Father Albert J. Hebert, S.M.

LITANIES
IN HONOR OF
ALMIGHTY GOD

"Blessed art thou, O Lord the God of our fathers: and worthy to be praised, and glorified, and exalted above all for ever: and blessed is the holy name of thy glory: and worthy to be praised, and exalted above all in all ages."

—Daniel 3:52

LITANY OF
THE MOST HOLY TRINITY

(For private use only.)

Blessed be the holy Trinity and undivided Unity;
We will give glory to Him, because He hath shown
His mercy to us.

V. O Lord our Lord, how wonderful is Thy Name in
all the earth!
R. *O the depth of the riches of the wisdom and of the*
knowledge of God!

Lord, have mercy.
Lord, have mercy.
Christ, have mercy.
Christ, have mercy.
Lord, have mercy.
Lord, have mercy.
Blessed Trinity, hear us.
Adorable Unity, graciously hear us.

God the Father of Heaven,
Have mercy on us.
God the Son, Redeemer of the world,
Have mercy on us.
God the Holy Ghost, *etc.*
Holy Trinity, One God,
Father from Whom are all things,
Son through Whom are all things,
Holy Ghost in Whom are all things,
Holy and undivided Trinity,
Father everlasting,
Only-begotten Son of the Father,
Spirit Who proceedeth from the Father and the Son,

Co-eternal Majesty of Three Divine Persons,
Father, the Creator,
Son, the Redeemer,
Holy Ghost, the Comforter,
Holy, holy, holy, Lord God of hosts,
Who art, Who wast, and Who art to come,
God Most High, Who inhabitest eternity,
To Whom alone are due all honor and glory,
Who alone doest great wonders,
Power infinite,
Wisdom incomprehensible,
Love unspeakable,

Be merciful,
   Spare us, O Holy Trinity.
Be merciful,
   Graciously hear us, O Holy Trinity.

From all evil,
   Deliver us, O Holy Trinity.
From all sin,
   Deliver us, O Holy Trinity.
From all pride, *etc.*
From all love of riches,
From all uncleanness,
From all sloth,
From all inordinate affection,
From all envy and malice,
From all anger and impatience,
From every thought, word, and deed contrary to Thy
   holy law,
From Thine everlasting malediction,
Through Thine almighty power,
Through Thy plenteous loving kindness,
Through the exceeding treasure of Thy goodness and
   love,
Through the depths of Thy wisdom and knowledge,
Through all Thy unspeakable perfections,

We sinners
Beseech Thee, hear us.

That we may ever serve Thee alone,
We beseech Thee, hear us.
That we may worship Thee in spirit and in truth,
We beseech Thee, hear us.
That we may love Thee with all our heart, with all our
soul, and with all our strength, *etc*
That, for Thy sake, we may love our neighbor as
ourselves,
That we may faithfully keep Thy holy
commandments,
That we may never defile our bodies and souls with
sin,
That we may go from grace to grace, and from virtue
to virtue,
That we may finally enjoy the sight of Thee in glory,
That Thou wouldst vouchsafe to hear us,

O Blessed Trinity,
We beseech Thee, deliver us.
O Blessed Trinity,
We beseech Thee, save us.
O Blessed Trinity,
Have mercy on us.
Lord, have mercy,
Christ, have mercy.
Lord, have mercy.

Our Father *(silently).* Hail Mary *(silently).*

V. Blessed art Thou, O Lord, in the firmament of
Heaven,
R. *And worthy to be praised, and glorious, and highly
exalted forever.*

Let Us Pray

Almighty and everlasting God, Who hast granted Thy servants in the confession of the True Faith, to acknowledge the glory of an Eternal Trinity, and in the power of Thy majesty to adore a Unity: we beseech Thee that by the strength of this faith we may be defended from all adversity. Through Jesus Christ Our Lord. R. *Amen.*

LITANY OF THE
LOVE OF GOD

(For private use only.)

Lord, have mercy on us.
  Christ, have mercy on us.
Lord, have mercy on us. Christ, hear us.
  Christ, graciously hear us.
God the Father of Heaven,
  Have mercy on us.
God the Son, Redeemer of the world,
  Have mercy on us.
God the Holy Ghost,
  Have mercy on us.
Holy Trinity, One God,
  Have mercy on us.

Thou Who art Infinite Love,
  I Love Thee, O my God.
Thou Who didst first love me,
  I Love Thee, O my God.
Thou Who dost command me to love Thee, *etc.*
With all my heart,
With all my soul,
With all my mind,
With all my strength,
Above all possessions and honor,
Above all pleasures and enjoyments,
More than myself and all that belongs to me,
More than all my relatives and friends,
More than all men and angels,
Above all created things in Heaven or on earth,
Only for Thyself,
Because Thou art the sovereign Good,
Because Thou art infinitely worthy of being loved,

Because Thou art infinitely perfect,
Even hadst Thou not promised me Heaven,
Even hadst Thou not menaced me with Hell,
Even shouldst Thou try me by want and misfortune,
In wealth and in poverty,
In prosperity and in adversity,
In health and in sickness,
In life and in death,
In time and in eternity,
In union with that love wherewith all the Saints and
    all the Angels love Thee in Heaven,
In union with that love wherewith the Blessed Virgin
    Mary loveth Thee,
In union with that infinite love wherewith Thou lovest
    Thyself eternally,

Let Us Pray

My God, Who dost possess in incomprehensible abundance all that is perfect and worthy of love, annihilate in me all guilty, sensual, and undue love for creatures; kindle in my heart the pure flame of Thy love, so that I may love nothing but Thee or in Thee, until, being entirely consumed by holy love of Thee, I may go to love Thee eternally with the elect in Heaven, the country of pure love. R. *Amen.*

This litany was composed by Pope Pius VI (1775-1799).

LITANY OF DIVINE PROVIDENCE

(For private use only.)

Lord, have mercy on us.
   Christ, have mercy on us.
Lord, have mercy on us. Christ, hear us.
   Christ, graciously hear us.
God the Father of Heaven,
   Have mercy on us.
God the Son, Redeemer of the world,
   Have mercy on us.
God the Holy Ghost,
   Have mercy on us.
Holy Trinity, one God,
   Have mercy on us.

God, all-knowing and all-wise,
   Have mercy on us.
God, all-powerful and all-good,
   Have mercy on us.
God, most patient and most merciful, *etc.*
Father of mercy and consolation,
God, wonderful and inscrutable in Thy plans,
God, in Whose hands is our life,
God, from Whom all good things and every perfect
   gift comes,
Thou Who hast made all things for the service of man,
Thou Who governest all with wisdom and love,
Thou Who fillest all living things with blessing,
Thou Who dost clothe the lilies of the field and feed
   the birds of the air,
Thou Who dost number the hairs of our head,
Thou Who seest in secret,
Thou Who makest the sun to shine upon the good and
   the bad,

9

Thou Who allowest it to rain upon the just and the
   unjust,
Thou Who workest all things for the benefit of those
   who love Thee,
Thou Who sendest temporal sufferings for our
   correction and good,
Thou Who dost reward Christian patience with an
   eternal reward,
God, our sole refuge and hope,
God, our only consoler and helper,

Be merciful,
   Spare us, O Lord.
Be merciful,
   Graciously hear us, O Lord.

From all evil,
   Deliver us, O Lord.
From all sin,
   Deliver us, O Lord.
From all murmurings and complaints against Thy
   holy decrees, *etc.*
From cowardice and impatience,
From mistrust in Thy divine Providence,
From too great trust in riches and the favor of men,
From immoderate concern for temporal things,
From misuse or neglect of Thy gifts and benefits,
From ingratitude toward Thy loving kindness,
From uncharitableness toward our neighbor,
From obduracy in sin,
From all dangers of body and soul,
From Thy well-merited chastisements,
From earthquake, pestilence, famine and distress,
From disease, hunger and war,
From a wicked and unprovided death,
On the day of judgment,

We sinners
   Beseech Thee, hear us.

That we may always trust in Thy divine Providence,
  We beseech Thee, hear us.
That in good fortune we may not become proud and
  godless,
  We beseech Thee, hear us.
That in misfortune we may not become discouraged
  and impatient, *etc.*
That we may submit simply to all Thy decrees,
That we may praise Thy name whether Thou givest or
  takest away,
That Thy will may be done on earth as it
  is in Heaven,
That we may seek consolation from Thee in time of
  trial,
That Thou mayest give us what is necessary for the
  support of our life,
That in all adversities we may grow in patience and
  humility,
That Thou mayest accompany all our labors with Thy
  blessing,
That Thou mayest reward our temporal sufferings
  with eternal joys,
That Thou mayest fill our spiritual and civil rulers
  with the spirit of truth and the fear of God,
That Thou mayest pity all who suffer want,
That Thou mayest console and raise up all the
  abandoned and oppressed,
That Thou mayest reward our benefactors with
  eternal goods,
That we may praise and glorify Thy divine
  Providence now and forever,

Lamb of God, Who takest away the sins of the world,
  Spare us, O Lord.
Lamb of God, Who takest away the sins of the world,
  Graciously hear us, O Lord.
Lamb of God, Who takest away the sins of the world,
  Have mercy on us.

Christ, hear us.
   Christ, graciously hear us.
Lord, have mercy on us.
   Christ, have mercy on us.
Lord, have mercy on us.

Our Father *(silently).* Hail Mary *(silently).*

All eyes are turned to Thee, O Lord,
   And Thou givest them food in season.
Thou openest Thy gentle hand,
   And fillest with blessing all living things.

V. Lord, show us Thy mercy,
R. *And grant us Thy salvation.*

Let Us Pray

O God, Whose Providence is never frustrated in its decrees, we beseech Thee to keep from us all harm and grant us every blessing, through Jesus Christ Our Lord. R. *Amen.*

LITANY OF RESIGNATION TO
THE WILL OF GOD
(For private use only.)

Lord, have mercy on us.
Christ, have mercy on us.
Lord, have mercy on us. Jesus, hear us.
Jesus, graciously hear us.
God the Father, Who hath created me,
Hallowed be Thy will.
God the Son, Who hath redeemed me,
Not my will but Thine be done.
God the Holy Ghost, Who hath offered sanctification,
Blessed be the Most Sweet Will of God.

Thou Who dost know and foresee all things,
Have mercy on us.
Thou Who dost govern and rule all things,
Have mercy on us.
Thou Who, according to Thy inscrutable designs,
dost effect all things in a wonderful manner,
Have mercy on us.
Thou Who dost permit evil in order thence to derive
good for the salvation of the elect,
Have mercy on us.

In all things and in all possible events,
Thy Holy Will be done, O my God.
In all circumstances and disgraces,
Thy Holy Will be done, O my God.
In my state and employment, *etc.*
In my affairs and occupations,
In all my actions,
In my health and strength,
In my body and soul,

13

In my life and death,
In myself and in those who belong to me,
In all men and angels,
In all creatures,
In all parts of the earth,
At all times,
For all eternity,
Although weak nature complains,
Although it costs much to self-love and sensuality,
Solely and only through love for Thee and Thy good
   pleasure,
Because Thou art my Creator,
Because Thou art the Supreme Lord of all things,
Because Thou art infinite perfection, therefore do I
   say, with all the saints in Heaven,

With the Blessed Virgin Mary,
   Thy Holy Will be done, O my God.
With Jesus in the Garden of Olives,
   Thy Holy Will be done, O my God.

Our Father *(silently).*

V. May the just, most amiable will of God be done in
   all things.
R. *May it be praised and magnified forever! Amen.*

Let Us Pray

Grant me Thy grace, O Father, that perfect resignation to Thy Holy Will may be with me, and labor
with me, and continue with me to the end. Grant me
always to desire and will that which is most acceptable to Thee and which pleaseth Thee best. Let Thy
will be mine, and let my will always follow Thine and
agree perfectly with it. Let me always will and not will
the same with Thee; let me not be able to will or not
will anything except what Thou willest or willest not.
R. *Amen.*

LITANIES DEVOTED TO
OUR LORD
JESUS CHRIST

"For God so loved the world, as to give his only begotten Son; that whosoever believeth in him, may not perish, but may have life everlasting."

—John *3:16*

LITANY OF THE
MOST HOLY NAME OF JESUS

(For public or private use.)

Lord, have mercy on us.
  Christ, have mercy on us.
Lord, have mercy on us. Jesus, hear us.
  Jesus, graciously hear us.
God the Father of Heaven,
  Have mercy on us.
God the Son, Redeemer of the world,
  Have mercy on us.
God the Holy Spirit,
  Have mercy on us.
Holy Trinity, One God,
  Have mercy on us.

Jesus, Son of the living God,
  Have mercy on us.
Jesus, splendor of the Father,
  Have mercy on us.
Jesus, brightness of eternal light, *etc.*
Jesus, King of glory,
Jesus, Sun of justice,
Jesus, Son of the Virgin Mary,
Jesus, most amiable,
Jesus, most admirable,
Jesus, mighty God,
Jesus, Father of the world to come,
Jesus, Angel of the great counsel,
Jesus, most powerful,
Jesus, most patient,
Jesus, most obedient,
Jesus, meek and humble of heart,
Jesus, Lover of chastity,

17

Jesus, Lover of us,
Jesus, God of peace,
Jesus, Author of life,
Jesus, Model of virtues,
Jesus, zealous for souls,
Jesus, our God,
Jesus, our Refuge,
Jesus, Father of the poor,
Jesus, Treasure of the faithful,
Jesus, Good Shepherd,
Jesus, true Light,
Jesus, eternal Wisdom,
Jesus, infinite Goodness,
Jesus, our Way and our Life,
Jesus, Joy of Angels,
Jesus, King of Patriarchs,
Jesus, Master of Apostles,
Jesus, Teacher of Evangelists,
Jesus, Strength of Martyrs,
Jesus, Light of Confessors,
Jesus, Purity of Virgins,
Jesus, Crown of all Saints,

Be merciful,
    Spare us, O Jesus.
Be merciful,
    Graciously hear us, O Jesus.

From all evil,
    Jesus, deliver us.
From all sin,
    Jesus, deliver us.
From Thy wrath, *etc.*
From the snares of the devil,
From the spirit of fornication,
From everlasting death,
From the neglect of Thine inspirations,
Through the mystery of Thy holy Incarnation,
Through Thy Nativity,

Through Thine Infancy,
Through Thy most divine life,
Through Thy labors,
Through Thine Agony and Passion,
Through Thy Cross and dereliction,
Through Thy faintness and weariness,
Through Thy death and burial,
Through Thy Resurrection,
Through Thine Ascension,
Through Thine institution of the Most Holy
    Eucharist,
Through Thy joys,
Through Thy glory,

Lamb of God, Who takest away the sins of the world,
    Spare us, O Jesus.
Lamb of God, Who takest away the sins of the world,
    Graciously hear us, O Jesus.
Lamb of God, Who takest away the sins of the world,
    Have mercy on us, O Jesus.

V. Jesus, hear us.
R. *Jesus, graciously hear us.*

Let Us Pray

O Lord Jesus Christ, Who hast said: "Ask and ye shall receive; seek, and ye shall find; knock, and it shall be opened unto you"; grant, we beseech Thee, to us who ask, the gift of Thy most divine love, that we may ever love Thee with all our heart, and in all our words and actions, and never cease from praising Thee.

Make us, O Lord, to have both a perpetual fear and love of Thy holy name, for Thou never failest to govern those whom Thou foundest upon the strength of Thy love, Who livest and reignest, world without end. R. *Amen.*

LITANY OF THE
MOST SACRED HEART
OF JESUS

(For public or private use.)

Lord, have mercy on us.
   Christ, have mercy on us.
Lord, have mercy on us. Christ, hear us.
   Christ, graciously hear us.
God the Father of Heaven,
   Have mercy on us.
God the Son, Redeemer of the world,
   Have mercy on us.
God the Holy Spirit,
   Have mercy on us.
Holy Trinity, One God,
   Have mercy on us.

Heart of Jesus, Son of the Eternal Father,
   Have mercy on us.
Heart of Jesus, formed by the Holy Spirit in the womb
   of the Virgin Mother,
   Have mercy on us.
Heart of Jesus, substantially united to the Word of
   God, *etc.*
Heart of Jesus, of infinite majesty,
Heart of Jesus, holy Temple of God,
Heart of Jesus, Tabernacle of the Most High,
Heart of Jesus, House of God and
   Gate of Heaven,
Heart of Jesus, burning Furnace of charity,
Heart of Jesus, Vessel of justice and love,
Heart of Jesus, full of goodness and love,
Heart of Jesus, Abyss of all virtues,
Heart of Jesus, most worthy of all praise,

20

Heart of Jesus, King and center of all hearts,
Heart of Jesus, in Whom are all the treasures of
   wisdom and knowledge,
Heart of Jesus, in Whom dwelleth all the
   fullness of the divinity,
Heart of Jesus, in Whom the Father
   was well pleased,
Heart of Jesus, of whose fullness we have
   all received,
Heart of Jesus, desire of the everlasting hills,
Heart of Jesus, patient and abounding in mercy,
Heart of Jesus, rich unto all who call
   upon Thee,
Heart of Jesus, Fountain of life and
   holiness,
Heart of Jesus, Propitiation for our sins,
Heart of Jesus, filled with reproaches,
Heart of Jesus, bruised for our offenses,
Heart of Jesus, made obedient unto death,
Heart of Jesus, pierced with a lance,
Heart of Jesus, Source of all consolation,
Heart of Jesus, our Life and Resurrection,
Heart of Jesus, our Peace and Reconciliation,
Heart of Jesus, Victim for our sins,
Heart of Jesus, Salvation of those who
   hope in Thee,
Heart of Jesus, Hope of those who die in Thee,
Heart of Jesus, Delight of all the saints,

Lamb of God, Who takest away the sins of the world,
   Spare us, O Lord.
Lamb of God, Who takest away the sins of the world,
   Graciously hear us, O Lord.
Lamb of God, Who takest away the sins of the world,
   Have mercy on us.

V. Jesus meek and humble of heart,
R. *Make our hearts like unto Thine.*

Let Us Pray

Almighty and eternal God, consider the Heart of Thy well-beloved Son and the praises and satisfaction He offers Thee in the name of sinners; appeased by worthy homage, pardon those who implore Thy mercy, in the name of the same Jesus Christ Thy Son, Who lives and reigns with Thee, world without end. R. *Amen.*

LITANY OF THE
MOST PRECIOUS BLOOD OF JESUS
(For public or private use.)

Lord, have mercy on us.
 Christ, have mercy on us.
Lord, have mercy on us. Christ, hear us.
 Christ, graciously hear us.
God the Father of Heaven,
 Have mercy on us.
God the Son, Redeemer of the world,
 Have mercy on us.
God the Holy Spirit,
 Have mercy on us.
Holy Trinity, One God,
 Have mercy on us.

Blood of Christ, only-begotten Son of the Eternal
 Father, *save us.*
Blood of Christ, Incarnate Word of God, *save us.*
Blood of Christ, of the New and Eternal Testament,
 etc.
Blood of Christ, falling upon the earth in the Agony,
Blood of Christ, shed profusely in the Scourging,
Blood of Christ, flowing forth in the Crowning with
 Thorns,
Blood of Christ, poured out on the Cross,
Blood of Christ, Price of our salvation,
Blood of Christ, without which there is no
 forgiveness,
Blood of Christ, Eucharistic drink and refreshment of
 souls,
Blood of Christ, river of mercy,
Blood of Christ, Victor over demons,
Blood of Christ, Courage of martyrs,

Blood of Christ, Strength of confessors,
Blood of Christ, bringing forth virgins,
Blood of Christ, Help of those in peril,
Blood of Christ, Relief of the burdened,
Blood of Christ, Solace in sorrow,
Blood of Christ, Hope of the penitent,
Blood of Christ, Consolation of the dying,
Blood of Christ, Peace and Tenderness of hearts,
Blood of Christ, Pledge of Eternal Life,
Blood of Christ, freeing souls from Purgatory,
Blood of Christ, most worthy of all glory and honor,

Lamb of God, Who takest away the sins of the world,
Spare us, O Lord.
Lamb of God, Who takest away the sins of the world,
Graciously hear us, O Lord.
Lamb of God, Who takest away the sins of the world,
Have mercy on us.

V. Thou hast redeemed us, O Lord, in Thy Blood,
R. *And made of us a kingdom for our God.*

Let Us Pray

Almighty and Eternal God, Thou hast appointed
Thine only-begotten Son the Redeemer of the world,
and willed to be appeased by His Blood. Grant, we
beseech Thee, that we may worthily adore this Price
of our salvation, and through its power be
safeguarded from the evils of this present life, so that
we may rejoice in its fruits forever in Heaven.
Through the same Christ Our Lord. R. *Amen.*

LITANY OF
THE HOLY FACE
OF JESUS

(For private use only.)

Lord, have mercy on us.
  Jesus Christ, have mercy on us.
Lord, have mercy on us. Jesus Christ,
  Have mercy on us.
Holy Virgin Mary,
  Pray for us.

O Jesus, Whose adorable Face Mary and Joseph
  worshiped with profoundest reverence,
  have mercy on us.
O Jesus, Whose adorable Face is the masterpiece of
  the Holy Ghost, in which the Father was well
  pleased, *have mercy on us.*
O Jesus, Whose adorable Face ravished with joy the
  angels, shepherds and Magi in the stable of
  Bethlehem, *etc.*
O Jesus, Whose adorable Face wounded with a dart of
  love the aged Simeon and the Prophetess Anna in
  the temple,
O Jesus, Whose adorable Face was bathed in tears in
  Thy Holy Infancy,
O Jesus, Whose adorable Face at the age of twelve
  astonished the doctors in the temple,
O Jesus, Whose adorable Face is white with purity
  and ruddy with charity,
O Jesus, Whose adorable Face is more beautiful than
  the sun, brighter than the moon and more brilliant
  than the stars,
O Jesus, Whose adorable Face is lovelier than the
  roses of spring,

25

O Jesus, Whose adorable Face is more precious than
    gold, silver and gems,

O Jesus, Whose adorable Face wins all hearts by Its
    charms and grace,

O Jesus, Whose adorable Face is most noble in Its
    heavenly features,

O Jesus, Whose adorable Face is contemplated by the
    angels,

O Jesus, Whose adorable Face is the sweet delight of
    the saints,

O Jesus, Whose adorable Face was the joy of Thy
    Virgin Mother and Thy foster-father,

O Jesus, Whose adorable Face is the ineffable mirror
    of the Divine perfections,

O Jesus, the beauty of Whose adorable Face is ever
    ancient and ever new,

O Jesus, the modesty and mildness of Whose adorable
    Face attracteth both just and sinners,

O Jesus, Whose adorable Face appeaseth the Divine
    wrath,

O Jesus, Whose adorable Face is the terror of the evil
    spirits,

O Jesus, Whose adorable Face is the treasure of grace
    and blessings,

O Jesus, Whose adorable Face was exposed to the
    inclemency of the weather in the wilderness,

O Jesus, Whose adorable Face was bathed with sweat
    in Thy journeys and scorched with the heat of the
    sun,

O Jesus, the expression of Whose adorable Face is
    wholly Divine,

O Jesus, Whose adorable Face gave a holy kiss and
    blessing to the little children,

O Jesus, Whose adorable Face sorrowed and wept at
    the grave of Lazarus,

O Jesus, Whose adorable Face was brilliant as the sun
    and radiant with glory on Mount Tabor,

V. The light of Thy Face has been shed upon us, O Lord.

R. *Thou hast given joy to our hearts.*

O Adorable Face, worthy of all reverence, veneration and worship, *have mercy on us.*

O Adorable Face, sorrowful at the sight of Jerusalem and shedding tears over that ungrateful city, *have mercy on us.*

O Adorable Face, bowed to the earth in the Garden of Olives and covered with confusion for our sins, *etc.*

O Adorable Face, bathed in a bloody sweat,

O Adorable Face, kissed by the traitor Judas,

O Adorable Face, Whose sanctity and majesty smote the soldiers with fear and cast them to the ground,

O Adorable Face, struck by an infamous servant, blindfolded and profaned by the sacrilegious hands of Thine enemies,

O Adorable Face, defiled with spittle and bruised by so many buffets and blows,

O Adorable Face, Whose Divine look wounded the heart of Peter with repentance, sorrow and love,

O Adorable Face, humbled for us at the tribunals of Jerusalem,

O Adorable Face, which didst preserve Thy serenity when Pilate pronounced the fatal sentence,

O Adorable Face, covered with sweat and blood and forced into the mire under the weight of the Cross,

O Adorable Face, the brow crowned with deep and piercing thorns,

O Adorable Face, wiped with a veil by a pious woman on the way to Calvary,

O Adorable Face, raised on the instrument of the most shameful punishment,

O Adorable Face, Whose eyes shed tears of blood,

O Adorable Face, Whose mouth was tormented with vinegar and gall,

O Adorable Face, Whose hair and beard were plucked out by executioners,

O Adorable Face, disfigured like the face of a leper,

O Adorable Face, Whose incomparable beauty was obscured under the fearful cloud of the sins of the world,

O Adorable Face, covered with the sad shades of death,

O Adorable Face, washed and anointed by Mary and the holy women, and covered with a shroud,

O Adorable Face, enclosed in the sepulcher,

O Adorable Face, all resplendent with glory and beauty on the day of Thy Resurrection,

O Adorable Face, all dazzling with light at the moment of Thine Ascension,

O Adorable Face, hidden in the Most Blessed Sacrament of the Altar,

O Adorable Face, which will appear at the End of Time in the clouds, with great power and majesty,

O Adorable Face, which will cause sinners to tremble with terror,

O Adorable Face, which will fill the just with joy for all eternity,

V. O Lord, show us Thy Face,
R. *And we shall be saved.*

Lamb of God, Who takest away the sins of the world, *Spare us, O Lord.*

Lamb of God, Who takest away the sins of the world, *Graciously hear us, O Lord.*

Lamb of God, Who takest away the sins of the world, *Have mercy on us, O Lord.*

Let Us Pray

I salute Thee, I adore Thee, I love Thee, O adorable Face of Jesus my beloved, noble seal of the Divinity! With all the powers of my soul I apply myself to Thee, and most humbly pray Thee to imprint in me all the features of Thy divine countenance. R. *Amen.*

We beseech Thee, O Almighty and merciful God, grant to us and to all who venerate the countenance of Thy dearly beloved Son, all disfigured by our sins, the grace to behold It throughout eternity in the glory of Its majesty, through the same Jesus Christ Our Lord, Who is, with Thee and the Holy Spirit, ever one God, world without end. R. *Amen.*

O my Jesus, cast upon us a look of mercy! Turn Thy Face toward each of us as Thou didst to Veronica, not that we may see It with our bodily eyes, for this we do not deserve, but turn It toward our hearts, so that remembering Thee, we may ever draw from this fountain of strength the vigor necessary to sustain the combats of life. R. *Amen.*

LITANY OF THE PASSION

(For private use only.)

Lord, have mercy on us.
  Christ, have mercy on us.
Lord, have mercy on us. Christ, hear us.
  Christ, graciously hear us.
God the Father of Heaven,
  Have mercy on us.
God the Son, Redeemer of the world,
  Have mercy on us.
God the Holy Spirit,
  Have mercy on us.
Holy Trinity, One God,
  Have mercy on us.

Jesus, the Eternal Wisdom, *have mercy on us.*
Jesus, sold for thirty pieces of silver, *have mercy on us.*
Jesus, prostrate on the ground in prayer, *etc.*
Jesus, strengthened by an angel,
Jesus, in Thine agony bathed in a bloody sweat,
Jesus, betrayed by Judas with a kiss,
Jesus, bound by the soldiers,
Jesus, forsaken by Thy disciples,
Jesus, brought before Annas and Caiphas,
Jesus, struck in the face by a servant,
Jesus, accused by false witnesses,
Jesus, declared guilty of death,
Jesus, spat upon,
Jesus, blindfolded,
Jesus, smitten on the cheek,
Jesus, thrice denied by Peter,
Jesus, despised and mocked by Herod,
Jesus, clothed in a white garment,

Jesus, rejected for Barabbas,

Jesus, torn with scourges,

Jesus, bruised for our sins,

Jesus, esteemed a leper,

Jesus, covered with a purple robe,

Jesus, crowned with thorns,

Jesus, struck with a reed upon the Head,

Jesus, demanded for crucifixion by the Jews,

Jesus, condemned to an ignominious death,

Jesus, given up to the will of Thine enemies,

Jesus, loaded with the heavy weight of the Cross,

Jesus, led like a sheep to the slaughter,

Jesus, stripped of Thy garments,

Jesus, fastened with nails to the cross,

Jesus, reviled by the malefactors,

Jesus, promising Paradise to the penitent thief,

Jesus, commending St. John to Thy Mother as her
    son,

Jesus, declaring Thyself forsaken by Thy Father,

Jesus, in Thy thirst given gall and vinegar to drink,

Jesus, testifying that all things written concerning
    Thee were accomplished,

Jesus, commending Thy spirit into the hands of Thy
    Father,

Jesus, obedient even to the death of the cross,

Jesus, pierced with a lance,

Jesus, made a propitiation for us,

Jesus, taken down from the cross,

Jesus, laid in the sepulcher,

Jesus, rising gloriously from the dead,

Jesus, ascending into Heaven,

Jesus, our Advocate with the Father,

Jesus, sending down on Thy disciples the Holy Spirit,
    the Paraclete,

Jesus, exalting Thy Mother above the choirs of
    angels,

Jesus, Who shall come to judge the living and the
    dead,

Be merciful, *spare us, O Lord.*
Be merciful, *graciously hear us, O Lord.*

From all evil, *Lord Jesus, deliver us.*
From all sin, *Lord Jesus, deliver us.*
From anger, hatred, and every evil will, *etc.*
From war, famine, and pestilence,
From all dangers of mind and body,
From everlasting death,
Through Thy most pure Conception,
Through Thy miraculous Nativity,
Through Thy humble Circumcision,
Through Thy baptism and holy fasting,
Through Thy labors and watchings,
Through Thy cruel scourging and crowning,
Through Thy thirst, and tears, and nakedness,
Through Thy precious death and Cross,
Through Thy glorious Resurrection and Ascension,
Through Thy sending forth the Holy Spirit, the
    Paraclete,
In the Day of Judgment,

We sinners beseech Thee, *hear us.*
That Thou wilt spare us, *we beseech Thee, hear us.*
That Thou wilt pardon us, *we beseech Thee, hear us.*
That Thou wilt bring us to true penance, *etc.*
That Thou wilt mercifully pour into our hearts the
    grace of the Holy Spirit,
That Thou wilt defend and propagate Thy holy
    Church,
That Thou wilt preserve and increase all societies
    assembled in Thy Holy Name,
That Thou wilt bestow upon us true peace,
That Thou wilt give us perseverance in grace and in
    Thy holy service,
That Thou wilt deliver us from unclean thoughts,
    from the temptations of the devil, and from
    everlasting damnation,
That Thou wilt unite us to the company of Thy saints,

That Thou wilt graciously hear us,

Lamb of God, Who takest away the sins of the world,
   Spare us, O Lord.
Lamb of God, Who takest away the sins of the world,
   Graciously hear us, O Lord.
Lamb of God, Who takest away the sins of the world,
   Have mercy on us.

V. Christ, hear us.
R. *Christ, graciously hear us.*
V. We adore Thee, O Christ, and we bless Thee,
R. *Because by Thy Holy Cross Thou hast redeemed the world.*

Let Us Pray

Almighty and eternal God, Who didst appoint Thine only-begotten Son the Saviour of the world and willed to be appeased by His blood, grant that we may so venerate this Price of our Salvation, and by its might be so defended upon earth from the evils of this present life, that in Heaven we may rejoice in its everlasting fruit. Through Christ Our Lord Who lives and reigns with Thee in the unity of the Holy Spirit, world without end. R. *Amen.*

LITANY OF THE
HOLY CROSS

(For private use only.)

Lord, have mercy.
Lord, have mercy.
Christ, have mercy.
Christ, have mercy.
Lord, have mercy.
Lord, have mercy.
Christ, hear us.
Christ, graciously hear us.
God the Father of Heaven,
Have mercy on us.
God the Son, Redeemer of the world,
Have mercy on us.
God the Holy Ghost, our Advocate,
Have mercy on us.
Holy Trinity, one God,
Have mercy on us.

Holy Cross whereon the Lamb of God was offered,
Save us, O Holy Cross.
Hope of Christians,
Save us, O Holy Cross.
Pledge of the resurrection of the dead, *etc.*
Shelter of persecuted innocence,
Guide of the blind,
Way of those who have gone astray,
Staff of the lame,
Consolation of the poor,
Restraint of the powerful,
Destruction of the proud,
Refuge of sinners,
Trophy of victory over Hell,

Terror of demons,
Mistress of youth,
Succor of the distressed,
Hope of the hopeless,
Star of the mariner,
Harbor of the wrecked,
Rampart of the besieged,
Father of orphans,
Defense of widows,
Counsel of the just,
Judge of the wicked,
Rest of the afflicted,
Safeguard of childhood,
Strength of manhood,
Last hope of the aged,
Light of those who sit in darkness,
Splendor of kings,
Civilizer of the world,
Shield impenetrable,
Wisdom of the foolish,
Liberty of slaves,
Knowledge of the ignorant,
Sure rule of life,
Heralded by prophets,
Preached by apostles,
Glory of martyrs,
Study of hermits,
Chastity of virgins,
Joy of priests,
Foundation of the Church,
Salvation of the world,
Destruction of idolatry,
Stumbling block to the Jews,
Condemnation of the ungodly,
Support of the weak,
Medicine of the sick,
Health of the leprous,
Strength of the paralytic,
Bread of the hungry,

Fountain of those who thirst,
Clothing of the naked,

Lamb of God, Who takest away the sins of the world,
   Spare us, O Lord.
Lamb of God, Who takest away the sins of the world,
   Hear us, O Lord.
Lamb of God, Who takest away the sins of the world,
   Have mercy on us.

Christ, hear us.
   Christ, graciously hear us.
Lord, have mercy.
   Christ, have mercy.
Lord, have mercy.

V. We adore Thee, O Christ, and we bless Thee,
R. *Because by Thy Holy Cross Thou hast redeemed the world.*

(Together) Behold the Cross of the Lord! Begone ye evil powers! The Lion of the tribe of Juda, the Root of David, has conquered! + Alleluia!

Let Us Pray

O God, Who for the redemption of the world, wast pleased to be born in a stable and to die upon a cross; O Lord Jesus Christ, by Thy holy sufferings, which we, Thy unworthy servants, call to mind: by Thy Holy Cross, and by Thy death, deliver us from the pains of Hell, and vouchsafe to conduct us whither Thou didst conduct the good thief who was crucified with Thee, Who livest and reignest eternally in Heaven. R. *Amen.*

Sweet the wood, sweet the nails, sweet the Burden which thou bearest, for thou alone, O Holy Cross, wast worthy to bear the King and Lord of Heaven. R. *Amen.*

This litany, which has come down to us from the Middle Ages and from many countries, should not be thought to be addressed to an inanimate object, great relic though it is, but rather, to Him who hung upon it and thereby redeemed us all. By our salutation to the chief instrument of Our Lord's Passion and death, we hope and we trust that He will show mercy to us.

LITANY OF
CHRIST THE KING
(For private use only.)

The Lamb that was slain is worthy to receive power
and divinity and wisdom and strength and honor;
To Him be glory and empire forever and ever.

V. He shall rule from sea to sea, and from the river to
the ends of the earth.
R. *All kings shall adore Him, all nations shall serve
Him.*

Lord, have mercy upon us.
Christ, have mercy upon us.
Lord, have mercy upon us. Christ the King, hear us.
Christ the King, graciously hear us.

Thou Who didst receive crowns and tribute from the
Magi, *May all nations serve Thee, O Lord.*
Who didst rule by love the Holy Family of Nazareth,
May all nations serve Thee, O Lord.
Who as King, served Thy people in the example of
filial obedience, *etc.*
Who drawest to Thy realm the fishermen to be fishers
of men,
Whose Kingdom is not of the spirit of this world,
Who art King not of the Jews alone but of all creation,
Who wast mocked in false purple by the little rulers,
Who wast crowned with piercing thorns,
Who wast nailed to Thy throne on Golgotha,
Who didst ransom Thy people by the royal Sacrifice
of Calvary,
Who didst purchase Thy Kingdom with the Blood of
the Atonement,

Who in Thy Resurrection wert the First-born from the
    dead,
Who in Thy glorified body art risen triumphant,
Who art throned and crowned at the right hand of Thy
    Father,
In Whom are all created things in Heaven and on
    earth, visible and invisible,
Beneath Whom are all thrones and dominations,
Beneath Whom are all principalities and powers,
By Whom all things subsist,
To Whom all the nations of the earth are subject,
Through Whom all things are reconciled unto Thy
    Father,

V. His power shall be an everlasting power,
R. *And His Kingdom a kingdom that shall not be
    destroyed.*

That the peoples of this world may know themselves
    subject to Thee, *We beseech Thee, hear us.*
That they may put off their vainglory, *We beseech
    Thee, hear us.*
That they may dispel the evils laicism has brought
    upon society, *etc.*
That they may hearken to Thy *fiat,*
That they may bow their heads before Thee,
That they may know Thy reign is eternal,
That they may submit to Thy just and gentle rule,
That they may recognize Thy Vicar on earth,
That they may freely accept his rule for Thy sake,
That they may know that Thy Church, being Thee
    Thyself, cannot die as nations die,
That the Gentiles may be restored to mercy,
That to Christ the King all things may be restored,
That in the Prince of Peace true peace may by all be
    found,

Lamb of God, Who takest away the sins of the world,
    Spare us, O Christ our King.

Lamb of God, Who takest away the sins of the world,
  Hear us, O Christ our King.
Lamb of God, Who takest away the sins of the world,
  Have mercy on us.

V. His power shall be an everlasting power, which
  shall not be taken away,
R. *And His Kingdom shall not decay. Alleluia.*

Let Us Pray

Almighty, everlasting God, Who in Thy beloved
Son, King of the whole world, hast willed to restore all
things anew, grant in Thy mercy that all the families
of nations, rent asunder by the wound of sin, may be
subjected to His most gentle rule, Who with Thee
liveth and reigneth in the unity of the Holy Ghost,
God, world without end. R. *Amen.*

EUCHARISTIC LITANIES

"I am the living bread which came down from heaven. If any man eat of this bread, he shall live forever; and the bread that I will give, is my flesh, for the life of the world."

—John 6:51-52

LITANY OF THE
BLESSED SACRAMENT

(For private use only.)

Lord, have mercy on us.
  Christ, have mercy on us.
Lord, have mercy on us. Christ, hear us.
  Christ, graciously hear us.
God the Father of Heaven,
  Have mercy on us.
God the Son, Redeemer of the world,
  Have mercy on us.
God the Holy Spirit,
  Have mercy on us.
Holy Trinity, One God,
  Have mercy on us.

Living Bread, that came down from Heaven,
  have mercy on us.
Hidden God and Saviour, *have mercy on us.*
Wheat of the elect, *etc.*
Wine of which virgins are the fruit,
Bread of fatness and royal dainties,
Perpetual Sacrifice,
Clean oblation,
Lamb without spot,
Most pure feast,
Food of angels,
Hidden manna,
Memorial of the wonders of God,
Super-substantial Bread,
Word made Flesh, dwelling in us,
Sacred Host,
Chalice of benediction,
Mystery of Faith,

Most high and adorable Sacrament,
Most holy of all sacrifices,
True Propitiation for the living and the dead,
Heavenly antidote against the poison of sin,
Most wonderful of all miracles,
Most holy Commemoration of the Passion of Christ,
Gift transcending all fullness,
Special Memorial of divine love,
Affluence of divine bounty,
Most august and holy Mystery,
Medicine of immortality,
Tremendous and life-giving Sacrament,
Bread made Flesh by the omnipotence of the Word,
Unbloody Sacrifice,
At once our Feast and our Guest,
Sweetest Banquet, at which angels minister,
Sacrament of piety,
Bond of charity,
Priest and Victim,
Spiritual Sweetness tasted in its proper source,
Refreshment of holy souls,
Viaticum of such as die in the Lord,
Pledge of future glory,

Be merciful, *Spare us, O Lord,*
Be merciful, *Graciously hear us, O Lord.*

From an unworthy reception of Thy Body and Blood,
     O Lord, deliver us.
From the lust of the flesh, *O Lord, deliver us.*
From the lust of the eyes, *etc.*
From the pride of life,
From every occasion of sin,
Through the desire with which Thou didst long to eat
     this Passover with Thy disciples,
Through that profound humility with which Thou
     didst wash their feet,
Through that ardent charity by which Thou didst
     institute this Divine Sacrament,

Through Thy Precious Blood, which Thou didst leave us on our altars,

Through the five wounds of this Thy most holy Body, which Thou didst receive for us,

We sinners beseech Thee, *hear us.*

That Thou wilt preserve and increase our faith, reverence, and devotion toward this admirable Sacrament, *we beseech Thee, hear us.*

That Thou wilt conduct us, through a true confession of our sins, to a frequent reception of the Holy Eucharist, *we beseech Thee, hear us.*

That Thou wilt deliver us from all heresy, perfidy, and blindness of heart, *etc.*

That Thou wilt impart to us the precious and heavenly fruits of this most holy Sacrament,

That at the hour of death Thou wilt strengthen and defend us by this heavenly Viaticum,

Son of God,

Lamb of God, Who takest away the sins of the world, *Spare us, O Lord.*

Lamb of God, Who takest away the sins of the world, *Graciously hear us, O Lord.*

Lamb of God, Who takest away the sins of the world, *Have mercy on us.*

V. Christ, hear us.

R. *Christ, graciously hear us.*

V. Thou didst give them Bread from Heaven. Alleluia.

R. *Containing in Itself all sweetness. Alleluia.*

Let Us Pray

O God, Who in this wonderful Sacrament hast left us a memorial of Thy Passion, grant us the grace, we beseech Thee, so to venerate the Sacred Mysteries of Thy Body and Blood, that we may ever continue to feel within ourselves the blessed fruit of Thy Redemption, Who livest and reignest, God forever and ever. R. *Amen.*

LITANY FOR HOLY COMMUNION

(For private use only.)

Lord, have mercy on us.
Christ, have mercy on us.
Lord, have mercy on us. Christ, hear us.
Christ, graciously hear us.
God the Father of Heaven,
Have mercy on us.
God the Son, Redeemer of the world,
Have mercy on us.
God the Holy Spirit,
Have mercy on us.
Holy Trinity, One God,
Have mercy on us.

Jesus, living Bread which came down from Heaven,
Have mercy on us.
Jesus, Bread from Heaven giving life to the world,
Have mercy on us.
Jesus, hidden God and Saviour, *etc.*
Jesus, Who has loved us with an everlasting love,
Jesus, Whose delights are to be with the children of men,
Jesus, Who has given Thy Flesh for the life of the world,
Jesus, Who invites all to come to Thee,
Jesus, Who promises eternal life to those who receive Thee,
Jesus, Who with desire desires to eat this Pasch with us,
Jesus, ever ready to receive and welcome us,
Jesus, Who stands at our door knocking,
Jesus, Who has said that if we will open to Thee the door, Thou wilt come in and sup with us,

Jesus, Who receives us into Thy arms and blesses us
    with the little children,

Jesus, Who suffers us to sit at Thy feet with
    Magdalen,

Jesus, Who invites us to lean on Thy bosom with the
    beloved disciple,

Jesus, Who has not left us orphans,

Most dear Sacrament,

Sacrament of love,

Sacrament of sweetness,

Life-giving Sacrament,

Sacrament of strength,

My God and my all,

That our hearts may pant after Thee as the hart after
    the fountains of water, *we beseech Thee, hear us.*

That Thou wouldst manifest Thyself to us as to the
    two disciples in the breaking of bread, *we beseech*
    Thee, hear us.

That we may know Thy voice like Magdalen, *etc.*

That with a lively faith we may confess with the
    beloved disciple, "It is the Lord,"

That Thou wouldst bless us who have not seen and yet
    have believed,

That we may love Thee in the Blessed Sacrament with
    our whole heart, with our whole soul, with all our
    mind, and with all our strength,

That the fruit of each Communion may be fresh love,

That our one desire may be to love Thee and to do
    Thy will,

That we may ever remain in Thy love,

That Thou wouldst teach us how to receive and
    welcome Thee,

That Thou wouldst teach us to pray, and Thyself pray
    within us,

That with Thee every virtue may come into
    our souls,

That throughout this day Thou wouldst keep us
    closely united to Thee,

That Thou wouldst give us grace to persevere to the
　end,

That Thou wouldst then be our support and
　Viaticum,

That with Thee and leaning on Thee we may safely
　pass through all dangers,

That our last act may be one of perfect love and our
　last breath a long deep sigh to be in Our Father's
　house,

That Thy sweet face may smile upon us when we
　appear before Thee,

That our banishment from Thee, dearest Lord, may
　not be very long,

That when the time is come, we may fly up from our
　prison to Thee, and in Thy Sacred Heart find our
　rest forever,

Lamb of God, Who takest away the sins of the world,
　Spare us, O Lord.

Lamb of God, Who takest away the sins of the world,
　Graciously hear us, O Lord.

Lamb of God, Who takest away the sins of the world,
　Have mercy on us.

V. Stay with us, Lord, because it is toward evening,
R. *And the day is now far spent.*

Let Us Pray

We come to Thee, dear Lord, with the Apostles,
saying, "Increase our faith." Give us a strong and
lively faith in the mystery of Thy Real Presence in the
midst of us. Give us the splendid faith of the cen-
turion, which drew from Thee such praise. Give us
the faith of the beloved disciple to know Thee in the
dark and say, "It is the Lord!" Give us the faith of
Martha to confess, "Thou art the Christ, the Son of
the living God." Give us the faith of Magdalen to fall
at Thy feet crying, "Rabboni, Master." Give us the
faith of all Thy saints, to whom the Blessed Sacrament

has been Heaven begun on earth. In every Communion increase our faith; for with faith, love and humility and reverence and all good will come into our souls. Dearest Lord, increase our faith. R. *Amen.*

LITANY OF REPARATION
TO OUR LORD
IN THE BLESSED EUCHARIST
(For private use only.)

Lord, have mercy on us.
Christ, have mercy on us.
Lord, have mercy on us. Christ, hear us.
Christ, graciously hear us.
God the Father of Heaven,
Have mercy on us.
God the Son, Redeemer of the world,
Have mercy on us.
God the Holy Spirit,
Have mercy on us.
Holy Trinity, One God,
Have mercy on us.

Sacred Host, offered for the salvation of sinners,
Have mercy on us.
Sacred Host, annihilated on the altar for us and by us,
Have mercy on us.
Sacred Host, despised by lukewarm Christians, *etc.*
Sacred Host, mark of contradiction,
Sacred Host, delivered over to Jews and heretics,
Sacred Host, insulted by blasphemers,
Sacred Host, Bread of angels, given to animals,
Sacred Host, flung into the mud and trampled
  underfoot,
Sacred Host, dishonored by unfaithful priests,
Sacred Host, forgotten and abandoned in Thy
  churches,

Be merciful unto us,
Pardon us, O Lord.

Be merciful unto us,
  Hear us, O Lord.

For the outrageous contempt of this most wonderful
  Sacrament,
  We offer Thee our reparation.
For Thine extreme humiliation in Thine admirable
  Sacrament,
  We offer Thee our reparation.
For all unworthy Communions, *etc.*
For the irreverences of wicked Christians,
For the profanation of Thy sanctuaries,
For the holy ciboriums dishonored and carried away
  by force,
For the continual blasphemies of impious men,
For the obduracy and treachery of heretics,
For the unworthy conversations carried on in Thy
  holy temples,
For the profaners of Thy churches which they have
  desecrated by their sacrileges,

That it may please Thee to increase in all Christians
  the reverence due to this adorable Mystery, *we
  beseech Thee, hear us.*
That it may please Thee to manifest the Sacrament of
  Thy Love to heretics, *we beseech Thee, hear us.*
That it may please Thee to grant us the grace to atone
  for their hatred by our burning love for Thee, *etc.*
That it may please Thee that the insults of those who
  outrage Thee may rather be directed against
  ourselves,
That it may please Thee graciously to receive this our
  humble reparation,
That it may please Thee to make our adoration
  acceptable to Thee,

Pure Host, *hear our prayer.*
Holy Host, *hear our prayer.*
Immaculate Host, *hear our prayer.*

Lamb of God, Who takest away the sins of the world,
  Spare us, O Lord.
Lamb of God, Who takest away the sins of the world,
  Graciously hear us, O Lord.
Lamb of God, Who takest away the sins of the world,
  Have mercy on us.

Lord, have mercy on us.
  Christ, have mercy on us.

V. See, O Lord, our affliction,
R. *And give glory to Thy Holy Name.*

Let Us Pray

O Lord Jesus Christ, Who dost deign to remain with us in Thy wonderful Sacrament to the end of the world, in order to give to Thy Father, by the memory of Thy Passion, eternal glory, and to give to us the Bread of life everlasting: Grant us the grace to mourn, with a heart full of sorrow, over the injuries which Thou hast received in this adorable Mystery, and over the many sacrileges which are committed by the impious, by heretics and by bad Catholics.

Inflame us with an ardent zeal to repair all these insults to which, in Thine infinite mercy, Thou hast preferred to expose Thyself rather than deprive us of Thy Presence on our altars, Who with God the Father and the Holy Spirit livest and reignest one God, world without end. R. *Amen.*

LITANIES OF
THE CHILD JESUS

"And this shall be a sign unto you. You shall find the infant wrapped in swaddling clothes, and laid in a manger. And suddenly there was with the angel a multitude of the heavenly army, praising God, and saying: Glory to God in the highest; and on earth peace to men of good will."

—Luke *2:12-14*

LITANY OF THE
MIRACULOUS INFANT
OF PRAGUE

(For private use only.)

Lord, have mercy on us.
   Christ, have mercy on us.
Lord, have mercy on us. Christ, hear us.
   Christ, graciously hear us.
God the Father of Heaven,
   Have mercy on us.
God the Son, Redeemer of the world,
   Have mercy on us.
God the Holy Spirit,
   Have mercy on us.
Holy Trinity, One God,
   Have mercy on us.

O merciful Infant Jesus, *have mercy on us.*
O Infant Jesus, true God, *have mercy on us.*
O Infant Jesus, Whose omnipotence is shown in
   miracles, *etc.*
O Infant Jesus, Whose wisdom searches our hearts
   and minds,
O Infant Jesus, Whose kindness is ever ready to send
   us aid,
O Infant Jesus, Whose providence leads us to our
   final end,
O Infant Jesus, Whose truth enlightens the darkness
   of our hearts,
O Infant Jesus, Whose generosity enriches the poor,
O Infant Jesus, Whose friendship is comfort to the sad
   of heart,
O Infant Jesus, Whose mercy forgives the sins
   of men,

O Infant Jesus, Whose strength invigorates us,
O Infant Jesus, Whose power protects us from harm,
O Infant Jesus, Whose justice deters us
　　from evil,
O Infant Jesus, Whose power conquers Hell,
O Infant Jesus, Whose lovely image draws our hearts
　　and minds,
O Infant Jesus, Whose magnificence embraces the
　　entire world with Thy hand,
O Infant Jesus, Whose Heart aflame with love
　　enkindles our cold hearts,
O Infant Jesus, Whose outstretched little hand of
　　mercy fills us with all blessings,
O Infant Jesus, Whose sweetest and most holy Name
　　rejoices the hearts of the faithful,
O Infant Jesus, Whose glory fills all the world,

Be merciful, *spare us, O Infant Jesus.*
Be merciful, *hear us, O Infant Jesus.*

From all evil, *deliver us, O Infant Jesus.*
From all sin, *deliver us, O Infant Jesus.*
From all distrust of Thine infinite goodness, *etc.*
From all doubts about Thy miraculous power,
From all lukewarmness in worshiping Thee,
From all want and need,
By all the mysteries of Thy Holy Childhood,

We poor sinners pray to Thee, *hear us.*
Through the help of Mary, Thy Virgin Mother, and
　　Joseph, Thy foster father,
　　　We pray Thee, please hear us.
That Thou wouldst bring us to true repentance,
　　　We pray Thee, please hear us.
That Thou wouldst forgive us our sins, *etc.*
That Thou wouldst absolve us from punishment for
　　our sins,
That Thou wouldst preserve and increase in us love
　　and devotion to Thy holy Infancy,

That Thou wouldst never withdraw Thy merciful
hand from us,
That Thou wouldst keep us eternally grateful for the
many graces we have received,
That Thou wouldst move us more and more to love
Thy divine Heart,
That Thou wouldst graciously hear all who call upon
Thee with confidence,
That Thou wouldst preserve peace for our country,
That Thou wouldst deliver us fom any evil that
threatens us,
That Thou wouldst repay with eternal life those who
are generous toward Thee,
That Thou wouldst grant us blessings at the hour of
death,
That Thou wouldst pronounce a merciful sentence on
us at the Judgment,
That Thou wouldst remain our comfort through Thy
holy image,

Jesus, Son of God and holy Mary,
Hear us, we pray.

Lamb of God, Who takest away the sins of the world,
Spare us, O Infant Jesus.
Lamb of God, Who takest away the sins of the world,
Graciously hear us, O Infant Jesus.
Lamb of God, Who takest away the sins of the world,
Have mercy on us, O Infant Jesus.

V. Infant Jesus, hear us.
R. *Infant Jesus, graciously hear us.*

Our Father, *etc.*

Let Us Pray

O Miraculous Infant Jesus, prostrate before Thy
sacred image, we beseech Thee to look mercifully
upon our troubled hearts. Let Thy tender Heart, so in-

clined to pity, be softened at our prayers, and grant us that grace for which we ardently implore Thee. Take from us all affliction and despair, all trials and misfortunes with which we are laden. For Thy sacred Infancy's sake, hear our prayers and send us consolation and aid, that we may praise Thee, with the Father and the Holy Spirit, forever and ever. R. *Amen.*

LITANY OF THE
INFANT JESUS
(For private use only.)

Lord, have mercy on us.
Christ, have mercy on us.
Lord, have mercy on us. Jesus, hear us.
Jesus, graciously hear us.
God the Father of Heaven,
Have mercy on us.
God the Son, Redeemer of the world,
Have mercy on us.
God the Holy Spirit,
Have mercy on us.
Holy Trinity, One God,
Have mercy on us.

Infant, Jesus Christ,
Have mercy on us.
Infant, true God,
Have mercy on us.
Infant, Son of the living God, *etc.*
Infant, Son of the Virgin Mary,
Infant, strong in weakness,
Infant, powerful in tenderness,
Infant, Treasure of grace,
Infant, Fountain of love,
Infant, Renewer of the heavens,
Infant, Repairer of the evils of earth,
Infant, Head of the angels,
Infant, Root of the patriarchs,
Infant, Speech of prophets,
Infant, Desire of the Gentiles,
Infant, Joy of shepherds,
Infant, Light of the Magi,

59

Infant, Salvation of infants,
Infant, Expectation of the just,
Infant, Instructor of the wise,
Infant, First-fruit of all saints,

Be merciful, *spare us, O Infant Jesus.*
Be merciful, *graciously hear us, O Infant Jesus.*

From the slavery of the children of Adam,
    Infant Jesus, deliver us.
From the slavery of the devil,
    Infant Jesus, deliver us.
From the evil desires of the flesh, *etc.*
From the malice of the world,
From the pride of life,
From the inordinate desire of knowing,
From blindness of spirit,
From an evil will,
From our sins,
Through Thy most pure Conception,
Through Thy most humble Nativity,
Through Thy tears,
Through Thy most painful Circumcision,
Through Thy most glorious Epiphany,
Through Thy most pious Presentation,
Through Thy most divine life,
Through Thy poverty,
Through Thy many sufferings,
Through Thy labors and travels,

Lamb of God, Who takest away the sins of the world,
    Have mercy on us, O Infant Jesus.
Lamb of God, Who takest away the sins of the world,
    Graciously hear us, O Infant Jesus.
Lamb of God, Who takest away the sins of the world,
    Have mercy on us.

V. Jesus, Infant, hear us.
R. *Jesus, Infant, graciously hear us.*

Let Us Pray

O Lord Christ, Thou wert pleased so to humble Thyself in Thine incarnate divinity and most sacred humanity as to be born in time and become a little child. Grant that we may acknowledge infinite wisdom in the silence of a child, power in weakness, and majesty in humiliation. Adoring Thy humiliations on earth, may we contemplate Thy glories in Heaven, Who with the Father and the Holy Spirit livest and reignest forever. R. *Amen.*

LITANY OF THE
HOLY CHILDHOOD
OF JESUS

(For private use only.)

Lord, have mercy on us.
  Christ, have mercy on us.
Lord, have mercy on us. Christ hear us.
  Christ, graciously hear us.
God the Father of Heaven,
  Have mercy on us.
God the Son, Redeemer of the world,
  Have mercy on us.
God the Holy Spirit,
  Have mercy on us.
Holy Trinity, One God,
  Have mercy on us.

O Divine Infant Jesus, sent to earth from Heaven,
  Have mercy on us.
O Divine Infant Jesus, born of Mary in Bethlehem,
  Have mercy on us.
O Divine Infant Jesus, wrapped in swaddling clothes,
  etc.
O Divine Infant Jesus, placed in the crib,
O Divine Infant Jesus, praised by the angels,
O Divine Infant Jesus, adored by the shepherds,
O Divine Infant Jesus, proclaimed as Saviour through
  Thy adorable Name,
O Divine Infant Jesus, announced by the star,
O Divine Infant Jesus, worshipped by the Magi with
  symbolic gifts,
O Divine Infant Jesus, presented in the Temple by the
  Virgin,
O Divine Infant Jesus, embraced by the aged Simeon,

O Divine Infant Jesus, revealed in the Temple by the
   prophetess Anna,
O Divine Infant Jesus, persecuted by King Herod,
O Divine Infant Jesus, fleeing into the exile
   of Egypt,
O Divine Infant Jesus, crowning with martyrdom the
   infants of Bethlehem,
O Divine Infant Jesus, rejoicing the heart of Mary
   with Thy first words,
O Divine Infant Jesus, learning to take Thy first steps
   in exile,
O Divine Infant Jesus, returning from Egypt to be
   reared in Nazareth,
O Divine Infant Jesus, loved by all as a shining
   example of obedience,
O Divine Infant Jesus, brought to the Temple at the
   age of twelve,
O Divine Infant Jesus, lost by Mary and Joseph on
   their return home,
O Divine Infant Jesus, sought for three days with
   great sorrow,
O Divine Infant Jesus, found with great delight,

Be merciful, *O Jesus.*
Be merciful, *hear us, O Jesus.*

From all evil, *deliver us, O Jesus.*
From all sin, *deliver us, O Jesus.*
From misconduct in the Church, *etc.*
From quarrels and anger,
From lies and thievery,
From evil talk and bad example,
From bad habits,
By Thine Incarnation,
By Thy birth,
By Thy most bitter poverty,
By Thy persecution and sufferings,
Through the intercession of Thy most holy Mother,
Through the intercession of Thy holy foster father,

Through the intercession of the Holy Innocents,
Through the intercession of all the angels and saints,

We, Thy sinful children, *beseech Thee to hear us,*
Hear our prayer for the salvation of the unfortunate heathen, *we beseech Thee to hear us.*
With pity, *we beseech Thee to hear us.*
That Thou wouldst look kindly upon our small gifts, *etc.*
That Thou wouldst number the men of God among Thy saints,
That Thou wouldst richly bless their apostolic works,
That all the world may kneel before Thee,
That we may be zealous to convert all unbelievers, in the Name of Thy Holy Childhood,
That we may keep our baptismal vows faithfully,
That we may rejoice to be children of Thy Father in Heaven,
That we may ever honor and love our Father in Heaven,
That we may pray as Christian children, freely and devoutly,
That we may willingly obey Thy commandments,
That we may inscribe in our hearts the Fourth Commandment: "Honor thy father and thy mother,"
That we may grow in wisdom and virtue as we grow in years,
That Thou wilt keep us innocent,
That Thou wilt deliver us from temptation,
That Thou wilt instill in us great love and devotion for Thy Mother, Mary,
That we may never make an unworthy Confession,
That we may receive Holy Communion with sincerity,
That Thou wilt grant our parents a long life,
That Thou wilt grant them Thy best gifts,
That Thou wilt enlighten our pastors and give them strength,

That Thou wilt repay our benefactors with eternal
   gifts,
That Thou wilt have mercy upon the poor souls in
   Purgatory,

Lamb of God, Who takest away the sins of the world,
   Spare us, O Lord.
Lamb of God, Who takest away the sins of the world,
   Hear our prayer, O Lord.
Lamb of God, Who takest away the sins of the world,
   Have mercy on us, O Lord.

V. Christ, hear us.
R. *Christ, graciously hear us.*

Our Father, *etc.*

Let Us Pray

We pray to Thee, heavenly Father, Who for the Infant Jesus' sake adopted us as Thy children and as
heirs of Heaven, look kindly upon children not of the
Faith and let them participate in our unearned and
priceless fortune. We ask this through the Infant Jesus
Christ, Thy Son Our Lord, Who liveth and reigneth
with Thee and the Holy Spirit forever and ever. R.
Amen.

Some of the invocations in this litany are especially suited to
children.

LITANIES OF
THE HOLY SPIRIT

"But the Paraclete, the Holy Ghost, whom the Father will send in my name, he will teach you all things, and bring all things to your mind, whatsoever I shall have said to you."

—John *14:26*

LITANY OF THE HOLY SPIRIT
Litany One
(For private use only.)

Lord, have mercy on us.
Christ, have mercy on us.
Lord, have mercy on us. Father all powerful,
Have mercy on us.
Jesus, Eternal Son of the Father, Redeemer of the
world,
Save us.
Spirit of the Father and the Son, boundless
Life of both,
Sanctify us.
Holy Trinity,
Hear us.

Holy Spirit, Who proceedest from the Father and the
Son, *enter our hearts.*
Holy Spirit, Who art equal to the Father and the Son,
enter our hearts.
Promise of God the Father, *have mercy on us.*
Ray of heavenly light, *have mercy on us.*
Author of all good, *etc.*
Source of heavenly water,
Consuming Fire,
Ardent Charity,
Spiritual Unction,
Spirit of love and truth,
Spirit of wisdom and understanding,
Spirit of counsel and fortitude,
Spirit of knowledge and piety,
Spirit of the fear of the Lord,
Spirit of grace and prayer,
Spirit of peace and meekness,
Spirit of modesty and innocence,

Holy Spirit, the Comforter,
Holy Spirit, the Sanctifier,
Holy Spirit, Who governest the Church,
Gift of God the Most High,
Spirit Who fillest the universe,
Spirit of the adoption of the children of God,

Holy Spirit, *inspire us with horror of sin.*
Holy Spirit, *come and renew the face of the earth.*
Holy Spirit, *shed Thy light into our souls.*
Holy Spirit, *engrave Thy law in our hearts.*
Holy Spirit, *inflame us with the flame of Thy love.*
Holy Spirit, *open to us the treasures of Thy graces.*
Holy Spirit, *teach us to pray well.*
Holy Spirit, *enlighten us with Thy heavenly
    inspirations.*
Holy Spirit, *lead us in the way of salvation.*
Holy Spirit, *grant us the only necessary knowledge.*
Holy Spirit, *inspire in us the practice of good.*
Holy Spirit, *grant us the merits of all virtues.*
Holy Spirit, *make us persevere in justice.*
Holy Spirit, *be our everlasting reward.*

Lamb of God, Who takest away the sins of the world,
    Send us Thy Holy Spirit.
Lamb of God, Who takest away the sins of the world,
    Pour down into our souls the gifts of the Holy Spirit.
Lamb of God, Who takest away the sins of the world,
    Grant us the Spirit of wisdom and piety.

V. Come, Holy Spirit! Fill the hearts of Thy faithful,
R. *And enkindle in them the fire of Thy love.*

Let Us Pray

Grant, O merciful Father, that Thy Divine Spirit may enlighten, inflame and purify us, that He may penetrate us with His heavenly dew and make us fruitful in good works, through Our Lord Jesus Christ, Thy Son, Who with Thee, in the unity of the same Spirit, liveth and reigneth forever and ever. R. *Amen.*

LITANY OF THE HOLY SPIRIT
Litany Two
(For private use only.)

Lord, have mercy on us.
  Christ, have mercy on us.
Lord, have mercy on us. God the Father of Heaven,
  Have mercy on us.
God the Son, Redeemer of the world,
  Have mercy on us.
God the Holy Spirit,
  Have mercy on us.
Holy Trinity, One God,
  Have mercy on us.

Divine Essence, one true God,
  Have mercy on us.
Spirit of truth and wisdom,
  Have mercy on us.
Spirit of holiness and justice, *etc.*
Spirit of understanding and counsel,
Spirit of love and joy,
Spirit of peace and patience,
Spirit of longanimity and meekness,
Spirit of benignity and goodness,
Love substantial of the Father and the Son,
Love and life of saintly souls,
Fire ever burning,
Living water to quench the thirst of hearts,

From all evil, *deliver us, O Holy Spirit.*
From all impurity of soul and body, *deliver us, O Holy Spirit.*
From all gluttony and sensuality, *etc.*
From all attachments to the things of the earth,

From all hypocrisy and pretence,
From all imperfections and deliberate faults,
From self-love and self-judgment,
From our own will,
From slander,
From deceiving our neighbors,
From our passions and disorderly appetites,
From our inattentiveness to Thy holy inspirations,
From despising little things,
From debauchery and malice,
From love of comfort and luxury,
From wishing to seek or desire anything other than
    Thee,
From everything that displeases Thee,

Most loving Father, *forgive us.*
Divine Word, *have pity on us.*
Holy and divine Spirit, *leave us not until we are in
    possession of the Divine Essence, Heaven of
    heavens.*

Lamb of God, Who takest away the sins of the world,
    Send us the divine Consoler.
Lamb of God, Who takest away the sins of the world,
    Fill us with the gifts of Thy Spirit.
Lamb of God, Who takest away the sins of the world,
    Make the fruits of the Holy Spirit increase within us.

Come, O Holy Spirit, fill the hearts of Thy faithful,
    And enkindle in them the fire of Thy love.
Send forth Thy Spirit and they shall be created,
    And Thou shalt renew the face of the earth.

Let Us Pray

O God, Who by the light of the Holy Spirit didst instruct the hearts of the faithful, grant us by the same
Spirit to be truly wise and ever to rejoice in His consolation. Through Jesus Christ Our Lord. R. *Amen.*

LITANY OF THE HOLY SPIRIT
Litany Three
(For private use only.)

God the Eternal Father,
Bless me, I adore Thee.
God the Eternal Son,
Bless me, I adore Thee.
God the Eternal Spirit,
Bless me, I adore Thee.

Teach me to live for the glory of the
Eternal Trinity alone.
Amen.

Blessed Mother Mary, Virgin spouse of the Holy
Ghost, intercede for me that I may obtain through
thy intercession the graces I desire through this
litany, which I offer to thy Divine Spouse by thy
Immaculate Heart.
Amen.

Holy Spirit, Who created me,
I thank Thee.
Holy Spirit, Who redeemed me,
I thank Thee.
Holy Spirit, Who sanctified me,
I thank Thee.

Holy Spirit of God,
I adore Thee.
Holy Spirit, without Whom the Father and the Son do
nothing in Heaven or on earth,
I adore Thee.
Holy Spirit, Who in the beginning moved over the
waters, *etc.*

Holy Spirit, Who made Mary immaculate,
Holy Spirit, by Whom the Mystery of the Incarnation was accomplished,
Holy Spirit, Source of all holiness,
Holy Spirit, Who made me a child of God,
Holy Spirit, Who made me a soldier of God,
(Holy Spirit, Who made me a religious of God,)
Holy Spirit, Who wishes to make me a saint of God,
Holy Spirit, Source of my every good thought,
Holy Spirit, Inspirer of my every good word,
Holy Spirit, Spring of my every good action,
Holy Spirit, Who dwellest in the bosom of the Father,
Holy Spirit, Who dwellest in the bosom of Jesus,
Holy Spirit, Who dwellest in the heart of Mary,
Holy Spirit, Who dwellest in the Church,
Holy Spirit, Who dwellest in the souls of the faithful,
Holy Spirit, Who dwellest in my unworthy heart,
(Holy Spirit, Who speaketh to me through my superiors,)
Holy Spirit, Who hast been so patient with me,
Holy Spirit, Who hast been so forgiving to me,
Holy Spirit, Who hast inspired my contrition,
Holy Spirit, Who hast inspired my resolutions,
Holy Spirit, Light of my mind,
Holy Spirit, Strength of my will,
Holy Spirit, Sweetness of my heart,
Holy Spirit, Divine Guardian of my virtue,
Holy Spirit, my Beginning,
Holy Spirit, my Last End,
Holy Spirit, without Whom I can do nothing,
Holy Spirit, without Whom I desire to do nothing,
Holy Spirit, Who leadest me to Jesus,
Holy Spirit, Who bringest the Father and Jesus to me,
Holy Spirit, my God and my all,
Holy Spirit, Who hast set a seal upon my soul,
Holy Spirit, Who protectest me at this moment,
Holy Spirit, Who watchest over me whether I wake or sleep,
Holy Spirit, Who keepest my soul in life,

Holy Spirit, Who wilt claim my soul in death,

Holy Spirit, my Eternal Love,
  I thank Thee.
Holy Spirit, my Eternal Love,
  I adore Thee.
Holy Spirit, my Eternal Love,
  I love Thee.

Lamb of God, Who takest away the sins of the world,
  Pour down Thy Spirit upon us, O Lord.
Lamb of God, Who takest away the sins of the world,
  Pour down Thy Spirit upon us, O Lord.
Lamb of God, Who takest away the sins of the world,
  Pour down Thy Spirit upon us, O Lord.

V. Pray for us, sweet spouse of the Holy Ghost,
R. *That we may be more worthy of His indwelling.*

Let Us Pray

O Sweet Holy Spirit, Who dwellest as the Bond of Love in the Adorable Unity of the Eternal Trinity, dwell evermore in our souls; grant that we may never more grieve Thee, but that we may be ever docile to Thine inspirations; and in the unutterable condescension of Thy love, fulfill the desire of Our Sweet Jesus that we should be one in Him as He is in His Father, Thou Who livest and reignest with Them, One Eternal Lord and God, world without end. R. *Amen.*

The invocations in parentheses are for use by members of religious orders.

LITANIES OF THE
BLESSED VIRGIN MARY

*"And the angel being come in, said
unto her: Hail, full of grace, the Lord is
with thee: blessed art thou among
women."*

—Luke *1:28*

THE LITANY OF THE BLESSED VIRGIN MARY
(The Litany of Loreto)
(For public or private use.)

Lord, have mercy on us.
  Christ, have mercy on us.
Lord, have mercy on us. Christ, hear us.
  Christ, graciously hear us.
God the Father of Heaven,
  Have mercy on us.
God the Son, Redeemer of the world,
  Have mercy on us.
God the Holy Spirit,
  Have mercy on us.
Holy Trinity, One God,
  Have mercy on us.

Holy Mary, *pray for us.*
Holy Mother of God, *pray for us.*
Holy Virgin of virgins, *etc.*
Mother of Christ,
Mother of divine grace,
Mother most pure,
Mother most chaste,
Mother inviolate,
Mother undefiled,
Mother most amiable,
Mother most admirable,
Mother of good counsel,
Mother of our Creator,
Mother of our Saviour,
Mother of the Church,
Virgin most prudent,
Virgin most venerable,

Virgin most renowned,
Virgin most powerful,
Virgin most merciful,
Virgin most faithful,
Mirror of justice,
Seat of wisdom,
Cause of our joy,
Spiritual vessel,
Vessel of honor,
Singular vessel of devotion,
Mystical rose,
Tower of David,
Tower of ivory,
House of gold,
Ark of the covenant,
Gate of Heaven,
Morning star,
Health of the sick,
Refuge of sinners,
Comforter of the afflicted,
Help of Christians,
Queen of angels,
Queen of patriarchs,
Queen of prophets,
Queen of apostles,
Queen of martyrs,
Queen of confessors,
Queen of virgins,
Queen of all saints,
Queen conceived without Original Sin,
Queen assumed into Heaven,
Queen of the most holy Rosary,
Queen of peace,

Lamb of God, Who takest away the sins of the world,
    Spare us, O Lord.
Lamb of God, Who takest away the sins of the world,
    Graciously hear us, O Lord.

Lamb of God, Who takest away the sins of the world,
Have mercy on us.

V. Pray for us, O holy Mother of God,
R. *That we may be made worthy of the promises of Christ.*

Let Us Pray

Grant, we beseech Thee, O Lord God, that we Thy servants may enjoy perpetual health of mind and body, and by the glorious intercession of the Blessed Mary, ever Virgin, be delivered from present sorrow and enjoy everlasting happiness. Through Christ Our Lord. R. *Amen.*

LITANY OF THE
HOLY NAME OF MARY
(For private use only.)

Lord, have mercy.
   Lord, have mercy.
Christ, have mercy.
   Christ, have mercy.
Lord, have mercy.
   Lord, have mercy.
Son of Mary, hear us.
   Son of Mary, graciously hear us.
Heavenly Father, of Whom Mary is the Daughter,
   Have mercy on us.
Eternal Word, of Whom Mary is the Mother,
   Have mercy on us.
Holy Spirit, of Whom Mary is the spouse,
   Have mercy on us.
Divine Trinity, of Whom Mary is the Handmaid,
   Have mercy on us.

Mary, Mother of the Living God, *pray for us.*
Mary, daughter of the Light Eternal, *pray for us.*
Mary, our light, *etc.*
Mary, our sister,
Mary, flower of Jesse,
Mary, issue of kings,
Mary, chief work of God,
Mary, the beloved of God,
Mary, Immaculate Virgin,
Mary, all fair,
Mary, light in darkness,
Mary, our sure rest,
Mary, house of God,
Mary, sanctuary of the Lord,

Mary, altar of the Divinity,
Mary, Virgin Mother,
Mary, embracing thy Infant God,
Mary, reposing with Eternal Wisdom,
Mary, ocean of bitterness,
Mary, Star of the Sea,
Mary, suffering with thine only Son,
Mary, pierced with a sword of sorrow,
Mary, torn with a cruel wound,
Mary, sorrowful even to death,
Mary, bereft of all consolation,
Mary, submissive to the law of God,
Mary, standing by the Cross of Jesus,
Mary, Our Lady,
Mary, Our Queen,
Mary, Queen of glory,
Mary, glory of the Church Triumphant,
Mary, Blessed Queen,
Mary, advocate of the Church Militant,
Mary, Queen of Mercy,
Mary, consoler of the Church Suffering,
Mary, exalted above the angels,
Mary, crowned with twelve stars,
Mary, fair as the moon,
Mary, bright as the sun,
Mary, distinguished above all,
Mary, seated at the right hand of Jesus,
Mary, our hope,
Mary, our sweetness,
Mary, glory of Jerusalem,
Mary, joy of Israel,
Mary, honor of our people,
Mary, Our Lady of the Immaculate Conception,
Mary, Our Lady of the Assumption,
Mary, Our Lady of Loreto,
Mary, Our Lady of Lourdes,
Mary, Our Lady of Fatima,
Mary, Our Lady of Czestochowa,
Mary, Our Lady of the Miraculous Medal,

Mary, Our Lady of Mount Carmel,
Mary, Our Lady of the Angels,
Mary, Our Lady of Dolors,
Mary, Our Lady of Mercy,
Mary, Our Lady of the Rosary,
Mary, Our Lady of Victory,
Mary, Our Lady of La Trappe,
Mary, Our Lady of Divine Providence,

Lamb of God, Who takest away the sins of the world,
Spare us, O Lord Jesus.
Lamb of God, Who takest away the sins of the world,
Graciously hear us, O Lord Jesus.
Lamb of God, Who takest away the sins of the world,
Have mercy on us, O Lord Jesus.

Son of Mary, hear us.
Son of Mary, graciously hear us.

V. I will declare thy name unto my brethren.
R. *I will praise thee in the assembly of the faithful.*

Let Us Pray

O Almighty God, Who beholdest Thy servants earnestly desirous of placing themselves under the shadow of the name and protection of the Most Holy Virgin Mary, vouchsafe, we beseech Thee, that by her charitable intercession, we may be delivered from all evil on earth, and may arrive at everlasting joys in Heaven, through Jesus Christ Our Lord. R. *Amen.*

LITANY OF THE
LIFE OF MARY
(For private use only.)

Lord, have mercy.
  Christ, have mercy.
Lord, have mercy. Christ, hear us.
  Christ, graciously hear us.
God the Father of Heaven,
  Have mercy on us.
God the Son, Redeemer of the world,
  Have mercy on us.
God the Holy Ghost, dwelling in the souls of the just,
  Have mercy on us.
Holy Trinity, One God,
  Have mercy on us.

Holy Mary, *pray for us.*
Holy Virgin, sprung from the race of David,
  pray for us.
Holy Virgin, of the root of Jesse, *etc.*
Holy Virgin, conceived without Original Sin,
Holy Virgin, presented in childhood in the temple,
Holy Virgin, espoused to the just Joseph,
Holy Virgin, bound by an inviolable vow of chastity,
Holy Virgin, gloriously saluted by the Angel,
Holy Virgin, full of grace,
Holy Virgin, blessed among all women,
Holy Virgin, consenting to the plea of Heaven,
Holy Virgin, conceiving by the operation of the Holy
  Ghost,
Holy Virgin, bearing in thy womb the Man-God,
Holy Virgin, Mother of the Lord,
Holy Virgin, Mother of the true Solomon,
Holy Virgin, Mother of God,

Holy Virgin, visiting thy cousin Elizabeth,

Holy Virgin, blest land, whence sprung the Saviour,

Holy Virgin, holy gate, through which the King of Heaven alone may pass,

Holy Virgin, journeying to Bethlehem with thy spouse Joseph,

Holy Virgin, bringing into the world thy Divine Son,

Holy Virgin, Mother of thine own Creator,

Holy Virgin, laying God the Son in a manger,

Holy Virgin, visited by the shepherds,

Holy Virgin, saluted by the Magi,

Holy Virgin, presenting thy Son to be circumcized,

Holy Virgin, submitting to the law of purification,

Holy Virgin, offering thy dear Son in the temple,

Holy Virgin, flying into Egypt to save thy Child,

Holy Virgin, returning into the land of Israel,

Holy Virgin, leading an obscure life at Nazareth,

Holy Virgin, keeping the feasts prescribed by the law,

Holy Virgin, afflicted at the loss of thy Child, when He was twelve years old,

Holy Virgin, sorrowfully seeking thy Child for three days,

Holy Virgin, honoring with thy presence the marriage feast of Cana,

Holy Virgin, graciously representing to thy Son the want of wine,

Holy Virgin, obtaining Christ's first public miracle by thy intercession,

Holy Virgin, following thy Son in His ministrations,

Holy Virgin, sharing the sorrows of thy Son,

Holy Virgin, standing at the foot of the Cross,

Holy Virgin, confided by thy Son to John the Beloved Disciple,

Holy Virgin, pierced with a sword of sorrow,

Holy Virgin, filled with the Holy Spirit on the day of Pentecost,

Holy Virgin, assumed by thy Son into Heaven,

Holy Virgin, reigning in Heaven, our Queen,

Holy Virgin, called Blessed by all generations,

Lamb of God, Who takest away the sins of the world,
Spare us, O Lord.
Lamb of God, Who takest away the sins of the world,
Graciously hear us, O Lord.
Lamb of God, Who takest away the sins of the world,
Have mercy on us.

V. Pray for us, O Holy Mother of God,
R. *That we may be made worthy of the promises of Christ.*

Let Us Pray

Protect, O Lord, Thy servants by Thy gracious and abundant help, and grant that our confidence in the protection of Blessed Mary ever Virgin, and our humble imitation of her holy life, may obtain for us security against all enemies and all dangers, through Our Lord Jesus Christ. R. *Amen.*

LITANY OF THE
IMMACULATE HEART OF MARY
Litany One
(For private use only.)

Lord, have mercy on us.
Christ, have mercy on us.
Lord, have mercy on us. Christ, hear us.
Christ, graciously hear us.
God the Father of Heaven,
Have mercy on us.
God the Son, Redeemer of the world,
Have mercy on us.
God the Holy Ghost,
Have mercy on us.
Holy Trinity, One God,
Have mercy on us.

Heart of Mary, *pray for us.*
Heart of Mary, like unto the Heart of God,
pray for us.
Heart of Mary, united to the Heart of Jesus, *etc.*
Heart of Mary, instrument of the Holy Ghost,
Heart of Mary, sanctuary of the Divine Trinity,
Heart of Mary, tabernacle of God Incarnate,
Heart of Mary, immaculate from thy creation,
Heart of Mary, full of grace,
Heart of Mary, blessed among all hearts,
Heart of Mary, throne of glory,
Heart of Mary, most humble,
Heart of Mary, holocaust of Divine Love,
Heart of Mary, fastened to the Cross with Jesus
    Crucified,
Heart of Mary, comfort of the afflicted,
Heart of Mary, refuge of sinners,
Heart of Mary, hope of the agonizing,

Heart of Mary, seat of mercy,

Lamb of God, Who takest away the sins of the world,
 Spare us, O Lord.
Lamb of God, Who takest away the sins of the world,
 Graciously hear us, O Lord.
Lamb of God, Who takest away the sins of the world,
 Have mercy on us.

Christ, hear us.
 Christ, graciously hear us.

V. Immaculate Mary, meek and humble of heart,
R. *Make our hearts like unto the Heart of Jesus.*

Let Us Pray

O most merciful God, Who, for the salvation of sinners and the refuge of the miserable, wast pleased that the Most Pure Heart of Mary should be most like in charity and pity to the Divine Heart of Thy Son, Jesus Christ, grant that we who commemorate this sweet and loving Heart may, by the merits and intercession of the same Blessed Virgin, merit to be found like to the Heart of Jesus, through the same Christ Our Lord.
R. *Amen.*

This litany was composed by John Henry (Cardinal) Newman shortly after he converted to Catholicism in 1845.

LITANY OF THE
IMMACULATE HEART OF MARY
Litany Two

(For private use only.)

Immaculate Heart of Mary,
Pray for our dear country.
Immaculate Heart of Mary,
Sanctify our clergy.
Immaculate Heart of Mary,
Make our Catholics more fervent.
Immaculate Heart of Mary,
Guide and inspire those who govern us.
Immaculate Heart of Mary,
Cure the sick who confide in thee.
Immaculate Heart of Mary,
Console the sorrowful who trust in thee.
Immaculate Heart of Mary,
Help those who invoke thine aid.
Immaculate Heart of Mary,
Deliver us from all dangers.
Immaculate Heart of Mary,
Help us to resist temptations.
Immaculate Heart of Mary,
Obtain for us all we lovingly ask of thee.
Immaculate Heart of Mary,
Make our family life holy.
Immaculate Heart of Mary,
Help those who are dear to us.
Immaculate Heart of Mary,
Bring back to the right road our erring brothers.
Immaculate Heart of Mary,
Give us back our ancient fervor.
Immaculate Heart of Mary,
Obtain for us pardon of our manifold sins and offenses.

Immaculate Heart of Mary,
  Bring all men to the feet of thy Divine Child.
Immaculate Heart of Mary,
  Obtain peace for the world.

Let Us Pray

O God of infinite goodness and mercy, fill our hearts with a great confidence in our Most Holy Mother, whom we invoke under the title of the Immaculate Heart of Mary, and grant us by her most powerful intercession all the graces, spiritual and temporal, which we need. Through Christ Our Lord. R. *Amen.*

LITANY OF THE
BLESSED VIRGIN MARY,
MEDIATRIX OF ALL GRACES
(For private use only.)

Lord, have mercy on us.
   Christ, have mercy on us.
Lord, have mercy on us. Christ, hear us.
   Christ, graciously hear us.
God the Father of Heaven,
   Have mercy on us.
God the Son, Redeemer of the world,
   Have mercy on us.
God the Holy Ghost,
   Have mercy on us.
Holy Trinity, One God,
   Have mercy on us.

Holy Mary, *pray for us.*
Mother of God, and our Mother, *pray for us.*
True Mother of the living, *etc.*
Mother regenerating men in Christ unto God,
Mother of piety and of grace,
Mother of pardon and remission,
Partner in human redemption,
Recoverer of a lost world,
Restorer of the ages,
Petitioner of all graces,
Suppliant all-powerful,
Advocate with thy Son for thy sons,
Obtainer of the divine mercy,
Dispenser of heavenly treasures,
Handmaid of divine blessings,
Fullness of grace to overflow upon all,
Succor of the Church Militant,

Ready helper of those in peril,
Devoted consoler of the sorrowful,
Conqueress of all error,
Protectress of the world,
Impregnable protection,
Propitiation of the divine wrath,
Refuge of all the unhappy,
Shelter of orphans,
Assured safety of the faithful,
Hope of all who despair,
Stay of the falling,
Uplifter of the fallen,
Cheer and comfort of the dying,
Peace and joy of mankind,
Our life, our sweetness and our hope,
Gate of Paradise,
Mystical stair of Jacob,
Key of the heavenly kingdom,
Channel of divine graces,
Throne of divine clemency,
Fountain of living waters,
Fountain sealed by the Holy Spirit,
Unfailing stream of mercy,
Asylum of the erring,
Haven of the shipwrecked,
Shining star of the sea,
Light of those who sit in darkness,
Chamber of spiritual nuptials,
Mediatrix of men with God,
Mediatrix after the Mediator,
Mediatrix reconciling us to the Son,
Mediatrix of sinners, staunch and true,
Mediatrix of all beneath the sky,
Mediatrix ever pleading for us,
Mediatrix set between Christ and His Church,
Mediatrix who hast found favor with God,
Mediatrix to win salvation for the world,
Mediatrix of the mysteries of God,
Mediatrix of all graces,

Lamb of God, Who takest away the sins of the world,
Spare us, O Lord.
Lamb of God, Who takest away the sins of the world,
Graciously hear us, O Lord.
Lamb of God, Who takest away the sins of the world,
Have mercy on us, O Lord.

V. Pray for us, our powerful Mediatrix,
R. *That we may be made worthy of the promises of Christ.*

Let Us Pray

O Lord Jesus Christ, our Mediator with the Father, Who hast deigned to appoint the Blessed Virgin, Thy Mother, to be our Mother also and our Mediatrix with Thee, graciously grant that whosoever goes to Thee in quest of blessings may be gladdened by obtaining them all through her, Thou Who livest and reignest with the Father and the Holy Ghost, ever one God, world without end. R. *Amen.*

LITANY OF
OUR LADY OF PERPETUAL HELP
(For private use only.)

Lord, have mercy on us.
Christ, have mercy on us.
Lord, have mercy on us. Christ, hear us.
Christ, graciously hear us.
God the Father of Heaven,
Have mercy on us.
God the Son, Redeemer of the world,
Have mercy on us.
God the Holy Ghost,
Have mercy on us.
Holy Trinity, One God,
Have mercy on us.

Holy Mary, *pray for us.*
Holy Mother of God, *pray for us.*
Holy Virgin of virgins, *etc.*
Mother of Christ,
Queen conceived without the stain
  of Original Sin,
Queen of the most Holy Rosary,
Our Lady of Perpetual Help,

O Mother of Perpetual Help, whose very name
  inspires confidence,
Come to my aid, O loving Mother.
That I may love God with all my heart,
Come to my aid, O loving Mother.
That I may in all things conform my will to that of thy
  Divine Son, *etc.*
That I may always shun sin, the only real evil,
That I may always remember my last end,

That I may often and devoutly receive the
Sacraments,

That I may avoid every proximate occasion of sin,

That I may never neglect prayer,

That I may ever remember to invoke thee,
particularly in time of temptation,

That I may always be victorious in the hour of
temptation,

That I may generously pardon my enemies,

That I may arise quickly, should I have the
misfortune of falling into mortal sin,

That I may courageously resist the seductions of evil
companions,

That I may be strong against my own inconstancy,

That I may not delay my conversion from day to day,

That I may labor zealously to eradicate my evil
habits,

That I may ever love to serve thee,

That I may lead others to love and serve thee,

That I may live and die in the friendship of God,

In all necessities of body and soul,

In sickness and pain,

In poverty and distress,

In persecution and abandonment,

In grief and dereliction of mind,

In time of war, famine and contagion,

In every danger of sin,

When assailed by the evil spirits,

When tempted by the allurements of a deceitful world,

When struggling against the inclinations of my
corrupt nature,

When tempted against the holy virtue of purity,

When death is nigh,

When the loss of my senses shall warn me that my
earthly career is at an end,

When the thought of my approaching dissolution shall
fill me with fear and terror,

When at the decisive hour of death, the evil spirit will
endeavor to plunge my soul into despair,

When the priest of God shall give me his last
   absolution and his last blessing,

When my friends and relations, surrounding my bed,
   moved with compassion, shall invoke thy clemency
   on my behalf,

When the world will vanish from my sight, and my
   heart will cease to beat,

When I shall yield my soul into the hands of its
   Creator,

When my soul will appear before its Sovereign Judge,

When the irrevocable sentence will be pronounced,

When I will be suffering in Purgatory, and sighing for
   the vision of God,

Lamb of God, Who takest away the sins of the world,
   Spare us, O Lord.

Lamb of God, Who takest away the sins of the world,
   Graciously hear us, O Lord.

Lamb of God, Who takest away the sins of the world,
   Have mercy on us.

Let Us Pray

O Almighty and merciful God, Who, in order to
succor the human race, hast willed the Blessed Virgin
Mary to become the Mother of Thy only-begotten
Son, grant, we beseech Thee, that by her intercession
we may avoid the contagion of sin and serve Thee
with a pure heart, through the same Christ Our Lord.
R. *Amen.*

LITANY OF
OUR LADY OF GOOD COUNSEL

(For private use only.)

Lord, have mercy on us.
  Christ, have mercy on us.
Lord, have mercy on us. Christ, hear us.
  Christ, graciously hear us.
God the Father of Heaven,
  Have mercy on us.
God the Son, Redeemer of the world,
  Have mercy on us.
God the Holy Ghost,
  Have mercy on us.
Holy Trinity, One God,
  Have mercy on us.

Beloved Daughter of the Eternal Father, *pray for us.*
August Mother of God the Son, *pray for us.*
Blessed Spouse of God the Holy Ghost, *etc.*
Living temple of the Holy Trinity,
Queen of Heaven and earth,
Seat of Divine wisdom,
Depositary of the secrets of the Most High,
Virgin most prudent,
In our doubts and difficulties,
In our tribulations and anguish,
In our discouragements,
In perils and temptations,
In all our undertakings,
In all our needs,
At the hour of death,
By thine Immaculate Conception,
By thy happy nativity,
By thine admirable presentation,

By thy glorious Annunciation,
By thy charitable Visitation,
By thy Divine Maternity,
By thy holy Purification,
By the sorrows and anguish of thy maternal heart,
By thy precious death,
By thy triumphant Assumption,

Lamb of God, Who takest away the sins of the world,
Spare us, O Lord.
Lamb of God, Who takest away the sins of the world,
Graciously hear us, O Lord.
Lamb of God, Who takest away the sins of the world,
Have mercy on us.

V. Pray for us, O holy Mother of God,
R. *And obtain for us the gift of good counsel.*

Let Us Pray

Lord Jesus, Author and Dispenser of all good, Who in becoming incarnate in the womb of the Blessed Virgin hast communicated to her lights above those of all the heavenly intelligences, grant that in honoring her under the title of Our Lady of Good Counsel, we may merit always to receive from her goodness counsels of wisdom and salvation, which will conduct us to the port of a blessed eternity. R. *Amen.*

LITANY OF THE
SORROWFUL MOTHER

(For private use only.)

Lord, have mercy on us.
  Christ, have mercy on us.
Lord, have mercy on us. Christ, hear us.
  Christ, graciously hear us.
God the Father of Heaven,
  Have mercy on us.
God the Son, Redeemer of the world,
  Have mercy on us.
God the Holy Ghost,
  Have mercy on us.
Holy Trinity, One God,
  Have mercy on us.

Holy Mary, conceived without sin,
  Pray for us.
Holy Mother of God,
  Pray for us.
Mother of Christ, *etc.*
Mother of Our Saviour Crucified,
Mother most Sorrowful,
Mother most tearful,
Mother most afflicted,
Mother most lonely,
Mother most desolate,
Mother pierced by the sword of sorrow,
Queen of martyrs,
Comfort of the sorrowful,
Help of the needy,
Protectress of the forsaken,
Support of widows and orphans,
Health of the sick,

100

Hope of the troubled,
Haven of the ship-wrecked,
Refuge of sinners,
Hope of the despairing,
Mother of mercy,

Through thy poverty in the stable of Bethlehem,
Through thy sorrow at the prophecy of Simeon,
Through thy sad flight into Egypt,
Through thy anxiety when seeking thy lost Child,
Through thy grief when seeing thy divine Son
    persecuted,
Through thy fear and anxiety when Jesus was
    apprehended,
Through thy pain caused by the treason of Judas and
    the denial of Peter,
Through thy sad meeting with Jesus on the way of the
    Cross,
Through the tortures of thy loving Heart at the
    Crucifixion of Jesus,
Through thy agony at the death of Jesus,
Through the sword of sorrow that pierced thy heart
    when the side of Jesus was transfixed by the lance,
Through thy lamentations over the dead Body of thy
    divine Son lying on thy bosom,
Through thy deep mourning at His tomb,
Through thy desolation after the burial of Jesus,
Through the tears thou didst shed for
    thy beloved Son,
Through thy wonderful resignation to the will of God
    in all thy sufferings,

O Queen of peace,
In all our tribulations,
In our illnesses and pains,
In our sorrows and afflictions,
In our need and destitution,
In our fears and dangers,
In the hour of our death,

On the Day of Judgment,

Lamb of God, Who takest away the sins of the world,
  Spare us, O Lord.
Lamb of God, Who takest away the sins of the world,
  Graciously hear us, O Lord.
Lamb of God, Who takest away the sins of the world,
  Have mercy on us, O Lord.

V. Pray for us, O Sorrowful Virgin,
R. *That we may be made worthy of the promises of Christ.*

Let Us Pray

We beseech Thee, O Lord Jesus Christ, let Thy Mother, the Blessed Virgin Mary, whose holy soul was pierced by a sword of sorrow at the hour of Thy Passion, implore Thy mercy for us, both now and at the hour of our death, Who livest and reignest, world without end. R. *Amen.*

LITANY OF
OUR LADY OF SORROWS

(For private use only.)

Lord, have mercy on us.
  Christ, have mercy on us.
Lord, have mercy on us. Christ, hear us.
  Christ, graciously hear us.
God the Father of Heaven,
  Have mercy on us.
God the Son, Redeemer of the world,
  Have mercy on us.
God the Holy Spirit,
  Have mercy on us.
Holy Trinity, One God,
  Have mercy on us.

Holy Mary,
  Pray for us.
Holy Mother of God,
  Pray for us.
Holy Virgin of virgins, *etc.*
Mother crucified,
Mother sorrowful,
Mother tearful,
Mother afflicted,
Mother forsaken,
Mother desolate,
Mother bereft of thy Child,
Mother transfixed with the sword,
Mother consumed with grief,
Mother filled with anguish,
Mother crucified in heart,
Mother most sad,
Fountain of tears,

Abyss of suffering,
Mirror of patience,
Rock of constancy,
Anchor of confidence,
Refuge of the forsaken,
Shield of the oppressed,
Subduer of the unbelieving,
Comfort of the afflicted,
Medicine of the sick,
Strength of the weak,
Harbor of the wrecked,
Allayer of tempests,
Resource of mourners,
Terror of the treacherous,
Treasure of the faithful,
Eye of the Prophets,
Staff of the Apostles,
Crown of martyrs,
Light of confessors,
Pearl of virgins,
Consolation of widows,
Joy of all saints,

Lamb of God, Who takest away the sins of the world,
  Spare us, O Lord.
Lamb of God, Who takest away the sins of the world,
  Graciously hear us, O Lord.
Lamb of God, Who takest away the sins of the world,
  Have mercy on us.

Look down upon us, deliver us, and save us from all
  trouble, in the power of Jesus Christ.
  Amen.

Let Us Pray

Imprint, O Lady, thy wounds upon my heart, that I
may read therein sorrow and love—sorrow to endure
every sorrow for thee, love to despise every love for
thee. R. *Amen.*

(Conclude with the *Apostles Creed, Hail Holy Queen*, and three *Hail Marys*, in honor of the Most Holy Heart of Mary).

This litany was written in Latin by Pope Pius VII in 1809 during his captivity under Napoleon Bonaparte.

LITANY OF THE
SEVEN SORROWS OF
THE BLESSED VIRGIN MARY

(For private use only.)

Lord, have mercy.
  Lord, have mercy.
Christ, have mercy.
  Christ, have mercy.
Lord, have mercy.
  Lord, have mercy.
Christ, hear us.
  Christ, graciously hear us.
God the Father of Heaven,
  Have mercy on us.
God the Son, Redeemer of the world,
  Have mercy on us.
God the Holy Spirit,
  Have mercy on us.
Holy Trinity, One God,
  Have mercy on us.

Mother of Sorrows,
  Pray for us.
Mother whose soul was pierced by the sword,
  Pray for us.
Mother who fled with Jesus into Egypt, *etc.*
Mother who sought Him sorrowing for
  three days,
Mother who saw Him scourged and crowned with
  thorns,
Mother who stood by Him while He hung upon
  the Cross,
Mother who received Him into thine arms when He
  was dead,

Mother who saw Him buried in the tomb,

O Mary, Queen of Martyrs,
   Save us by thy prayers.
O Mary, comfort of the sorrowful,
   Save us by thy prayers.
O Mary, help of the weak, *etc.*
O Mary, strength of the fearful,
O Mary, light of the despondent,
O Mary, nursing mother of the sick,
O Mary, refuge of sinners,
Through the bitter Passion of thy Son,
Through the piercing anguish of thy heart,
Through thy heavy weight of woe,
Through thy sadness and desolation,
Through thy maternal pity,
Through thy perfect resignation,
Through thy meritorious prayers,
From immoderate sadness,
From a cowardly spirit,
From an impatient temper,
From fretfulness and discontent,
From sullenness and gloom,
From despair and unbelief,
From final impenitence,

We sinners, *beseech thee, hear us.*

Preserve us from sudden death,
   we beseech thee, hear us.
Teach us how to die, *we beseech thee, hear us.*
Succor us in our last agony, *etc.*
Guard us from the enemy,
Bring us to a happy end,
Gain for us the gift of perseverance,
Aid us before the Judgment Seat,
Mother of God,
Mother, most sorrowful,
Mother, most desolate,

Lamb of God, Who takest away the sins of the world,
   Spare us, O Lord.
Lamb of God, Who takest away the sins of the world,
   Graciously hear us, O Lord.
Lamb of God, Who takest away the sins of the world,
   Have mercy on us.

Christ, hear us.
   Christ, graciously hear us.
Lord, have mercy.
   Christ, have mercy.
Lord, have mercy.

V. Succor us, O Blessed Virgin Mary,
R. *In every time, and in every place.*

Let Us Pray

O Lord Jesus Christ, God and Man, grant, we
beseech Thee, that Thy dear Mother Mary, whose
soul the sword pierced in the hour of Thy Passion,
may intercede for us, now, and in the hour of our
death, through Thine own merits, O Saviour of the
world, Who with the Father and the Holy Spirit livest
and reignest, God, world without end. R. *Amen.*

LITANY OF
OUR LADY OF THE SACRED HEART

(For private use only.)

Lord, have mercy on us.
Christ, have mercy on us.
Lord, have mercy on us. Christ, hear us.
Christ, graciously hear us.
God the Father of Heaven,
Have mercy on us.
God the Son, Redeemer of the world,
Have mercy on us.
God the Holy Spirit,
Have mercy on us.
Holy Trinity, One God,
Have mercy on us.

Our Lady of the Sacred Heart, *pray for us.*
Our Lady of the Sacred Heart, Queen of peace and clemency, *pray for us.*
Our Lady of the Sacred Heart, dispensatrix of God's gifts, *etc.*
Our Lady of the Sacred Heart, subduer of hearts,
Our Lady of the Sacred Heart, Mother of mercy,
Our Lady of the Sacred Heart, Mother of divine grace,
Our Lady of the Sacred Heart, sweet gift from Heaven,
Our Lady of the Sacred Heart, sovereign benefactress,
Our Lady of the Sacred Heart, incomparable treasurer,
Our Lady of the Sacred Heart, august Mediatrix,
Our Lady of the Sacred Heart, refuge in danger,
Our Lady of the Sacred Heart, help of the abandoned,

Our Lady of the Sacred Heart, Mother of the orphan and the destitute,

Our Lady of the Sacred Heart, Hope of the hopeless,

Our Lady of the Sacred Heart, blessed by all generations,

Our Lady of the Sacred Heart, sweeter than honey and the honeycomb,

Our Lady of the Sacred Heart, immaculate lily perfuming the universe with thy perfumes,

Our Lady of the Sacred Heart, mysterious fountain,

Our Lady of the Sacred Heart, safe asylum amid the dangers of the world,

Our Lady of the Sacred Heart, the purest and loveliest of creatures,

May Heaven revere thee, *Our Lady of the Sacred Heart.*

May the earth publish thy benefits, *Our Lady of the Sacred Heart.*

May the young take refuge under thy virginal mantle, *etc.*

May mothers confide to thee their children,

May the aged invoke and bless thee,

Triumph over the insensibility of our hearts,

Draw from our eyes fountains of tears,

Convert the most hardened sinners,

Be our defense when Satan assaults us,

Help us to sanctify our trials,

Bless and fertilize our labors,

Guard us under thy shield,

Be moved by our misfortunes and our dangers,

In thy charity give us refuge in thine arms,

In thy compassion cover our sins and our faults,

In thy tenderness never abandon us,

By thy humility overcome our pride,

By thy prayers assist us in our last hour,

In thy love lead us to the Heart of Jesus,

Protect us at the tribunal of God,

Preserve our Sovereign Pontiff,

Preserve the faith in our land which loves thee,
Guide the bishops and the clergy in the way of
    holiness,
Protect the Catholic world against the efforts of the
    impious,
Bring back to the Church heretics and schismatics,
Make the light of the Gospel to shine among infidels,

Lamb of God, Who takest away the sins of the world,
    Spare us, O Lord.
Lamb of God, Who takest away the sins of the world,
    Graciously hear us, O Lord.
Lamb of God, Who takest away the sins of the world,
    Have mercy on us.

V. Pray for us, O invincible Lady of the Sacred Heart,
R. *That through thee, O sublime Hope of the hopeless,*
    we may become worthy of the promises of Jesus
    Christ, Our Saviour.

Let Us Pray

O God, Who for the triumph of Thy mercy and the
salvation of souls hast granted to the Immaculate
Virgin Mary boundless powers over the Heart of
Jesus, grant by her prayers and intercession that we
may live and die in Thy holy love. We ask this of Thee
through the same Jesus Christ Our Lord. R. *Amen.*

LITANY OF
OUR LADY OF MOUNT CARMEL
(For private use only.)

Lord, have mercy on us.
Christ, have mercy on us.
Lord, have mercy on us. Christ, hear us.
Christ, graciously hear us.
God the Father of Heaven,
Have mercy on us.
God the Son, Redeemer of the world,
Have mercy on us.
God the Holy Ghost,
Have mercy on us.
Holy Trinity, One God,
Have mercy on us.

Holy Mary, *pray for us.*
Holy Mary, Mother of God, *pray for us.*
Holy Mary, Virgin of virgins, *etc.*
Holy Mary, Mother of Christ,
Holy Mary, Mother of beautiful love,
Holy Mary, Mother of mercy,
Holy Mary, dwelling-place of God,
Holy Mary, seat of wisdom,
Holy Mary, temple of the Holy Ghost,
Holy Mary, sun never setting,
Holy Mary, moon never waning,
Holy Mary, morning-star,
Holy Mary, tabernacle of God among men,
Holy Mary, lily among thorns,
Holy Mary, gate of Heaven,
Holy Mary, flawless mirror,
Holy Mary, garden enclosed,
Holy Mary, fountain of living waters,

Holy Mary, promised to the Patriarchs,

Holy Mary, foretold by the Prophets,

Holy Mary, envisioned by the upright,

Holy Mary, consolation of Adam through the crushing of the infernal serpent's head,

Holy Mary, symbolized by the appearance of the cloud to the Prophet Elias on Mount Carmel,

Holy Mary, spouse of the upright Joseph,

Holy Mary, unique glory of the Order of Carmel,

Holy Mary, who hast bestowed the peerless garment, the holy Scapular, upon St. Simon Stock,

Holy Mary, everlasting strength and mercy because of thy efficacious intercession,

(Holy Mary, who dost succor with motherly affection thy children who observe the rules of thy confraternity,)

Holy Mary, unequaled Sister of those who daily honor thee in the Order of Carmel with praise and prayer,

(Holy Mary, protectress of all who serve thee worthily in this confraternity,)

(Holy Mary, helper unto sanctity of those who wear thy garment piously,)

(Holy Mary, advocate of the members of the confraternity, who esteem thy holy scapular,)

(Holy Mary, consolation of those who die clothed in thy holy scapular,)

(Holy Mary, speedy redemptrix from the pains of Purgatory for all who have properly served thee in this confraternity,)

Holy Mary, health of the sick,

Holy Mary, refuge of sinners,

Holy Mary, help of Christians,

Holy Mary, ornament of Carmel,

Holy Mary, fruitful Mother of the Order of Carmel,

Holy Mary, friend of those who live according to the evangelical counsels,

Holy Mary, Queen of those who observe the teachings of the Apostles,

Holy Mary, Queen of Angels,
Holy Mary, Patroness and hope of all Carmelites,

V. Have mercy on us, O Blessed Lady.
R. *Have mercy on us, O Holy Mother.*

Through thy powerful intercession, *Deliver us, O Holy Mother of God.*
From all evil, *Deliver us, O Holy Mother of God.*
From all sin, *etc.*
From pestilence, war and famine,
From a sudden and unforeseen death,
From everlasting death,

Holy Mary, through thine Immaculate Conception, *Protect us, O Holy Mother of God.*
Holy Mary, through thy joyful birth, *Protect us, O Holy Mother of God.*
Holy Mary, through thy seven joys, *etc.*
Holy Mary, through thine observance of the evangelical counsels,
Holy Mary, through thy practice of the ten virtues prescribed in the Gospel,
Holy Mary, through the Annunciation by the Archangel Gabriel at Nazareth,
Holy Mary, through the birth of thine only-begotten Son, Jesus Christ, our Lord,
Holy Mary, through the adoration by the three Magi from the East,
Holy Mary, through the glorious Resurrection of thy Son, our Divine Saviour,
Holy Mary, through His splendid Ascension into Heaven,
Holy Mary, through the Descent of the Holy Ghost, the Comforter,
Holy Mary, through thy wondrous Assumption into Heaven,
Holy Mary, through thy sublime Coronation by the Most Holy Trinity,

(Holy Mary, through thine unspeakable love and tenderness for those who wear the holy scapular in thy confraternity,)

We sinners
Beseech thee to hear us.

That thou guide and protect the Order and Confraternity of Carmel, dedicated to thy special devotion, *we beseech thee, hear us.*

That thou preserve and assist all here present and the entire Christian people, *we beseech thee, hear us.*

That thou promote and protect all devotion to the service of God and thyself, *etc.*

That through thy holy intercession and particular assistance thou ward off eternal damnation from our souls (and the souls of our fellow members and benefactors),

That thou come to the speedy assistance in Purgatory of all deceased members of the Christian Faith (and of our confraternity) and obtain for them eternal rest,

That thou preserve and assist us,

That thou hearken to our petitions,

Chosen Bride of God,

Mother and Daughter of the everlasting King, Virgin of Carmel, our Mother, Sister, and Queen,

Lamb of God, Who takest away the sins of the world, *Spare us, O Lord.*

Lamb of God, Who takest away the sins of the world, *Graciously hear us, O Lord.*

Lamb of God, Who takest away the sins of the world, *Have mercy on us.*

Christ, hear us.
Christ, graciously hear us.

O mighty advocate in vicissitudes and anxieties,
Come to our aid.

V. Pray for us, O Holy Mother of God,
R. *That we may be made worthy of the promises of Christ.*

Let Us Pray

Almighty and eternal God, Who hast honored the Order of Mount Carmel with the glorious title of the most renowned Virgin and Mother of Thy Son, Our Lord Jesus Christ, we pray Thee that through her intercession we may be spared all misfortune of soul and body, and may attain to everlasting bliss, Who livest and reignest with the same Christ Our Lord and the Holy Ghost, one God, world without end. R. *Amen.*

The invocations in parentheses are particularly intended for use by Carmelites, Carmelite Tertiaries, and members of the Confraternity of the Scapular.

INTERCESSORY LITANY OF
OUR LADY OF MOUNT CARMEL
FOR THE CONVERSION OF SINNERS

(For private use only.)

Lord, have mercy on us.
Christ, have mercy on us.
Lord, have mercy on us. Christ, hear us.
Christ, graciously hear us.
God the Father of Heaven,
Have mercy on us.
God the Son, Redeemer of the world,
Have mercy on us.
God the Holy Ghost,
Have mercy on us.
Holy Trinity, One God,
Have mercy on us.

Holy Mary, *pray for us sinners.*
Our Lady of Mount Carmel, Queen of Heaven,
pray for us sinners.
Our Lady of Mount Carmel, vanquisher
of Satan, *etc.*
Our Lady of Mount Carmel, most
dutiful Daughter,
Our Lady of Mount Carmel, most pure
Virgin,
Our Lady of Mount Carmel, most
devoted Spouse,
Our Lady of Mount Carmel, most
tender Mother,
Our Lady of Mount Carmel, perfect
model of virtue,
Our Lady of Mount Carmel, sure
anchor of hope,

Our Lady of Mount Carmel, refuge
in affliction,
Our Lady of Mount Carmel, dispenser
of God's gifts,
Our Lady of Mount Carmel, tower of strength against
our foes,
Our Lady of Mount Carmel, our aid
in danger,
Our Lady of Mount Carmel, road
leading to Jesus,
Our Lady of Mount Carmel, our light
in darkness,
Our Lady of Mount Carmel, our consolation at the
hour of death,
Our Lady of Mount Carmel, advocate of the most
abandoned sinners,

For those hardened in vice,
With confidence we come to thee,
O Lady of Mount Carmel.
For those who grieve thy Son,
With confidence we come to thee,
O Lady of Mount Carmel.
For those who neglect to pray, *etc.*
For those who are in their agony,
For those who delay their conversion,
For those suffering in Purgatory,
For those who know thee not,

Lamb of God, Who takest away the sins of the world,
Spare us, O Lord.
Lamb of God, Who takest away the sins of the world,
Graciously hear us, O Lord.
Lamb of God, Who takest away the sins of the world,
Have mercy on us.

V. Our Lady of Mount Carmel, Hope of the
Despairing,
R. *Intercede for us with thy Divine Son.*

Let Us Pray

Our Lady of Mount Carmel, glorious Queen of Angels, channel of God's tenderest mercy to man, refuge and advocate of sinners, with confidence I prostrate myself before thee, beseeching thee to obtain for me *(pause to mention request silently)*. In return I solemnly promise to have recourse to thee in all my trials, sufferings and temptations, and I shall do all in my power to induce others to love and reverence thee and to invoke thee in all their needs. I thank thee for the numberless blessings which I have received from thy mercy and powerful intercession. Continue to be my shield in danger, my guide in life, and my consolation at the hour of death. R. *Amen.*

LITANY OF
OUR LADY OF FATIMA
(For private use only.)

Our Lady of Fatima,
Pray for our dear country.
Our Lady of Fatima,
Sanctify our clergy.
Our Lady of Fatima,
Make our Catholics more fervent.
Our Lady of Fatima,
Guide and inspire those who govern us.
Our Lady of Fatima,
Cure the sick who confide in thee.
Our Lady of Fatima,
Console the sorrowful who trust in thee.
Our Lady of Fatima,
Help those who invoke thine aid.
Our Lady of Fatima,
Deliver us from all dangers.
Our Lady of Fatima,
Help us to resist temptation.
Our Lady of Fatima,
Obtain for us all that we lovingly ask of thee.
Our Lady of Fatima,
Help those who are dear to us.
Our Lady of Fatima,
Bring back to the right road our erring brothers.
Our Lady of Fatima,
Give us back our ancient fervor.
Our Lady of Fatima,
*Obtain for us pardon of our manifold sins and
offenses.*
Our Lady of Fatima,
Bring all men to the feet of thy Divine Child.

Our Lady of Fatima,
Obtain peace for the world.

O Mary conceived without sin,
Pray for us who have recourse to thee.
Immaculate Heart of Mary,
Pray for us now and at the hour of our death. Amen.

Let Us Pray

O God of infinite goodness and mercy, fill our hearts with a great confidence in Thy dear Mother, whom we invoke under the title of Our Lady of the Rosary and Our Lady of Fatima, and grant us by her powerful intercession all the graces, spiritual and temporal, which we need. Through Christ Our Lord. R. *Amen.*

THE GAELIC LITANY
TO OUR LADY

(For private use only.)

O Great Mary, *pray for us.*
O Mary, greatest of Maries, *pray for us.*
O Greatest of women, *etc.*
O Queen of angels,
O Mistress of the heavens,
O Woman full and replete with the grace of the Holy
    Spirit,
O Blessed and most blessed,
O Mother of Eternal Glory,
O Mother of the heavenly and earthly Church,
O Mother of Love and Indulgence,
O Mother of the Golden Heights,
O Honor of the sky,
O Sign of tranquillity,
O Gate of Heaven,
O Golden Vessel,
O Couch of Love and Mercy,
O Temple of Divinity,
O Beauty of virgins,
O Mistress of the tribes,
O Fountain of gardens,
O Cleansing of sins,
O Purifying of souls,
O Mother of orphans,
O Breast of infants,
O Solace of the wretched,
O Star of the sea,
O Handmaid of the Lord,
O Mother of Christ,
O Resort of the Lord,
O Graceful like the dove,

O Serene like the moon,
O Resplendent like the sun,
O Cancelling Eve's disgrace,
O Regeneration of life,
O Beauty of women,
O Leader of virgins,
O Garden Enclosed,
O Fountain sealed up,
O Mother of God,
O Perpetual Virgin,
O Holy Virgin,
O Prudent Virgin,
O Serene Virgin,
O Chaste Virgin,
O Temple of the Living God,
O Royal Throne of the Eternal King,
O Sanctuary of the Holy Spirit,
O Virgin of the Root of Jesse,
O Cedar of Mount Lebanon,
O Cypress of Mount Sion,
O Crimson Rose of the Land of Jacob,
O Blooming like the palm tree,
O Fruitful like the olive tree,
O Glorious Son-bearer,
O Light of Nazareth,
O Glory of Jerusalem,
O Beauty of the world,
O Noblest-Born of the Christian flock,
O Queen of Life,
O Ladder of Heaven,

This litany was translated by Eugene O'Curry and appears in *The Catholic Anthology.* It dates from the middle of the Eighth Century.

LITANIES OF
THE ANGELS
AND ARCHANGELS

"Behold I will send my angel, who shall go before thee, and keep thee in thy journey, and bring thee into the place that I have prepared."

—Exodus *23:20*

LITANY OF THE HOLY ANGELS

(For private use only.)

Lord, have mercy.
Lord, have mercy.
Christ, have mercy.
Christ, have mercy.
Lord, have mercy.
Lord, have mercy.
Christ, hear us.
Christ, graciously hear us.
God the Father of Heaven,
Have mercy on us.
God the Son, Redeemer of the world,
Have mercy on us.
God the Holy Ghost,
Have mercy on us.
Holy Trinity, One God,
Have mercy on us.

Holy Mary, Queen of Angels, *pray for us.*
Holy Mother of God, *pray for us.*
Holy Virgin of virgins, *etc.*
Saint Michael, who wast ever the defender of the
    people of God,
St. Michael, who didst drive from Heaven Lucifer and
    his rebel crew,
St. Michael, who didst cast down to Hell the accuser
    of our brethren,
Saint Gabriel, who didst expound to Daniel the
    heavenly vision,
St. Gabriel, who didst foretell to Zachary the birth
    and ministry of John the Baptist,
St. Gabriel, who didst announce to Blessed Mary the
    Incarnation of the Divine Word,

127

Saint Raphael, who didst lead Tobias safely through
his journey to his home again,

St. Raphael, who didst deliver Sara from
the devil,

St. Raphael, who didst restore his sight to Tobias the
elder,

All ye holy Angels, who stand around the high and
lofty throne of God,

Who cry to Him continually: Holy, Holy, Holy,

Who dispel the darkness of our minds and give us
light,

Who are the messengers of heavenly things
to men,

Who have been appointed by God to be our
guardians,

Who always behold the Face of our Father Who is in
Heaven,

Who rejoice over one sinner doing penance,

Who struck the Sodomites with blindness,

Who led Lot out of the midst of the ungodly,

Who ascended and descended on the ladder
of Jacob,

Who delivered the Divine Law to Moses on Mount
Sinai,

Who brought good tidings when Christ was born,

Who ministered to Him in the desert,

Who comforted Him in His agony,

Who sat in white garments at His sepulcher,

Who appeared to the disciples as He went up into
Heaven,

Who shall go before Him bearing the standard of the
Cross when He comes to judgment,

Who shall gather together the elect at the End of the
World,

Who shall separate the wicked from among
the just,

Who offer to God the prayers of those who pray,

Who assist us at the hour of death,

Who carried Lazarus into Abraham's bosom,

Who conduct to Heaven the souls of the just,
Who perform signs and wonders by the power
of God,
Who are sent to minister for those who shall receive
the inheritance of salvation,
Who are set over kingdoms and provinces,
Who have often put to flight armies of enemies,
Who have often delivered God's servants from prison
and other perils of this life,
Who have often consoled the holy martyrs in their
torments,
Who are wont to cherish with peculiar care the
prelates and princes of the Church,
All ye holy orders of blessed spirits,

From all dangers, *deliver us, O Lord.*
From the snares of the devil, *deliver us O Lord.*
From all heresy and schism, *etc.*
From plague, famine and war,
From sudden and unlooked-for death,
From everlasting death,

We sinners
Beseech Thee to hear us.

Through Thy holy Angels, *we beseech Thee, hear us.*
That Thou wouldst spare us, *we beseech Thee, hear
us.*
That Thou wouldst pardon us, *etc.*
That Thou wouldst govern and preserve Thy Holy
Church,
That Thou wouldst protect our Apostolic Prelate and
all ecclesiastical orders,
That Thou wouldst grant peace and security to kings
and all Christian princes,
That Thou wouldst give and preserve the fruits of the
earth,
That Thou wouldst grant eternal rest to all the faithful
departed,

Lamb of God, Who takest away the sins of the world,
  Spare us, O Lord.
Lamb of God, Who takest away the sins of the world,
  Graciously hear us, O Lord.
Lamb of God, Who takest away the sins of the world,
  Have mercy on us.

Lord, have mercy.
  Christ, have mercy.
Lord, have mercy.

Our Father, *etc. (silently).*

V. Bless the Lord, all ye Angels:
R. *Ye who are mighty in strength, who fulfill His
  commandments, hearkening unto the voice of His
  words.*
V. He hath given His Angels charge concerning thee,
R. *To keep thee in all thy ways.*

Let Us Pray

O God, Who dost arrange the services of Angels
and men in a wonderful order, mercifully grant that
our life may be protected on earth by those who always do Thee service in Heaven, through Jesus Christ
Thy Son, Who with Thee and the Holy Ghost art one
God, now and forever. R. *Amen.*

O God, Who in Thine unspeakable Providence dost
send Thine Angels to keep guard over us, grant unto
Thy suppliants that we may be continually defended
by their protection and may rejoice eternally in their
society, through Jesus Christ Our Lord, Who liveth
and reigneth with Thee, in the unity of the Holy
Ghost, forever and ever. R. *Amen.*

LITANY OF SAINT MICHAEL
Litany One
(For private use only.)

Lord, have mercy on us.
Christ, have mercy on us.
Lord, have mercy on us. Christ, hear us.
Christ, graciously hear us.
God the Father of Heaven,
Have mercy on us.
God the Son, Redeemer of the world,
Have mercy on us.
God the Holy Spirit,
Have mercy on us.
Holy Trinity, One God,
Have mercy on us.

Holy Mary, Queen of Angels, *pray for us.*
St. Michael, *pray for us.*
St. Michael, filled with the wisdom of God, *etc.*
St. Michael, perfect adorer of the Incarnate Word,
St. Michael, crowned with honor and glory,
St. Michael, most powerful Prince of the armies of the Lord,
St. Michael, standard-bearer of the Most Holy Trinity,
St. Michael, victor over Satan,
St. Michael, guardian of Paradise,
St. Michael, guide and comforter of the people of Israel,
St. Michael, splendor and fortress of the Church Militant,
St. Michael, honor and joy of the Church Triumphant,
St. Michael, light of angels,
St. Michael, bulwark of orthodox believers,

St. Michael, strength of those who fight under the
standard of the Cross,
St. Michael, light and confidence of souls at the hour
of death,
St. Michael, our most sure aid,
St. Michael, our help in all adversities,
St. Michael, Herald of the Everlasting Sentence,
St. Michael, Consoler of souls detained in the flames
of Purgatory,
Thou whom the Lord has charged to receive souls
after death,
St. Michael, our Prince,
St. Michael, our Advocate,

Lamb of God, Who takest away the sins of the world,
Spare us, O Lord.
Lamb of God, Who takest away the sins of the world,
Graciously hear us, O Lord.
Lamb of God, Who takest away the sins of the world,
Have mercy on us.

Christ, hear us.
Christ, graciously hear us.

V. Pray for us, O glorious St. Michael, Prince of the
Church of Jesus Christ,
R. *That we may be made worthy of His promises.*

Let Us Pray

Sanctify us, we beseech Thee, O Lord, with Thy
holy blessing, and grant us, by the intercession of St.
Michael, that wisdom which teaches us to lay up
treasures in Heaven by exchanging the goods of this
world for those of eternity, Thou Who livest and
reignest, world without end. R. *Amen.*

LITANY OF SAINT MICHAEL
Litany Two
(For private use only.)

Lord, have mercy on us.
  Christ, have mercy on us.
Lord, have mercy on us. Christ, hear us.
  Christ, graciously hear us.
God the Father of Heaven,
  Have mercy on us.
God the Son, Redeemer of the world,
  Have mercy on us.
God the Holy Spirit,
  Have mercy on us.
Holy Trinity, One God,
  Have mercy on us.

Holy Mary, Queen of the Angels, *pray for us.*
St. Michael the Archangel, *pray for us.*
Most glorious attendant of the Triune Divinity, *etc.*
Standing at the right of the Altar of Incense,
Ambassador of Paradise,
Glorious Prince of the heavenly armies,
Leader of the angelic hosts,
Warrior who thrust Satan into Hell,
Defender against the wickedness and snares of the
  devil,
Standard-bearer of God's armies,
Defender of divine glory,
First defender of the Kingship of Christ,
Strength of God,
Invincible prince and warrior,
Angel of peace,
Guardian of the Christian Faith,
Champion of God's people,
Guardian angel of the Eucharist,

Defender of the Church,
Protector of the Sovereign Pontiff,
Angel of Catholic Action,
Powerful intercessor of Christians,
Bravest defender of those who hope in God,
Guardian of our souls and bodies,
Healer of the sick,
Help of those in their agony,
Consoler of the souls in Purgatory,
God's messenger for the souls of the just,
Terror of the evil spirits,
Victorious in battle against evil,
Guardian and Patron of the Universal Church,

Lamb of God, Who takest away the sins of the world,
    Spare us, O Lord.
Lamb of God, Who takest away the sins of the world,
    Graciously hear us, O Lord.
Lamb of God, Who takest away the sins of the world,
    Have mercy on us.

V. Pray for us, O glorious St. Michael,
R. *That we may be made worthy of the promises of
    Christ.*

Let Us Pray

Relying, O Lord, upon the intercession of Thy
blessed Archangel Michael, we humbly beg of Thee,
that the Sacrament of the Eucharist which we have
received may make our souls holy and pleasing to
Thee. Through Christ Our Lord. R. *Amen.*

LITANY OF SAINT GABRIEL

(For private use only.)

Lord, have mercy on us.
  Christ, have mercy on us.
Lord, have mercy on us. Christ, hear us.
  Christ, graciously hear us.
God the Father of Heaven,
  Have mercy on us.
God the Son, Redeemer of the world,
  Have mercy on us.
God the Holy Spirit,
  Have mercy on us.
Holy Trinity, One God,
  Have mercy on us.

Holy Mary, Queen of angels, *pray for us.*
Saint Gabriel, glorious archangel, *pray for us.*
St. Gabriel, strength of God, *etc.*
St. Gabriel, who stands before the throne of God,
St. Gabriel, model of prayer,
St. Gabriel, herald of the Incarnation,
St. Gabriel, who revealed the glories of Mary,
St. Gabriel, Prince of Heaven,
St. Gabriel, ambassador of the Most High,
St. Gabriel, guardian of the Immaculate Virgin,
St. Gabriel, who foretold the greatness of Jesus,
St. Gabriel, peace and light of souls,
St. Gabriel, scourge of unbelievers,
St. Gabriel, admirable teacher,
St. Gabriel, strength of the just,
St. Gabriel, protector of the faithful,
St. Gabriel, first adorer of the Divine Word,
St. Gabriel, defender of the Faith,
St. Gabriel, zealous for the honor of Jesus Christ,

St. Gabriel, whom the Scriptures praise as the angel
  sent by God to Mary, the Virgin,

Lamb of God, Who takest away the sins of the world,
  Spare us, O Lord.
Lamb of God, Who takest away the sins of the world,
  Graciously hear us, O Lord.
Lamb of God, Who takest away the sins of the world,
  Have mercy on us.

Christ, hear us.
  Christ, graciously hear us.

V. Pray for us, blessed Archangel Gabriel,
R. *That we may be made worthy of the promises of
  Jesus Christ.*

Let Us Pray

O blessed Archangel Gabriel, we beseech thee, intercede for us at the throne of divine Mercy in our present necessities, that as thou didst announce to Mary the mystery of the Incarnation, so through thy prayers and patronage in Heaven we may obtain the benefits of the same, and sing the praise of God forever in the land of the living. R. *Amen.*

LITANY OF SAINT RAPHAEL

(For private use only.)

Lord, have mercy on us.
   Christ, have mercy on us.
Lord, have mercy on us. Christ, hear us.
   Christ, graciously hear us.
God the Father of Heaven,
   Have mercy on us.
God the Son, Redeemer of the world,
   Have mercy on us.
God the Holy Spirit,
   Have mercy on us.
Holy Trinity, One God,
   Have mercy on us.

Holy Mary, Queen of Angels, *pray for us.*
Saint Raphael, *pray for us.*
St. Raphael, filled with the mercy of God, *etc.*
St. Raphael, perfect adorer of the Divine Word,
St. Raphael, terror of demons,
St. Raphael, exterminator of vices,
St. Raphael, health of the sick,
St. Raphael, our refuge in all our trials,
St. Raphael, guide of travellers,
St. Raphael, consoler of prisoners,
St. Raphael, joy of the sorrowful,
St. Raphael, filled with zeal for the
   salvation of souls,
St. Raphael, whose name means
   "Medicine of God,"
St. Raphael, lover of chastity,
St. Raphael, scourge of demons,
St. Raphael, in pest, famine and war,
St. Raphael, angel of peace and prosperity,

137

St. Raphael, endowed with the grace of healing,

St. Raphael, sure guide in the paths of virtue and sanctification,

St. Raphael, help of all those who implore thy assistance,

St. Raphael, who wert the guide and consolation of Tobias on his journey,

St. Raphael, whom the Scriptures praise: "Raphael, the holy angel of the Lord, was sent to cure,"

St. Raphael, our advocate,

Lamb of God, Who takest away the sins of the world, *Spare us, O Lord.*

Lamb of God, Who takest away the sins of the world, *Graciously hear us, O Lord.*

Lamb of God, Who takest away the sins of the world, *Have mercy on us.*

Christ, hear us.
  Christ, graciously hear us.

V. Pray for us, St. Raphael, to the Lord Our God,

R. *That we may be made worthy of the promises of Christ.*

Let Us Pray

Lord Jesus Christ, by the prayer of the Archangel Raphael, grant us the grace to avoid all sin and to persevere in every good work until we reach our heavenly country, Thou who livest and reignest world without end. R. *Amen.*

LITANY OF THE
HOLY GUARDIAN ANGEL
Litany One
(For private use only.)

Lord, have mercy on us.
 Christ, have mercy on us.
Lord, have mercy on us. Jesus, hear us.
 Jesus, graciously hear us.
God the Father of Heaven,
 Have mercy on us.
God the Son, Redeemer of the world,
 Have mercy on us.
God the Holy Ghost,
 Have mercy on us.
Holy Trinity, One God,
 Have mercy on us.

Holy Mary, Queen of Angels, *pray for me.*
Angel of Heaven, who art my guardian, *pray for me.*
Angel of Heaven, whom I revere as my superior, *etc.*
Angel of Heaven, who dost give me charitable
 counsel,
Angel of Heaven, who dost give me wise direction,
Angel of Heaven, who dost take the place of a tutor,
Angel of Heaven, who dost love me tenderly,
Angel of Heaven, who art my consoler,
Angel of Heaven, who art attached to me as a good
 brother,
Angel of Heaven, who dost instruct me in the duties
 and truth of salvation,
Angel of Heaven, who art to me a charitable
 shepherd,
Angel of Heaven, who art witness of all my actions,
Angel of Heaven, who dost help me in all my
 undertakings,

Angel of Heaven, who dost continually watch over
me,
Angel of Heaven, who dost intercede for me,
Angel of Heaven, who dost carry me in thy hand,
Angel of Heaven, who dost direct me in all my ways,
Angel of Heaven, who dost defend me with zeal,
Angel of Heaven, who dost conduct me with wisdom,
Angel of Heaven, who dost guard me from all danger,
Angel of Heaven, who dost dissipate the darkness and
enlighten the mind,

Lamb of God, Who takest away the sins of the world,
Spare us, O Lord.
Lamb of God, Who takest away the sins of the world,
Graciously hear us, O Lord.
Lamb of God, Who takest away the sins of the world,
Have mercy on us, O Lord.

Jesus, hear us.
Jesus, graciously hear us.

V. Pray for us, O Guardian Angel,
R. *That we may be made worthy of the promises of
Christ.*

Let Us Pray

Almighty and eternal God, Who by an effect of
Thine ineffable bounty hast given to each of the
faithful an angel to be the guardian of body and soul,
grant that I may have for him whom Thou hast given
me in Thy mercy so much respect and love, that, protected by the gifts of Thy graces and by his help, I
may merit to go to Thee in Heaven, there to contemplate Thee with him and the other happy spirits in the
brightness of Thy glory. R. *Amen.*

LITANY OF THE
HOLY GUARDIAN ANGEL
Litany Two
(For private use only.)

Lord, have mercy on us.
Christ, have mercy on us.
Lord, have mercy on us. Christ, hear us.
Christ, graciously hear us.
God the Father of Heaven,
Have mercy on us.
God the Son, Redeemer of the world,
Have mercy on us.
God the Holy Spirit,
Have mercy on us.
Holy Trinity, One God,
Have mercy on us.

Holy Mary, Queen of Angels, *pray for us.*
Holy Angel, my guardian, *pray for us.*
Holy Angel, my prince, *etc.*
Holy Angel, my monitor,
Holy Angel, my counselor,
Holy Angel, my defender,
Holy Angel, my steward,
Holy Angel, my friend,
Holy Angel, my negotiator,
Holy Angel, my intercessor,
Holy Angel, my patron,
Holy Angel, my director,
Holy Angel, my ruler,
Holy Angel, my protector,
Holy Angel, my comforter,
Holy Angel, my brother,
Holy Angel, my teacher,
Holy Angel, my shepherd,

Holy Angel, my witness,
Holy Angel, my helper,
Holy Angel, my watcher,
Holy Angel, my conductor,
Holy Angel, my preserver,
Holy Angel, my instructor,
Holy Angel, my enlightener,

Lamb of God, Who takest away the sins of the world,
Spare us, O Lord.
Lamb of God, Who takest away the sins of the world,
Graciously hear us, O Lord.
Lamb of God, Who takest away the sins of the world,
Have mercy on us.

Christ, hear us.
Christ, graciously hear us.
Lord, have mercy on us.

V. Pray for us, O holy Guardian Angel,
R. *That we may be made worthy of the promises of Christ.*

Let Us Pray

Almighty and everlasting God, Who in the counsel of Thine ineffable goodness hast appointed to all the faithful, from their mother's womb, a special Angel Guardian of their body and soul, grant that I may so love and honor him whom Thou hast so mercifully given me, that protected by the bounty of Thy grace and by his assistance, I may merit to behold, with him and all the angelic hosts, the glory of Thy countenance in the heavenly kingdom. Thou, Who livest and reignest world without end. R. *Amen.*

LITANY OF THE
HOLY GUARDIAN ANGEL
Litany Three
(For private use only.)

Lord, have mercy on us.
  Christ, have mercy on us.
Lord, have mercy on us. Christ, hear us.
  Christ, graciously hear us.
God the Father of Heaven,
  Have mercy on us.
God the Son, Redeemer of the world,
  Have mercy on us.
God the Holy Spirit,
  Have mercy on us.
Holy Trinity, One God,
  Have mercy on us.

Holy Mary, Queen of Heaven, *pray for us.*
Holy Angel, my guardian, *pray for us.*
Holy Angel, my protector in all dangers, *etc.*
Holy Angel, my defense in all afflictions,
Holy Angel, most faithful lover,
Holy Angel, my preceptor,
Holy Angel, my guide,
Holy Angel, witness of all my actions,
Holy Angel, my helper in all my difficulties,
Holy Angel, my negotiator with God,
Holy Angel, my advocate,
Holy Angel, lover of chastity,
Holy Angel, lover of innocence,
Holy Angel, most obedient to God,
Holy Angel, director of my soul,
Holy Angel, model of purity,
Holy Angel, model of docility,
Holy Angel, my counsellor in doubt,

Holy Angel, my guardian through life,
Holy Angel, my shield at the hour of death,

Lamb of God, Who takest away the sins of the world,
   Spare us, O Lord.
Lamb of God, Who takest away the sins of the world,
   Hear us, O Lord.
Lamb of God, Who takest away the sins of the world,
   Have mercy on us.

Let Us Pray

Almighty and everlasting God, Who in the counsel of Thine ineffable goodness hast appointed to all the faithful, from their mother's womb, a special Angel Guardian of their body and soul, grant that I may so love and honor him whom Thou hast so mercifully given me, that protected by the bounty of Thy grace and by his assistance, I may merit to behold, with him and all the angelic hosts, the glory of Thy countenance in the heavenly country. Thou, Who livest and reignest, world without end. R. *Amen.*

LITANY OF THE SAINTS AND LITANIES OF VARIOUS SAINTS

"For the continual prayer of a just man availeth much. Elias was a man passible like unto us: and with prayer he prayed that it might not rain upon the earth, and it rained not for three years and six months. And he prayed again: and the heaven gave rain, and the earth brought forth her fruit."

—James 5:16-18

LITANY OF THE SAINTS

(For public or private use.)

Lord, have mercy on us.
Christ, have mercy on us.
Lord, have mercy on us. Christ, hear us.
Christ, graciously hear us.
God the Father of Heaven,
Have mercy on us.
God the Son, Redeemer of the world,
Have mercy on us.
God the Holy Spirit,
Have mercy on us.
Holy Trinity, One God,
Have mercy on us.

Holy Mary, *pray for us.*
Holy Mother of God, *pray for us.*
Holy Virgin of virgins, *etc.*
Saint Michael,
Saint Gabriel,
Saint Raphael,
All ye holy angels and archangels,
All ye holy orders of blessed spirits,
Saint John the Baptist,
Saint Joseph,
All ye holy patriarchs and prophets,
Saint Peter,
Saint Paul,
Saint Andrew,
Saint James,
Saint John,
Saint Thomas,
Saint James,
Saint Philip,

Saint Bartholomew,
Saint Matthew,
Saint Simon,
Saint Thaddeus,
Saint Matthias,
Saint Barnabas,
Saint Luke,
Saint Mark,
All ye holy apostles and evangelists,
All ye holy disciples of Our Lord,
All ye holy innocents,
Saint Stephen,
Saint Lawrence,
Saint Vincent,
Saints Fabian and Sebastian,
Saints John and Paul,
Saints Cosmas and Damian,
Saints Gervase and Protase,
All ye holy martyrs,
Saint Sylvester,
Saint Gregory,
Saint Ambrose,
Saint Augustine,
Saint Jerome,
Saint Martin,
Saint Nicholas,
All ye holy bishops and confessors,
All ye holy doctors,
Saint Antony,
Saint Benedict,
Saint Bernard,
Saint Dominic,
Saint Francis,
All ye holy priests and levites,
All ye holy monks and hermits,
Saint Mary Magdalen,
Saint Agatha,
Saint Lucy,
Saint Agnes,

Saint Cecilia,
Saint Catherine,
Saint Anastasia,
All ye holy virgins and widows,

All ye holy men and women, saints of God,
Make intercession for us.
Be merciful,
Spare us, O Lord.
Be merciful,
Graciously hear us, O Lord.

From all evil, *O Lord, deliver us.*
From all sin, *O Lord, deliver us.*
From Thy wrath, *etc.*
From a sudden and unprovided death,
From the deceits of the devil,
From anger, hatred, and all ill-will,
From the spirit of fornication,
From lightning and tempest,
From the scourge of earthquake,
From plague, famine, and war,
From everlasting death,
Through the mystery of Thy Holy Incarnation,
Through Thy coming,
Through Thy Nativity,
Through Thy baptism and holy fasting,
Through Thy Cross and Passion,
Through Thy death and burial,
Through Thy holy Resurrection,
Through Thine admirable Ascension,
Through the coming of the Holy Spirit, the Paraclete,
In the Day of Judgment,

We sinners,
We beseech Thee, hear us.

That Thou wouldst spare us,
We beseech Thee, hear us.

That Thou wouldst pardon us,
We beseech Thee, hear us.

That Thou wouldst bring us to true penance, *etc.*

That Thou wouldst govern and preserve Thy holy
Church,

That Thou wouldst preserve our Apostolic Prelate
and all ecclesiastical Orders in holy religion,

That Thou wouldst humble the enemies of Thy holy
Church,

That Thou wouldst give peace and true concord to
Christian kings and princes,

That Thou wouldst grant peace and unity to all
Christian people,

That Thou wouldst bring back to the unity of the
Church all those who have strayed from the truth,
and lead to the light of the Gospel all unbelievers,

That Thou wouldst confirm and preserve us in Thy
holy service,

That Thou wouldst lift up our minds to heavenly
desires,

That Thou wouldst render eternal blessings to all our
benefactors,

That Thou wouldst deliver our souls and those of our
brethren, relations, and benefactors from eternal
damnation,

That Thou wouldst give and preserve the fruits of the
earth,

That Thou wouldst give eternal rest to all the faithful
departed,

That Thou wouldst graciously hear us,

Son of God,

Lamb of God, Who takest away the sins of the world,
Spare us, O Lord.

Lamb of God, Who takest away the sins of the world,
Graciously hear us, O Lord.

Lamb of God, Who takest away the sins of the world,
Have mercy on us.

Christ, hear us.
   Christ, graciously hear us.
Lord, have mercy on us.
   Christ, have mercy on us.
Lord, have mercy on us.

Our Father, *etc. (silently).*

V. And lead us not into temptation,
R. *But deliver us from evil.*

LITANY OF
SAINT JOSEPH
Litany One
(For public or private use.)

Lord, have mercy on us.
   Christ, have mercy on us.
Lord, have mercy on us. Christ, hear us.
   Christ, graciously hear us.
God the Father of Heaven,
   Have mercy on us.
God the Son, Redeemer of the world,
   Have mercy on us.
God the Holy Spirit,
   Have mercy on us.
Holy Trinity, One God,
   Have mercy on us.

Holy Mary, *pray for us.*
Saint Joseph, *pray for us.*
Illustrious son of David, *etc.*
Light of the patriarchs,
Spouse of the Mother of God,
Chaste guardian of the Virgin,
Foster-father of the Son of God,
Watchful defender of Christ,
Head of the Holy Family,
Joseph most just,
Joseph most chaste,
Joseph most prudent,
Joseph most valiant,
Joseph most obedient,
Joseph most faithful,
Mirror of patience,
Lover of poverty,
Model of workmen,

Glory of domestic life,
Guardian of virgins,
Pillar of families,
Solace of the afflicted,
Hope of the sick,
Patron of the dying,
Terror of demons,
Protector of Holy Church,

Lamb of God, Who takest away the sins of the world,
Spare us, O Lord.
Lamb of God, Who takest away the sins of the world,
Graciously hear us, O Lord.
Lamb of God, Who takest away the sins of the world,
Have mercy on us.

V. He made him the lord of His household,
R. *And prince over all His possessions.*

Let Us Pray

O God, Who in Thine ineffable providence didst choose Blessed Joseph to be the spouse of Thy most Holy Mother, grant that as we venerate him as our protector on earth, we may deserve to have him as our intercessor in Heaven, Thou Who livest and reignest forever and ever. R. *Amen.*

St. Joseph, Foster-Father of Jesus and Patron of the Universal Church: St. Joseph was of royal descent of the line of David, and was probably born in Bethlehem. He practiced carpentry in Nazareth, and there married the Blessed Virgin Mary. St. Joseph and Mary went to Bethlehem for a census, and there Our Lady gave birth to the Messiah, Jesus Christ, who had been conceived of the Holy Ghost. St. Joseph, foster-father of Our Lord, probably died before Our Lord's Passion and death. St. Joseph is the Patron of the Universal Church, Patron of the Dying, Patron of a Happy Death, etc.

LITANY OF
SAINT JOSEPH
Litany Two
(For private use only.)

Lord, have mercy on us.
Christ, have mercy on us.
Lord, have mercy on us. Christ, hear us.
Christ, graciously hear us.
God the Father of Heaven,
Have mercy on us.
God the Son, Redeemer of the world,
Have mercy on us.
God the Holy Spirit,
Have mercy on us.
Holy Trinity, One God,
Have mercy on us.

Holy Mary, spouse of St. Joseph,
Pray for us.
Saint Joseph, confirmed in grace,
Pray for us.
Saint Joseph, guardian of the Word Incarnate,
etc.
Saint Joseph, favorite of the King of Heaven,
Saint Joseph, ruler of the family of Jesus,
Saint Joseph, spouse of the ever-blessed Virgin,
Saint Joseph, foster father to the Son of God,
Saint Joseph, example of humility and obedience,
Saint Joseph, mirror of silence and resignation,
Saint Joseph, patron of innocence and youth,
Saint Joseph, exiled with Christ into Egypt,
Saint Joseph, intercessor for the afflicted,
Saint Joseph, advocate of the humble,
Saint Joseph, model of every virtue,
Saint Joseph, honored among men,

Saint Joseph, in whom is the union of all Christian perfections,

Lamb of God, Who takest away the sins of the world,
Spare us, O Lord.
Lamb of God, Who takest away the sins of the world,
Graciously hear us, O Lord.
Lamb of God, Who takest away the sins of the world,
Have mercy on us.

V. Pray for us, O holy Saint Joseph,
R. *That we may be made worthy of the promises of Christ.*

Let Us Pray

Assist us, O Lord, we beseech Thee, by the merits of the spouse of Thy most holy Mother, that what our unworthiness cannot obtain, may be given us by his intercession with Thee, Who livest and reignest with God the Father in the unity of the Holy Spirit, one God, world without end. R. *Amen.*

Prayer to Saint Joseph

O Saint Joseph, whose protection is so great, so strong, so prompt before the throne of God, I place in thee all my interests and desires. O thou Saint Joseph, do assist me by thy powerful intercession, and obtain for me from thy divine Son all spiritual blessings, through Jesus Christ, Our Lord; so that, having engaged here below thy heavenly power, I may offer my thanksgiving and homage to the most loving of fathers. O Saint Joseph, I never weary contemplating thee, and Jesus asleep in thy arms; I dare not approach while He reposes near thy heart. Press Him in my name and kiss His fine head for me, and ask Him to return the kiss when I draw my dying breath. Saint Joseph, Patron of departing souls, pray for me. R. *Amen.*

LITANY OF
SAINT ANNE

(For private use only.)

Saint Anne, Grandmother of Our Saviour, *pray for us.*
Saint Anne, Mother of Mary, the Blessed Virgin and
    Mother, *pray for us.*
Saint Anne, ark of Noah, *etc.*
Saint Anne, ark of the covenant,
Saint Anne, root of Jesse,
Saint Anne, fruitful vine,
Saint Anne, issue of royal race,
Saint Anne, joy of angels,
Saint Anne, daughter of the patriarchs,
Saint Anne, filled with grace,
Saint Anne, mirror of obedience,
Saint Anne, mirror of patience,
Saint Anne, mirror of mercy,
Saint Anne, mirror of piety,
Saint Anne, bulwark of the Church,
Saint Anne, liberator of captives,
Saint Anne, refuge of sinners,
Saint Anne, consoler of the married,
Saint Anne, mother of widows,
Saint Anne, mother of virgins,
Saint Anne, mother of the sick,
Saint Anne, harbor of salvation,
Saint Anne, light of the blind,
Saint Anne, tongue of the dumb,
Saint Anne, hearing of the deaf,
Saint Anne, consolation of the afflicted,
Saint Anne, help of all who have recourse to thee,

Our Father. Hail Mary.

V. God has loved Saint Anne,
R. *And delighted in her beauty.*

Let Us Pray

Almighty and Eternal God, Who didst choose Saint Anne to be the mother of the Mother of Thine only Son, grant, we beseech Thee, that we who keep her in remembrance, may, through her prayers, attain to everlasting life, through Jesus Christ Our Lord. R. *Amen.*

St. Anne, Mother of Our Lady: According to pious tradition, St. Anne's husband was St. Joachim; both were of the tribe of Juda and the royal house of David. They endured the terrible trial of childlessness for 20 years, but finally, after many prayers, St. Anne learned from an angel that she would bear a child. This child was the Blessed Virgin Mary, Mother of the Messiah. A tradition says that St. Anne spent the last years of her life in prayer and austerity in the desert.

LITANY OF
SAINT JOHN THE BAPTIST

(For private use only.)

Lord, have mercy on us.
Christ, have mercy on us.
Christ, hear us.
Christ, graciously hear us.
God the Father of Heaven,
Have mercy on us.
God the Son, Redeemer of the world,
Have mercy on us.
God the Holy Ghost,
Have mercy on us.
Holy Trinity, One God,
Have mercy on us.

Holy Mary, *pray for us.*
Queen of Prophets, *pray for us.*
Queen of Martyrs, *etc.*
Saint John the Baptist,
St. John the Baptist, precursor of Christ,
St. John the Baptist, glorious forerunner of the
    Sun of Justice,
St. John the Baptist, minister of baptism to Jesus,
St. John the Baptist, burning and shining lamp
    of the world,
St. John the Baptist, angel of purity before
    thy birth,
St. John the Baptist, special friend and favorite
    of Christ,
St. John the Baptist, heavenly contemplative, whose
    element was prayer,
St. John the Baptist, intrepid preacher of truth,
St. John the Baptist, voice crying in the wilderness,

St. John the Baptist, miracle of mortification and penance,

St. John the Baptist, example of profound humility,

St. John the Baptist, glorious martyr of zeal for God's holy law,

St. John the Baptist, gloriously fulfilling thy mission,

Lamb of God, Who takest away the sins of the world,
Spare us, O Lord.

Lamb of God, Who takest away the sins of the world,
Hear us, O Lord.

Lamb of God, Who takest away the sins of the world,
Have mercy on us.

Christ, hear us.
Christ, graciously hear us.

V. Pray for us, O glorious St. John the Baptist,

R. *That we may be made worthy of the promises of Christ.*

Let Us Pray

O God, Who hast honored this world by the birth of Saint John the Baptist, grant that Thy faithful people may rejoice in the way of eternal salvation, through Jesus Christ Our Lord. R. *Amen.*

St. John The Baptist, The Last of the Prophets, and The Precursor of Christ the Messiah: Sanctified in the womb of his mother, St. Elizabeth, St. John the Baptist was a kinsman of Jesus Christ. St. John spent his youth and early manhood until age 30 in prayer and penance in the desert, then he preached penance and baptism in preparation for the coming of the Redeemer, finally baptizing Our Lord Himself and proclaiming Him "the Lamb of God." St. John the Baptist was beheaded by order of Herod Antipas while enduring imprisonment by the same ruler for denouncing Herod's adulterous and incestuous marriage to his half-brother's wife.

LITANY OF SAINT PETER, PRINCE OF THE APOSTLES

(For private use only.)

Lord, have mercy.
Christ, have mercy.
Lord, have mercy. Christ, hear us.
Christ, graciously hear us.
God the Father of Heaven,
Have mercy on us.
God the Son, Redeemer of the world,
Have mercy on us.
God the Holy Ghost,
Have mercy on us.
Holy Trinity, One God,
Have mercy on us.

Holy Mary, Mother of God, *pray for us.*
Queen conceived without original sin, *pray for us.*
Queen of Apostles, *etc.*
Saint Peter,
Prince of the Apostles,
St. Peter, to whom were given the keys of the Kingdom of Heaven,
St. Peter, so ardent for the glory of Christ,
St. Peter, whose heart was pierced with one look from Jesus,
St. Peter, who ceased not to grieve for having denied the Son of God,
St. Peter, whose cheeks were furrowed by a stream of tears which flowed to the end of thy life,
St. Peter, who cried out, "Lord, Thou knowest that I love Thee!"
St. Peter, bound in chains for Christ,
St. Peter, delivered from prison by an angel,

St. Peter, who rejoiced to suffer for Christ,

St. Peter, whose very shadow healed the sick,

St. Peter, whose voice even the dead obeyed,

St. Peter, that we may have a constant and mutual charity among ourselves,

That we may taste and see more and more how sweet is the Lord,

That we may be zealous in loyalty to thy successor, the present Vicar of Christ,

That we may help, at least by prayer, to restore to the unity of thy Holy See the scattered sheep,

That we may be prudent and watchful in prayer,

That we may die the death of the just,

V. Let the mercies of the Lord give glory to him,

R. *And His wonderful works to the children of men.*

V. Pray for us, Saint Peter the Rock,

R. *That we may be worthy of the Vicar of Christ.*

Let Us Pray

O Lord Jesus Christ, Who upon blessed Peter, Thine Apostle, didst bestow the pontifical power of binding and loosing, and didst give to him the keys of the Kingdom of Heaven, grant that his intercession may ensure our deliverance from the bondage of sin, Thou Who livest and reignest with the Father and the Holy Ghost, ever one God, world without end. R. *Amen.*

St. Peter, Prince of the Apostles: Born at Bethsaida and by trade a fisherman, Peter was actually named "Simon bar Jona," i.e. "Simon, son of John." When Our Lord made him the first pope, He renamed him "Cephas" (Aramaic) or "Petros" (Greek) or "Peter," all of which mean "Rock." Peter was the first bishop of Rome and was crucified there, head downward, around 64 A.D. His tomb has been found in excavations under St. Peter's Basilica in Rome.

LITANY OF
SAINT PAUL THE APOSTLE
(For private use only.)

Thou hast proved me and known me;
Thou hast known my sitting down and my rising up.

V. The great Saint Paul, vessel of election, is indeed
worthy to be glorified,
R. *For he also deserved to possess the twelfth throne.*

Lord, have mercy.
Christ, have mercy.
Lord, have mercy.

Holy Mary, Mother of God, *pray for us.*
Queen conceived without Original Sin, *pray for us.*
Saint Paul, *etc.*
Apostle of the Gentiles,
Vessel of election,
St. Paul, who wast rapt to the third heaven,
St. Paul, who heard things not given to man to utter,
St. Paul, who knew nothing but Christ and Him
crucified,
St. Paul, whose love for Christ was stronger than
death,
St. Paul, who wished to be dissolved and to be with
Christ,
St. Paul, whose zeal knew no bounds,
St. Paul, who made thyself all to all, to gain all to
Christ,
St. Paul, who called thyself prisoner of Christ for us,
St. Paul, who wast jealous of us with the jealousy of
God,
St. Paul, who gloried only in the Cross of Christ,

St. Paul, who bore in thy body the mortification of Christ,

St. Paul, who exclaimed: "With Christ I am nailed to the cross!"

St. Paul, that we may awake and sin no more,

That we may not receive the grace of God in vain,

That we may walk in newness of life,

That we may work out our salvation with fear and trembling,

That we may put on the armor of God,

That we may stand against the deceits of the wicked one,

That we may stand fast to the last,

That we may press forward to the mark,

That we may win the crown,

Lamb of God, Who takest away the sins of the world,
Spare us, O Lord.

Lamb of God, Who takest away the sins of the world,
Graciously hear us, O Lord.

Lamb of God, Who takest away the sins of the world,
Have mercy on us.

Let Us Pray

O God, Who hast taught the whole world by the preaching of blessed Paul the Apostle, grant that we who celebrate his memory may, by following his example, be drawn unto Thee, Through Our Lord Jesus Christ Thy Son, Who with Thee liveth and reigneth in the unity of the Holy Ghost, God, world without end. R. *Amen.*

St. Paul, Apostle to the Gentiles: Originally named Saul of Tarsus, Paul was a Jewish persecutor of Christians until, on his way to Damascus, he was thrown from his horse and struck blind by lightning from Heaven. He became a Christian and made several great missionary journeys in western Asia Minor and Greece, and wrote many of the books of the New Testament. St. Paul was martyred in Rome around 65 A.D.

LITANY OF
SAINT JUDE THADDEUS
Litany One
(For private use only.)

Lord, have mercy on us.
Christ, have mercy on us.
Lord, have mercy on us. Christ, hear us.
Christ, graciously hear us.
God the Father of Heaven,
Have mercy on us.
God the Son, Redeemer of the world,
Have mercy on us.
God the Holy Ghost,
Have mercy on us.
Holy Trinity, One God,
Have mercy on us.

Saint Jude, relative of Jesus and Mary,
Pray for us.
St. Jude, deemed worthy while on earth to see Jesus
and Mary and to enjoy their company,
Pray for us.
St. Jude, raised to the dignity of an Apostle, *etc.*
St. Jude, who hadst the honor of beholding thy Divine
Master humble Himself to wash thy feet,
St. Jude, who at the Last Supper didst receive the
Holy Eucharist from the hands of Jesus,
St. Jude, who after the profound grief which the death
of thy beloved Master caused thee, hadst the
consolation of beholding Him risen from the dead,
and of assisting at His glorious Ascension,
St. Jude, who wast filled with the Holy Ghost on the
day of Pentecost,
St. Jude, who didst preach the Gospel
in Persia,

St. Jude, who didst convert many people
to the Faith,
St. Jude, who didst perform wonderful miracles in the
power of the Holy Ghost,
St. Jude, who didst restore an idolatrous king to health
of both soul and body,
St. Jude, who didst impose silence on demons and
didst confound their oracles,
St. Jude, who didst foretell to a weak prince an
honorable peace with his powerful enemy,
St. Jude, who didst take from deadly serpents the
power of injuring man,
St. Jude, who, disregarding the threats of the impious,
didst courageously preach the doctrine of Christ,
St. Jude, who didst gloriously suffer martyrdom for
the love of thy Divine Master,

Blessed Apostle,
With confidence we invoke thee.
Blessed Apostle,
With confidence we invoke thee.
Blessed Apostle,
With confidence we invoke thee.
St. Jude, help of the hopeless,
Aid me in my distress.
St. Jude, help of the hopeless,
Aid me in my distress.
St. Jude, help of the hopeless,
Aid me in my distress.

That by thy intercession, both priests and people of
the Church may obtain an ardent zeal for the Faith
of Jesus Christ,
We beseech thee, hear us.
That thou wouldst defend our Sovereign Pontiff and
obtain peace and unity for the Holy Church,
We beseech thee, hear us.
That all heathens and unbelievers may be converted
to the True Faith, *etc.*

That faith, hope and charity may increase in our hearts,

That we may be delivered from all evil thoughts and from all the snares of the devil,

That thou wouldst vouchsafe to aid and protect all those who honor thee,

That thou wouldst preserve us from all sin and from all occasions of sin,

That thou wouldst defend us at the hour of death against the fury of the devil and of his evil spirits,

Pray for us, that before death we may expiate all our sins by sincere repentance and the worthy reception of the holy Sacraments,

Pray for us, that we may appease the Divine Justice and obtain a favorable judgment,

Pray for us, that we may be admitted into the company of the blessed, to rejoice in the presence of our God forever,

Lamb of God, Who takest away the sins of the world, *Spare us, O Lord.*

Lamb of God, Who takest away the sins of the world, *Graciously hear us, O Lord.*

Lamb of God, Who takest away the sins of the world, *Have mercy on us.*

V. Saint Jude, pray for us,

R. *And for all who invoke thine aid.*

Let Us Pray

O God, Who through Thy blessed Apostle Jude Thaddeus hast brought us unto the knowledge of Thy Name, grant us both to celebrate his eternal glory by making progress in virtues, and by celebrating his glory, to advance in virtue, through Our Lord Jesus Christ, Who with Thee and the Holy Ghost art one God, now and forever. R. *Amen.*

St. Jude Thaddeus, Apostle, and Helper in Hopeless and Desperate Cases: One of the twelve Apostles, St. Jude was the brother of the Apostle James the Less and was a near relative of the Blessed Virgin Mary; he is one of "the brethren of the Lord" mentioned in *Matthew* 13:55. St. Jude firmly established the Church of Edessa, and then visited the whole of Mesopotamia. He was martyred in Persia, and his body was translated to Rome where it rests in St. Peter's Basilica. St. Bernard of Clairvaux venerated a relic of St. Jude throughout his life, and then asked that the relic be placed on his breast and buried with him when he died. St. Jude is often represented wearing a picture of Our Lord on his breast, to commemorate Our Lord's miraculous imprinting of His face on a cloth.

LITANY OF
SAINT JUDE THADDEUS
Litany Two
(For private use only.)

Lord, have mercy on us.
Christ, have mercy on us.
Lord, have mercy on us. Christ, hear us.
Christ, graciously hear us.
God the Father of Heaven,
Have mercy on us.
God the Son, Redeemer of the world,
Have mercy on us.
God the Holy Spirit,
Have mercy on us.
Holy Trinity, One God,
Have mercy on us.

Holy Mary, Mother of God, *pray for us.*
Holy Mary, Mother of the Church, *pray for us.*
Holy Mary, Queen of Apostles, *etc.*
Saint Jude, Apostle of Christ,
Saint Jude, surnamed Thaddeus,
Saint Jude, among "the brethren of the Lord,"
Saint Jude, cousin of the Lord,
Saint Jude, relative of Mary,
Saint Jude, brother of Saint James the Less,
Saint Jude, Zealot party member turned Disciple,
Saint Jude, spiritual heir of the Maccabees,
Saint Jude, one of the Twelve,
Saint Jude, honored by thy humble Master washing
    thy feet,
Saint Jude, who received thy Eucharistic Lord from
    His own hands at the Last Supper,
Saint Jude, Saint of the Impossible,
Saint Jude, Helper in Difficult Cases,

Saint Jude, in whom so many have confidence,
Saint Jude, redeemer of the name of Judas,
Saint Jude, one in whom we can trust,
Saint Jude, sent by Christ on missions of healing,
Saint Jude, sent by Our Lord to drive out demons,
Saint Jude, sent to cure sickness and disease,
Saint Jude, sent without silver, staff or sandals,
Saint Jude, sent to raise the dead,
Saint Jude, sent as a sheep among wolves,
Saint Jude, sent to announce the reign of God,
Saint Jude, promised the Holy Spirit under trial,
Saint Jude, filled with the Holy Spirit on
    Pentecost,
Saint Jude, witness to the Resurrection of Christ
    and His Ascension,
Saint Jude, miracle worker,
Saint Jude, to whom the epistle by that name is
    attributed,
Saint Jude, believed to have preached in
    Mesopotamia,
Saint Jude, thought to have been martyred with Saint
    Simon in Persia,
Saint Jude, saint for our needs,
Saint Jude, saint for our times,
Saint Jude, pictured with a burning flame,
Saint Jude, patron of many shrines in thy honor,
Saint Jude, beloved intercessor at novenas,
Saint Jude, inspirer of confidence,
Saint Jude, helper of the persistent,

Lamb of God, Who takest away the sins of the world,
    Spare us, O Lord.
Lamb of God, Who takest away the sins of the world,
    Graciously hear us, O Lord.
Lamb of God, Who takest away the sins of the world,
    Have mercy on us.

Christ, hear us.
    Christ, graciously hear us.

V. Pray for us, St. Jude, Apostle of Christ,
R. *That we may be made worthy of the promises of Christ.*

Let Us Pray

O glorious Saint Jude Thaddeus, by those sublime prerogatives wherewith thou wast ennobled in thy lifetime, namely, thy kinship with Our Lord Jesus Christ according to the flesh, and thy vocation to be an Apostle; by that glory which is now thine in Heaven as the reward of thine apostolic labors and thy martyrdom: Obtain for us from the Giver of every good and perfect gift all the graces we stand in need of in order to treasure up in our hearts the divinely inspired doctrines which thou hast transmitted to us in thine Epistle; that is to say, to build our edifice of perfection upon our most holy Faith, praying by the grace of the Holy Spirit; to keep ourselves in the love of God, looking for the mercy of Jesus Christ unto eternal life; to strive by all means to help those who go astray, exalting thus the glory and majesty, the dominion and power of Him Who is able to keep us without sin and to present us spotless with exceeding joy at the coming of our Divine Saviour, the Lord Jesus Christ. R. *Amen.*

This litany was composed by Fr. Albert J. Hebert, S.M., with ecclesiastical approval. The "Let Us Pray" prayer is from the old *Raccolta.*

LITANY OF
SAINT MARY MAGDALEN

(For private use only.)

Lord, have mercy on us.
> *Christ, have mercy on us.*

Lord, have mercy on us. Christ, hear us.
> *Christ, graciously hear us.*

Holy Mary, Mother of God, *pray for us.*

Saint Mary Magdalen, *pray for us.*

Sister of Martha and Lazarus, *etc.*

Thou who didst enter the Pharisee's house to anoint the feet of Jesus,

Who didst wash His feet with thy tears,

Who didst dry them with thy hair,

Who didst cover them with kisses,

Who wast vindicated by Jesus before the proud Pharisee,

Who from Jesus received the pardon of thy sins,

Who before darkness wast restored to light,

Mirror of penance,

Disciple of Our Lord,

Wounded with the love of Christ,

Most dear to the Heart of Jesus,

Constant woman,

Last at the Cross of Jesus, first at His tomb,

Thou who wast the first to see Jesus risen,

Whose forehead was sanctified by the touch of thy risen Master,

Apostle of apostles,

Who didst choose the "better part,"

Who lived for many years in solitude being miraculously fed,

Who wast visited by angels seven times a day,

Sweet advocate of sinners,
Spouse of the King of Glory,

V. Saint Mary Magdalen, earnestly intercede for us
    with thy Divine Master,
R. *That we may share thy happiness in Heaven.*

Let Us Pray

May the glorious merits of blessed Mary Magdalen,
we beseech Thee, O Lord, make our offerings acceptable to Thee, for Thine only-begotten Son vouchsafed
graciously to accept the humble service she rendered.
We ask this through Him Who liveth and reigneth
with Thee and the Holy Ghost, God forever and ever.
R. *Amen.*

May the prayers of blessed Mary Magdalen help us,
O Lord, for it was in answer to them that Thou didst
call her brother Lazarus, four days after death, back
from the grave to life, Who livest and reignest with the
Father and the Holy Ghost, Unity in Trinity, world
without end. R. *Amen.*

St. Mary Magdalen, Penitent: St. Mary Magdalen was probably
born in Magdala, near Tiberias. She is mentioned in all four
Gospels. Seven devils were cast out of her by Our Lord, and she
was later present at His crucifixion. With the other women, she
found Christ's empty tomb and saw the angels there, and she was
the first person to see Our Lord after His Resurrection. According
to the tradition of the Western Church, Mary Magdalen is identical
with "the woman who was a sinner" who poured ointment on Our
Lord's feet, drying them with her hair, and with the sister of
Martha and Lazarus—that is, the Mary who chose "the better
part." Liturgical devotion to this glorious penitent has been im-
memorial.

LITANY OF OUR LADY OF CONSOLATION, SAINT AUGUSTINE AND SAINT MONICA

commonly called
"The Litany of The Three Patrons"
(For private use only.)

Lord, have mercy on us.
Christ, have mercy on us.
Lord, have mercy on us. Christ, hear us.
Christ, graciously hear us.

God the Father of Heaven,
Have mercy on us.
God the Son, Redeemer of the world,
Have mercy on us.
God the Holy Ghost,
Have mercy on us.
Holy Trinity, One God,
Have mercy on us.

Mary, our Mother and the Mother of Jesus,
Pray for us.
Mary, our Mother of Consolation,
Pray for us.
Mary, the source of our hope, *etc.*
Mary, the refuge of sinners,
Mary, the guiding star of our lives,
Mary, source of strength in our weakness,
Mary, source of light in our darkness,
Mary, source of consolation in our sorrows,
Mary, source of victory in our temptations,
Mary, who leads us to Jesus,
Mary, who keeps us with Jesus,
Mary, who redeems us through Jesus,
Mary, Mother of Consolation, our Patroness,

Saint Augustine, triumph of divine grace,
  Pray for us.
St. Augustine, so faithful to grace,
  Pray for us.
St. Augustine, glowing with pure love of God, *etc.*
St. Augustine, filled with zeal for God's glory,
St. Augustine, bright star in the firmament of the
  Church,
St. Augustine, so great and so humble,
St. Augustine, dauntless defender of
  the Faith,
St. Augustine, vanquisher of heresy,
St. Augustine, prince of bishops and doctors,
St. Augustine, our father (and founder),
(St. Augustine, glorious Patron of the Confraternity),

Saint Monica, devout mother of St. Augustine,
  Pray for us.
St. Monica, whose prayers won Augustine from sin,
  Pray for us.
St. Monica, whose prayers gave Augustine to God,
  etc.
St. Monica, pattern for wives,
St. Monica, model of mothers and mother of saints,
St. Monica, exemplar of widows,
St. Monica, devoted to prayer,
St. Monica, so patient in trials,
St. Monica, so resigned in sorrow,
St. Monica, so happy in death,
St. Monica, devoted child of Mary, Mother of
  Consolation,
(St. Monica, our Patroness in the Confraternity),

Lamb of God, Who takest away the sins of the world,
  Spare us, O Lord.
Lamb of God, Who takest away the sins of the world,
  Graciously hear us, O Lord.
Lamb of God, Who takest away the sins of the world,
  Have mercy on us.

V. Pray for us, O holy Mother of Consolation,

R. *That we may be made worthy of the promises of Christ.*

V. Pray for us, O holy father, Saint Augustine,

R. *That we may be made worthy of the promises of Christ.*

V. Pray for us, O holy mother, Saint Monica,

R. *That we may be made worthy of the promises of Christ.*

Let Us Pray

O Lord Jesus Christ, Father of mercies and God of all consolation, grant propitiously to Thy servants that, joyfully venerating Thy most pure Mother Mary as Our Lady of Consolation (and wearing in her honor the holy Cincture), we may be consoled by her in our sorrows, fortified in our trials through life, and in dying, may merit the ineffable consolations of Heaven for all eternity. *Amen.*

St. Monica, Widow and Patroness of Married Women: St. Monica (c. 331-387) was one of the primary reasons her son, Augustine, became a Christian and a great saint, after spending years in wayward living and heresy. St. Monica had prayed for him for years. She also converted her husband and her mother-in-law. St. Monica is the Patroness of Married Women, and is also a model for Christian mothers. (See also the Litany of St. Augustine).

The invocations in parentheses are for use by Augustinian Secular Tertiaries and members of the Archconfraternity of the Cincture.

LITANY OF
SAINT AUGUSTINE

(For private use only.)

Lord, have mercy on us.
Christ, have mercy on us.
Lord, have mercy on us. Christ, hear us.
Christ, graciously hear us.

God the Father of Heaven,
Have mercy on us.
God the Son, Redeemer of the world,
Have mercy on us.
God the Holy Ghost,
Have mercy on us.
Holy Trinity, One God,
Have mercy on us.

Holy Mary, *pray for us.*
Holy Mother of God, *pray for us.*
Holy Virgin of virgins, *etc.*
Holy Father Augustine,
Saint Augustine, example of contrite souls,
St. Augustine, son of the tears of thy mother Monica,
St. Augustine, light of teachers,
St. Augustine, exterminator of heresies,
St. Augustine, illustrious warrior against the foes of
the Church,
St. Augustine, pillar of the True Faith,
St. Augustine, vessel of Divine Wisdom,
St. Augustine, rule of conduct for apostolic life,
St. Augustine, whose heart was inflamed with the fire
of Divine Love,
St. Augustine, humble and merciful father,
St. Augustine, zealous preacher of the Word of God,

St. Augustine, precious treasure of confessors,
St. Augustine, illumined expounder of Sacred
  Scripture,
St. Augustine, ornament of bishops,
St. Augustine, light of the True Faith,
St. Augustine, noble defender of Holy Church,
St. Augustine, refulgence of the glory of God,
St. Augustine, blossoming olive tree of the House of
  God,
St. Augustine, indefatigable adorer of the Most Holy
  Trinity,
St. Augustine, inexhaustible fountain of Christian
  eloquence,
St. Augustine, shining mirror of holiness,
St. Augustine, model of all virtues,
St. Augustine, consoler of the distressed,
St. Augustine, comforter of the forsaken,
St. Augustine, friend and helper of the poor,
St. Augustine, our father,

Lamb of God, Who takest away the sins of the world,
  Spare us, O Lord.
Lamb of God, Who takest away the sins of the world,
  Graciously hear us, O Lord.
Lamb of God, Who takest away the sins of the world,
  Have mercy on us, O Lord.

Christ, hear us.
  Christ, graciously hear us.

Let Us Pray

O God, Who didst disclose to Saint Augustine the hidden mysteries of Thy wisdom and didst enkindle in his heart the flame of Divine Love, thus renewing in Thy Church the pillar of cloud and fire, graciously grant that we may pass safely through the storms of this world and reach the eternal fatherland which Thou didst promise us, through Christ Our Lord. R. *Amen.*

St. Augustine, Father and Doctor of the Church: After spending his youth and early manhood in wayward living and in philosophical studies, searching for truth, St. Augustine (354-430) was converted (throuh the prayers of his mother and the preaching of St. Ambrose) and became one of the greatest and most brilliant theologians in the history of the Church. He was Bishop of Hippo in North Africa for 35 years, and he led the fight against three major heresies: Manichaeism, Donatism, and Pelagianism. St. Augustine's most famous books are his *Confessions* and *The City of God.* He is also one of the four great founders of religious orders.

LITANY OF
SAINT BENEDICT

(For private use only.)

Lord, have mercy on us.
  Christ, have mercy on us.
Lord, have mercy on us. Christ, hear us.
  Christ, graciously hear us.
God the Father of Heaven,
  Have mercy on us.
God the Son, Redeemer of the world,
  Have mercy on us.
God the Holy Spirit,
  Have mercy on us.
Holy Trinity, One God,
  Have mercy on us.

Holy Mary,
  Pray for us.
Holy Mother of God,
  Pray for us.
Holy Virgin of virgins, *etc.*
Holy Father, Saint Benedict,
Father most reverend,
Father most renowned,
Father most compassionate,
Man of great fortitude,
Man of venerable life,
Man of the most holy conversation,
True servant of God,
Light of devotion,
Light of prayer,
Light of contemplation,
Star of the world,
Best master of an austere life,

Leader of the holy warfare,
Leader and chief of monks,
Master of those who die to the world,
Protector of those who cry to thee,
Wonderful worker of miracles,
Revealer of the secrets of the
   human heart,
Master of spiritual discipline,
Companion of the patriarchs,
Equal of the prophets,
Follower of the Apostles,
Teacher of martyrs,
Father of many pontiffs,
Gem of abbots,
Glory of confessors,
Imitator of anchorites,
Associate of virgins,
Colleague of all the saints,

Lamb of God, Who takest away the sins of the world,
   Spare us, O Lord.
Lamb of God, Who takest away the sins of the world,
   Graciously hear us, O Lord.
Lamb of God, Who takest away the sins of the world,
   Have mercy on us.

V. Intercede for us, O holy father Saint Benedict,
R. *That we may be made worthy of the promises of
   Christ.*

Let Us Pray

O God, Who hast called us from the vanity of the
world, and Who dost incite us to the reward of a
heavenly vocation under the guidance of our holy
patriarch and founder, Saint Benedict, inspire and
purify our hearts and pour forth on us Thy grace,
whereby we may persevere in Thee. Through Jesus
Christ, Our Lord. R. *Amen.*

St. Benedict, Father of Western Monasticism: Born at Nursia in Umbria near Rome around 480, St. Benedict fled from the license of Rome and lived as a hermit in Subiaco. When a multitude of disciples gathered around him, he built the Monastery of Monte Cassino, the birthplace of western monasticism. For the monks there he wrote the Rule which bears his name and from which most monastic rules in the Church have been derived. St. Benedict made the Divine Office the center of monastic life. He was never ordained a priest. He was known for his holiness, wisdom, and miracles, including raising people from the dead. Benedictine monks taught the barbarians to work and pray, and they educated western Europe. St. Benedict died around 547. Monte Cassino was destroyed during World War II, but has been rebuilt.

LITANY OF
SAINT SCHOLASTICA

(For private use only.)

Lord, have mercy on us.
Lord, have mercy on us.
Christ, have mercy on us.
Christ, have mercy on us.
Lord, have mercy on us.
Lord, have mercy on us.
Christ, hear us.
Christ, graciously hear us.
God the Father of Heaven,
Have mercy on us.
God the Son, Redeemer of the world,
Have mercy on us.
God the Holy Ghost,
Have mercy on us.
Holy Trinity, One God,
Have mercy on us.

Holy Mary, *pray for us.*
Holy Mother of God, *pray for us.*
Holy Virgin of virgins, *etc.*
Saint Scholastica,
St. Scholastica, true sister of St. Benedict,
St. Scholastica, chosen by God from eternity,
St. Scholastica, predisposed to faith by the grace of
    Christ Our Lord,
St. Scholastica, consecrated to God from thine
    infancy,
St. Scholastica, always a virgin incorrupt,
St. Scholastica, espoused to Jesus Christ,
St. Scholastica, scholar of the Holy Ghost,
St. Scholastica, mirror of innocence,

St. Scholastica, model of perfection,

St. Scholastica, pattern of virtues,

St. Scholastica, glory of the monastic life,

St. Scholastica, mother of numberless virgins,

St. Scholastica, imitator of the angelic life,

St. Scholastica, full of faith in God,

St. Scholastica, replenished with hope of the goods of Heaven,

St. Scholastica, ever burning with the love of thy Spouse,

St. Scholastica, resplendent with humility,

St. Scholastica, trusting as a daughter in the Lord,

St. Scholastica, intent on prayer,

St. Scholastica, quickly heard by the Lord,

St. Scholastica, famed for the praise of perseverance,

St. Scholastica, who didst enter the courts of Heaven in the form of a dove,

St. Scholastica, who dost now follow the Lamb whithersoever He goeth,

St. Scholastica, who dost rejoice in the delights of thy Spouse forever,

St. Scholastica, adorned with a crown of glory,

St. Scholastica, advocate with God of those who invoke thee,

St. Scholastica, generous patron of those who imitate thee,

St. Scholastica, holy and innocent virgin,

We sinners
Beseech thee, Saint Scholastica, to hear us.

That thou wouldst deign to help us by thy most holy and efficacious prayers to God,
We beseech thee, hear us.

That thou wouldst deign to cherish and preserve, by thy protection, the Benedictine Order (and this monastery) and all who dwell therein,
We beseech thee, hear us.

(That thou wouldst admit us into the number of thy children,) *etc.*

That thou wouldst deign to raise up, increase, and preserve our devotion toward thee,

(That thou wouldst deign to preserve in us the perfect observance of the Rule of thy blessed brother, our most holy father Saint Benedict,)

That thou wouldst deign, by thy supplications, to moisten the dryness of our hearts with the dew of heavenly grace,

That by thy intercession thou mayest eternally unite us to Christ, the Spouse of our souls,

That thou mayest lead us to eternal joys, and to Jesus (our most sweet Spouse),

That thou wouldst vouchsafe to hear us,

Lamb of God, Who takest away the sins of the world, *Spare us, O Lord.*

Lamb of God, Who takest away the sins of the world, *Graciously hear us, O Lord.*

Lamb of God, Who takest away the sins of the world, *Have mercy on us.*

V. Pray for us, O holy Virgin Scholastica,
R. *That we may be made worthy of the promises of Christ.*

Let Us Pray

O God, Who, to show the innocence of her life, didst cause the soul of Thy blessed virgin Scholastica to ascend to Heaven in the form of a dove, grant, we beseech Thee, by her merits and prayers, that we may live so innocently as to deserve to arrive at eternal joys, through Jesus Christ, Thine only-begotten Son Our Lord, Who with Thee and the Holy Ghost liveth and reigneth, God, forever and ever. R. *Amen.*

St. Scholastica, Abbess: St. Scholastica, the sister of St. Benedict, and the first Benedictine nun, was born around 480 and was dedicated to God as an infant. At St. Scholastica's death (c. 543), her brother, St. Benedict, saw her soul fly to Heaven in the form of a dove.

The invocations in parentheses are for use by Benedictine nuns.

LITANY OF
SAINT AUGUSTINE OF CANTERBURY
(For private use only.)

Lord, have mercy on us.
  Christ, have mercy on us.
Lord, have mercy on us. Christ, hear us.
  Christ, graciously hear us.
God the Father of Heaven,
  Have mercy on us.
God, the Son, Redeemer of the world,
  Have mercy on us.
God the Holy Ghost,
  Have mercy on us.
Holy Trinity, One God,
  Have mercy on us.

Holy Mary, Mother of God,
  Pray for us.
Holy Mary, devoutly honored by Saint Augustine,
  Pray for us.
Saint Augustine, *etc.*
St. Augustine, glory of the Catholic Church,
St. Augustine, chosen vessel of the Holy Ghost,
Great Apostle of England,
Renowned Apostle of Gentiles,
Glorious defender of the Catholic Faith,
Worthy confessor of Christ Our Lord,
Thou faithful son of the holy Father St. Benedict,
Thou honorable disciple of thy holy master St.
  Gregory,
Thou perfect contemner of the world,
Example of humility,
Lover of poverty,
Strict observer of the holy Rule,

St. Augustine, curing the blind,
St. Augustine, restoring health to the sick,
St. Augustine, preaching the Gospel to our
    forefathers,
Zealous patron of immortal souls,
Powerful in need to all who take refuge in thee in their
    wants,
Powerful intercessor in Heaven,
Thou our patron saint,

In all our wants of body and soul,
    Help us by thy intercession.
In all dangers,
    Help us by thy intercession.
In all tribulations, *etc.*
In temptations of the world, the flesh, and the devil,
In case of sickness,
In poverty and famine,
In danger of losing the Catholic Faith,
In the hour of our death,

That God may humble the enemies of the Catholic
    Faith, *make intercession for us.*
That all heresies may be extinguished, *make
    intercession for us.*
That the spirit of infidelity may be checked, *etc.*
That all prodigal children may return to the true
    Church of Christ,
That our faith may never cease,
That our hope may continually increase,
That we may perpetually love God with a sincere
    heart,
That the English nation may return to the Catholic
    Faith which thou hast preached to their forefathers,
That we may escape eternal condemnation and the
    everlasting fire of Hell,
That we may be saved through Jesus Christ,
That we may be taken up to Heaven to see the eternal
    Glory of God,

That we may never lose the grace and love of our
  heavenly Father,

Lamb of God, Who takest away the sins of the world,
  Spare us, O Lord.
Lamb of God, Who takest away the sins of the world,
  Graciously hear us, O Lord.
Lamb of God, Who takest away the sins of the world,
  Have mercy on us, O Lord.

V. Intercede for us, O holy Augustine, great Apostle
  of England,
R. *That we may be made worthy of the promises of
  Christ.*

Let Us Pray

O God, Who in the conversion of the Gentiles, hast
mercifully granted the pious prayers of Saint
Augustine, Thy Confessor and Bishop, vouchsafe to
grant through his merits and intercession that we,
bewailing our sins, may be consoled by the gift of Thy
graces, through Jesus Christ Our Lord. R. *Amen.*

St. Augustine of Canterbury, Apostle of the English: Born in
Rome, Augustine became a Benedictine priest. In 596 he was sent
to England by Pope St. Gregory the Great with 40 monks to convert England. In 597 he baptized King Ethelbert of Kent (Canterbury). St. Augustine was consecrated a bishop, and on Christmas
Day of 597 he baptized 10,000 Saxons. In 601 he received the
pallium from Rome as Archbishop and father of the English
hierarchy. He erected the Archdiocese of Canterbury and the sees
of London and Rochester. St. Augustine died in 605. (He is sometimes also called St. Austin).

LITANY OF
SAINT BONIFACE

(For private use only.)

Lord, have mercy.
   Lord, have mercy.
Christ, have mercy.
   Christ, have mercy.
Lord, have mercy.
   Lord, have mercy.
Christ, hear us.
   Christ, graciously hear us.
God the Father of Heaven,
   Have mercy on us.
God the Son, Redeemer of the world,
   Have mercy on us.
God the Holy Ghost,
   Have mercy on us.
Holy Trinity, One God,
   Have mercy on us.

Holy Mary, *pray for us.*
Holy Mother of God, *pray for us.*
Holy Virgin of virgins, *etc.*
Queen of the Apostles,
Saint Boniface,
Apostle of Germany,
Worthy successor of the Apostles,
Worthy disciple of Saint Benedict,
Ornament of the Catholic Church,
Thou light, shining for the conversion of pagan
   nations,
Thou light, shining like the sun,
Thou great benefactor of many nations,
Thou zealous preacher of the Gospel,

Thou unwearied laborer in the vineyard of the Lord,
Thou founder of the Catholic Church in Germany,
Saint Boniface, our Father,
St. Boniface, teacher of truth and virtue,
St. Boniface, extirpator of heathenism,
St. Boniface, destroyer of heresy,
St. Boniface, great bishop and model of missionaries,
St. Boniface, protector of missions,
St. Boniface, founder of many monasteries,
St. Boniface, powerful advocate with God,
St. Boniface, who didst work many miracles,
St. Boniface, great martyr of faith,
That God may preserve and confirm us in our holy
    Catholic religion,
That God may grant us the grace to walk piously and
    faithfully before Him,
That God may humble the enemies of His Church,
That God may grant the grace of True Faith to all
    heretics and infidels,
That God may give us that spirit with which thou
    didst serve Him,
That God may restore the Faith to the whole of
    Germany,
That God may raise up zealous missionaries to
    convert all pagans and heretics,
That the Holy Spirit may enlighten all missionaries,

Lamb of God, Who takest away the sins of the world,
    Spare us, O Lord.
Lamb of God, Who takest away the sins of the world,
    Graciously hear us, O Lord.
Lamb of God, Who takest away the sins of the world,
    Have mercy on us.

Christ, hear us.
    Christ, graciously hear us.
Lord, have mercy.
    Christ, have mercy.
Lord, have mercy.

Our Father, *etc. (for the re-conversion of Germany and for the conversion of all heathens).*

Let Us Pray

Merciful God, Who hast shown compassion to so many heathen nations through Thy faithful servant St. Boniface, we humbly pray Thee to revive and preserve that Faith which he preached in Thy holy Name, that we may receive Thy revelation with a faithful heart, and so regulate our lives as to gain the Heavenly Kingdom, through Jesus Christ Our Lord. R. *Amen.*

Preserve and increase, we beseech Thee, O God, the faith of Thy children, and lead back to the True Fold all those who have been separated or have separated themselves from it, through Christ Our Lord. R. *Amen.*

St. Boniface, Apostle of Germany: St. Boniface was born of noble Anglo-Saxon parents in Devonshire, England around the year 680. He became a Benedictine priest and later a bishop. The pope authorized him as metropolitan of Germany beyond the Rhine, and he evangelized Upper Hessia, Hessia, Thuringia, and pagan Saxony. St. Boniface converted a huge group of pagans at Geismar after cutting down an oak tree considered sacred to the pagan god Thor without suffering any punishment from the god. St. Boniface founded nine episcopal sees, established the Catholic hierarchy in Germany, founded several monasteries, reformed the Frankish Church, crowned King Pepin, consecrated Archbishops for Rheims, Sens and Rouen, and was in charge of missionary work in The Netherlands. St. Boniface and 52 companions were martyred by pagans in 754. His body rests in the cathedral crypt at Fulda, Germany.

LITANY OF
SAINT WALBURGA

(For private use only.)

Lord, have mercy on us.
Christ, have mercy on us.
Lord, have mercy on us. Christ, hear us.
Christ, graciously hear us.
God the Father of Heaven,
Have mercy on us.
God the Son, Redeemer of the world,
Have mercy on us.
God the Holy Ghost,
Have mercy on us.
Holy Trinity, One God,
Have mercy on us.

Holy Mary, conceived without sin, *pray for us.*
Holy Mother of God, *pray for us.*
Holy Virgin of virgins, *etc.*
Saint Walburga,
St. Walburga, lily of purity,
St. Walburga, model of humility,
St. Walburga, model of obedience,
St. Walburga, perfect model of monastic discipline
  and modesty,
St. Walburga, ornament of virgins consecrated to
  God,
St. Walburga, model of mortification,
St. Walburga, conqueror of all temptations,
St. Walburga, perpetual sacrifice of Divine love,
St. Walburga, glorious example of perseverance in
  the service of God,
St. Walburga, zealous servant of Jesus and Mary,
St. Walburga, light and ornament of thy order,

St. Walburga, miraculous help in time of need,

St. Walburga, refuge of the afflicted,

St. Walburga, solace of the sick and sorrowful,

St. Walburga, powerful advocate of all who venerate thee,

St. Walburga, who through love of Jesus didst despise the pomps and vanities of the world,

St. Walburga, who through love for Jesus didst forsake thy home and country,

St. Walburga, who didst bring from afar the light of faith to heathen nations,

St. Walburga, who as a wise and prudent virgin didst make an entire offering of thyself to thy heavenly Spouse,

St. Walburga, who didst teach the true Faith both by thy word and example,

St. Walburga, who through works of charity poured out the oil of tender compassion,

St. Walburga, who through thy holy example didst gain many virgins to follow Jesus Christ,

St. Walburga, who, strong in faith, didst conquer the world,

St. Walburga, who didst at all times confide in the Lord,

St. Walburga, who didst faithfully serve God in perfect love,

St. Walburga, who didst restore sight to the blind and hearing to the deaf,

St. Walburga, who didst restore speech to the dumb and reanimate the paralyzed limbs of the lame,

St. Walburga, who through thy example and intercession didst convert so many sinners,

Lamb of God, Who takest away the sins of the world,
Spare us, O Lord.

Lamb of God, Who takest away the sins of the world,
Hear us, O Lord.

Lamb of God, Who takest away the sins of the world,
Have mercy on us, O Lord.

V. Pray for us, O holy Saint Walburga,

R. *That we may be made worthy of the promises of Christ.*

Let Us Pray

O God, Who art full of mercy and compassion toward all who call upon Thee, and Who dost not cast away anyone who approaches Thee with confidence and humility, grant that through the intercession of Thy holy virgin, Saint Walburga, we may partake of the plenitude of Thy mercies; help us, that as by Thy special grace we have known and praised Thee, through the holy virgin Walburga, as a God rich in miracles, we may also love and adore Thee as a merciful Father, through Jesus Christ Our Lord. R. *Amen.*

St. Walburga, Virgin and Abbess: Born around the year 710, in Devonshire, England, St. Walburga became a Benedictine nun and was sent to help her kinsman, St. Boniface, evangelize the Germans. She became supreme abbess of the great double monastery of Heidenheim, which had been founded by her brothers, Sts. Willibald and Winnebald; she wrote St. Winnebald's life. St. Walburga died in 779, and from the rocks on which her relics rest there exudes even to our day a miraculous oil through which many cures have been granted. St. Walburga is also known by other names, including Vaubourg, Walpurgis, and Falbourg.

LITANY OF
SAINT BERNARD OF CLAIRVAUX
(For private use only.)

Lord, have mercy on us.
Christ, have mercy on us.
Lord, have mercy on us. Christ, hear us.
Christ, graciously hear us.
God the Father of Heaven,
Have mercy on us.
God the Son, Redeemer of the world,
Have mercy on us.
God the Holy Ghost,
Have mercy on us.
Holy Trinity, One God,
Have mercy on us.

Holy Mary, Mother of God, *pray for us.*
Queen conceived without sin, *pray for us.*
Saint Bernard, *etc.*
St. Bernard, who in giving thyself to God, drew many souls to Him,
St. Bernard, prodigy of the eleventh age,
St. Bernard, ornament of the clergy,
St. Bernard, terror of heretics,
St. Bernard, oracle of the Church,
St. Bernard, light of bishops,
St. Bernard, most humble,
St. Bernard, burning with zeal for the glory of God,
St. Bernard, most ardent for the honor of Mary,
St. Bernard, most beloved son of the Queen of Angels,
St. Bernard, most pure in body and mind,
St. Bernard, perfect model of poverty and mortification,
St. Bernard, most ardent in charity to all,

St. Bernard, who feared God and not earthly powers,
St. Bernard, whose whole exterior breathed
holiness,
St. Bernard, whose very look spoke of God,
St. Bernard, flower of religious,
St. Bernard, who never lost sight of the presence of
God,
St. Bernard, angel of Clairvaux,
St. Bernard, always absorbed in God,

Lamb of God, Who takest away the sins of the world,
Hear us, O Lord.
Lamb of God, Who takest away the sins of the world,
Spare us, O Lord.
Lamb of God, Who takest away the sins of the world,
Have mercy on us, O Lord.

Let Us Pray

O great saint, who from the very dawn of life turned all the powers of thy soul and the noble affections of thy pure and loving heart toward thy Creator; O angel clothed in mortal flesh, who appeared in this valley of tears as a bright lily of purity to shed around thee the good odor of Christ, to show to all the beauty of virtue, and to point out to thousands the way to Heaven—O pray for us, that truly despising all earthly objects, we may live for God alone. R. *Amen.*

The Memorare of St. Bernard

Remember, O most gracious Virgin Mary, that never was it known that anyone who fled to thy protection, implored thy help, or sought thy intercession was left unaided. Inspired with this confidence, I fly unto thee, O Virgin of virgins, my Mother. To thee I come, before thee I stand, sinful and sorrowful. O Mother of the Word Incarnate, despise not my petitions, but in thy mercy, hear and answer me. R. *Amen.*

St. Bernard of Clairvaux, Oracle of the 12th Century, and Doctor of the Church: St. Bernard was born around 1091 of a noble family at Castle Fontaines near Dijon, France. At age 22 he took 32 of his relatives with him to join the Cistercian monastery of Citeaux. St. Bernard is considered the second founder of the Cistercian Order, and he was the first abbot of the abbey of Clairvaux. He became the greatest preacher of his time, performed innumerable miracles (including raising many people from the dead), preached the second Crusade, and dominated political and ecclesiastical events all over Europe from age 25 to his death in 1153. Yet he also reached the heights of contemplation and left some of the Church's greatest mystical writings, particularly *On the Necessity of Loving God*, and his *Sermons on the Song of Songs*. St. Bernard is known as "The Mellifluous Doctor" and is considered the last of the Fathers of the Church.

LITANY OF
SAINT DOMINIC

(For private use only.)

Lord, have mercy on us.
   Christ, have mercy on us.
Lord, have mercy on us. Christ, hear us.
   Christ, graciously hear us.
God the Father of Heaven,
   Have mercy on us.
God the Son, Redeemer of the world,
   Have mercy on us.
God the Holy Spirit,
   Have mercy on us.
Holy Trinity, One God,
   Have mercy on us.

Holy Mary, *pray for us.*
Holy Mother of God, *pray for us.*
Holy Virgin of virgins, *etc.*
Our glorious father, Saint Dominic,
Follower of Jesus Christ,
Eminently endowed with the virtues of His Sacred
   Heart,
Adorer of the Blessed Sacrament,
Singularly devoted to our Blessed Lady,
Promoter of her honor,
Promulgator of the Holy Rosary,
Splendor of the priesthood,
Founder of the Friars Preachers,
Confounder of the Albigenses,
Reviver of ecclesiastical discipline,
Rose of patience,
Most ardent for the salvation of souls,
Most desirous of martyrdom,

Evangelical man,
Doctor of truth,
Ivory of chastity,
Man of truly apostolic heart,
Poor in the midst of riches,
Rich in an unspotted life,
Burning with zeal for perishing souls,
Preacher of the Gospel,
Rule of abstinence,
Herald of heavenly things,
Salt of the earth,
Thou who didst water the earth with thy precious
    blood,
Shining in the choir of virgins,
Saint Dominic most humble,
Saint Dominic most obedient,
Saint Dominic most chaste,
Saint Dominic most charitable,

That at the hour of death we may be received into
    Heaven with thee, *pray for us.*

Be merciful unto us, O Lord, *and pardon us.*
Be merciful unto us, O Lord, *and graciously hear us.*

From all sin and evil, *O Lord, deliver us.*
From the snares of the devil, *O Lord, deliver us.*
From eternal death, *etc.*
By the merits of our holy father, Saint Dominic,
By his ardent love,
By his indefatigable zeal,
By his extraordinary labors,
By his inexpressible penances,
By his voluntary poverty,
By his perpetual chastity,
By his perfect obedience,
By his profound humility,
By his rare constancy,
By all his other virtues,

Lamb of God, Who takest away the sins of the world,
Spare us, O Lord.

Lamb of God, Who takest away the sins of the world,
Graciously hear us, O Lord.

Lamb of God, Who takest away the sins of the world,
Have mercy on us.

V. Pray for us, O holy father, Saint Dominic,

R. *That we may be made worthy of the promises of Christ.*

Let Us Pray

Grant, we beseech Thee, O Almighty God, that we who are weighed down by the burden of our sins may be relieved by the patronage of Saint Dominic, Thy confessor and our father. Through Christ Our Lord. R. *Amen.*

St. Dominic, Founder of the Dominican Order: St. Dominic was born to the Guzman family in Spain around 1170. He was ordained a priest, and at Prouille, France he founded a convent whose first nuns were converts from the Albigensian heresy; this was the germ of the Dominican Order. After 10 years of preaching, St. Dominic established the Friars Preachers (the Dominicans), for the conversion of the Albigensians. The Dominicans made innumerable converts. The most Holy Rosary was given to the world by Our Lady through St. Dominic. St. Dominic died in 1221; after his death, the Dominican Order spread at a phenomenal rate; it has given the Church many of her greatest saints.

LITANY OF
SAINT ALBERT THE GREAT

(For private use only.)

Lord, have mercy on us.
  Christ, have mercy on us.
Lord, have mercy on us. Christ, hear us.
  Christ, graciously hear us.
God the Father of Heaven,
  Have mercy on us.
God the Son, Redeemer of the world,
  Have mercy on us.
God the Holy Spirit,
  Have mercy on us.
Holy Trinity, One God,
  Have mercy on us.

Holy Mary, *pray for us.*
Holy Mother of God, *pray for us.*
Holy Virgin of virgins, *etc.*
Saint Albert,
Man after the heart of God,
Zealous client of Mary,
Worthy son of Saint Dominic,
Mighty defender of the Faith,
Solid rock of hope,
Burning seraph of love,
Enlightened cherub of wisdom,
Valiant defender of justice,
Sure norm of prudence,
Bright mirror of temperance,
Unshakable pillar of fortitude,
Living model of humility,
Shining example of poverty,
Pure lily of chastity,

True model of obedience,
Precious vessel of all virtues,
Zealous imitator of the Apostles,
Bright gem of bishops,
Singular ornament of doctors,
Special glory of thy order,
Golden treasure of thy fatherland,
Certain protector of thy clients,
Albert the Great,
In anguish and in need,
In tribulation and in persecution,
In the hour of death,

Lamb of God, Who takest away the sins of the world,
   Spare us, O Lord.
Lamb of God, Who takest away the sins of the world,
   Graciously hear us, O Lord.
Lamb of God, Who takest away the sins of the world,
   Have mercy on us.

Christ, have mercy on us.
   Lord, have mercy on us.
Pray for us, Saint Albert,
   *That we may be made worthy of the promises
   of Christ.*

Let Us Pray

O God, Who richly adorned Saint Albert with Thy
heavenly gifts and decorated him with all virtues,
grant us, Thy servants, that we may follow in his
footsteps, may persevere in Thy service until death
and may securely obtain an everlasting reward,
through Jesus Christ, Thy Son Our Lord. R. *Amen.*

This litany dates from the sixteenth century.

St. Albert the Great, Doctor of the Church: Born in 1205 near
Augsburg, Germany, St. Albert received the Dominican habit in
1222. He was consecrated a bishop, but after two years he
resigned his see to devote the rest of his life to writing and to ac-

tivities of the Dominican Order. A tradition says that Our Lady appeared to him and offered him the gift of great knowledge—either human or divine. When he chose the former, she granted it, but told him that because he had not chosen knowledge of divine things, the gift would be retracted before his death. (St. Albert did lose his mental powers two years before his death.) Albert the Great was the forerunner and teacher of St. Thomas Aquinas, and is known as "The Universal Doctor" because of his vast learning in numerous varied fields. He wrote a proof that the earth was round, and because of his immense knowledge on all subjects, he was accused of acquiring it through magic. St. Albert the Great died in 1280.

LITANY OF
SAINT THOMAS AQUINAS
(For private use only.)

Lord, have mercy on us.
Christ, have mercy on us.
Lord, have mercy on us. Christ, hear us.
Christ, graciously hear us.
God the Father of Heaven,
Have mercy on us.
God the Son, Redeemer of the world,
Have mercy on us.
God the Holy Ghost,
Have mercy on us.
Holy Trinity, One God,
Have mercy on us.

Holy Mary,
Pray for us.
Glorious Mother of the King of kings,
Pray for us.
Saint Thomas of Aquin, *etc.*
Worthy child of the Queen of virgins,
St. Thomas most chaste,
St. Thomas most patient,
Prodigy of science,
Silently eloquent,
Reproach of the ambitious,
Lover of that life which is hidden with Christ in God,
Fragrant flower in the garden of Saint Dominic,
Glory of the Friars Preachers,
Illumined from on high,
Angel of the Schools,
Oracle of the Church,
Incomparable scribe of the Man-God,

Satiated with the odor of
    His perfumes,
Perfect in the school of His Cross,
Intoxicated with the strong wine
    of His charity,
Glittering gem in the cabinet
    of the Lord,
Model of perfect obedience,
Endowed with the true spirit of
    holy poverty,

Lamb of God, Who takest away the sins of the world,
    Spare us, O Lord.
Lamb of God, Who takest away the sins of the world,
    Graciously hear us, O Lord.
Lamb of God, Who takest away the sins of the world,
    Have mercy on us.

Oh, how beautiful is the chaste generation
    with glory,
    For the memory thereof is immortal.
Because it is known with God and man,
    And it triumpheth crowned forever.

V. What have I in Heaven, or what do I desire on
    earth!
R. *Thou art the God of my heart, and my portion
    forever.*

Let Us Pray

O God, Who hast ordained that blessed Thomas
should enlighten Thy Church, grant that through his
prayers we may practice what he taught, through
Christ Our Lord. R. *Amen.*

St. Thomas Aquinas, The Angelic Doctor: Born around 1225 in
the castle of Rocca Sicca near Naples, St. Thomas was opposed by
his family when he tried to become a Dominican; they imprisoned
him for 15 months and even tried to distract him with a

prostitute—whom he repelled with a blazing firebrand in his hand. An angel then girded him with a mystical cincture and he was thenceforth entirely free from all temptations of the flesh. He escaped from imprisonment and became a Dominican priest. Taught by St. Albert the Great, and deriving much light from meditations on the crucifix, St. Thomas was one of the most brilliant intellects in the history of Christianity. His *Summa Theologica* continues to be the greatest work of theology ever written, yet St. Thomas remained deeply humble. Shortly before he died, he had a mystical experience, after which he declared, "I can write no more; everything I have written seems like so much straw." St. Thomas died in 1274. He is the Church's official theologian—*The Common Doctor,* or Universal Teacher.

LITANY OF
SAINT LOUIS, KING OF FRANCE
(For private use only.)

Lord, have mercy on us.
Christ, have mercy on us.
Lord, have mercy on us. Christ, hear us.
Christ, graciously hear us.
God the Father of Heaven,
Have mercy on us.
God the Son, Redeemer of the world,
Have mercy on us.
God the Holy Ghost,
Have mercy on us.
Holy Trinity, One God,
Have mercy on us.

Holy Mary, *pray for us.*
Holy Mother of God, *pray for us.*
Holy Virgin of virgins, *etc.*
Saint Louis of France,
St. Louis, scion of devout parents,
St. Louis, constant protector of the children of God,
St. Louis, steadfast teacher of piety,
St. Louis, true model of Christian virtue,
St. Louis, faithful confessor of the living Christ,
St. Louis, kingly bearer of humiliations,
St. Louis, staunch defender of the glorified Christ,
St. Louis, true martyr of the flesh by mortification,
St. Louis, detester of worldly pride and honor,
St. Louis, saviour of souls,
St. Louis, ardent lover of God,
St. Louis, kind friend of enemies,
St. Louis, rapt in prayer to God,
St. Louis, hope of sinners,

St. Louis, giver of gifts,
St. Louis, founder of charitable institutions for the
    afflicted,
St. Louis, generous giver of alms,
St. Louis, lavish dispenser of riches,
St. Louis, guard of the holy places of pilgrimage,
St. Louis, detester of immoderation,
St. Louis, protector of widows and orphans,
St. Louis, defender of the sepulcher of
    Our Lord Jesus Christ,
St. Louis, victor over the Saracens,
St. Louis, protector of those in pagan slavery,
St. Louis, converter of unbelievers to the
    Christian Faith,
St. Louis, visitor of hospitals and dispenser of
    favors to the infirm,
St. Louis, healer of the sick,
St. Louis, intercessor and patron of the
    French kings,
St. Louis, from whom those who flee to thee obtain
    the infallible help of God,
St. Louis, at whose request various diseases are
    miraculously cured,

Lamb of God, Who takest away the sins of the world,
    Spare us, O Lord.
Lamb of God, Who takest away the sins of the world,
    Graciously hear us, O Lord.
Lamb of God, Who takest away the sins of the world,
    Have mercy on us.

Christ, hear us.
    Christ, graciously hear us.
Lord, have mercy on us.
    Christ, have mercy on us.
Lord, have mercy on us.

Our Father, *etc. (silently).* Hail, Mary, *etc. (silently).*

V. Pray for us, Saint Louis,

R. *That we may be made worthy of the promises of Christ.*

Let Us Pray

O Lord, King of kings, Jesus Christ, Who didst love Saint Louis and didst lead him into the heavenly kingdom, grant that by his intercession and good works we may participate in his glory for all eternity, Who livest and reignest, world without end. R. *Amen.*

St. Louis, King of France: Son of Louis VIII and the pious but domineering Queen Blanche of Castille, Louis was born in 1215. He was proclaimed King Louis IX at age 11. He was a most Christian ruler—ascetical, kind, and just. Louis and his wife had 11 children. Louis built the Chapel Royal to enshrine the relics of the True Cross and the Crown of Thorns. He died of the plague on a crusade in 1270. His relics were destroyed by the French revolutionists. St. Louis is Co-Patron (along with St. Elizabeth of Hungary) of the Third Order of St. Francis.

LITANY OF
SAINT ELIZABETH OF HUNGARY

(For private use only.)

Lord, have mercy on us.
  Christ, have mercy on us.
Lord, have mercy on us. Christ, hear us.
  Christ, graciously hear us.
God the Father of Heaven,
  Have mercy on us.
God the Son, Redeemer of the world,
  Have mercy on us.
God the Holy Ghost,
  Have mercy on us.
Holy Trinity, One God,
  Have mercy on us.

Holy Mary, Mother of Mercy, *pray for us.*
Holy Elizabeth, mother of the poor, *pray for us.*
Saint Elizabeth, who didst fear God from thy heart,
  etc.
St. Elizabeth, most fervent in devotion,
St. Elizabeth, devout and beloved disciple of Jesus,
St. Elizabeth, imitator of blessed Francis,
St. Elizabeth, of noblest faith and birth,
St. Elizabeth, devoted to all pious offices,
St. Elizabeth, whose nights were spent in prayer and
  contemplation,
St. Elizabeth, who wast consoled with heavenly
  visions,
St. Elizabeth, beloved of God and man,
St. Elizabeth, full of contempt of this world,
St. Elizabeth, example of poverty, chastity and
  obedience,
St. Elizabeth, solace of thy husband,

St. Elizabeth, mirror of widows,
St. Elizabeth, holocaust of penance and humility,
St. Elizabeth, admirable preacher of meekness,
St. Elizabeth, despiser of the luxuries of the regal house,
St. Elizabeth, lover of the Cross of Christ,
St. Elizabeth, light of all pious women,
St. Elizabeth, nourisher of the orphans,
St. Elizabeth, always intent on works of mercy,
St. Elizabeth, consoler of all sorrows,
St. Elizabeth, teacher of the poor,
St. Elizabeth, seeker of contumely and affronts,
St. Elizabeth, distributor of thy riches to thy poor neighbors,
St. Elizabeth, patient in adversity,
St. Elizabeth, maker of garments for the poor,
St. Elizabeth, hospitable receiver of pilgrims and the sick,
St. Elizabeth, succor of the needy,
St. Elizabeth, formidable to demons,
St. Elizabeth, example of all spiritual perfection,
St. Elizabeth, repressor of all vain and dissolute conversation,
St. Elizabeth, cheered by angelic choirs in thy last agony,
St. Elizabeth, miraculous in life,
St. Elizabeth, helper of our devotions,
St. Elizabeth, our sweetest patron,

Lamb of God, Who takest away the sins of the world,
   Spare us, O Lord.
Lamb of God, Who takest away the sins of the world,
   Graciously hear us, O Lord.
Lamb of God, Who takest away the sins of the world,
   Have mercy on us, O Lord.

Christ, hear us.
   Christ, graciously hear us.

V. Pray for us, blessed Elizabeth,

R. *That we may be made worthy of the promises of Christ.*

Let Us Pray

Enlighten, O God of compassion, the hearts of Thy faithful servants, and through the glorious prayers of blessed Elizabeth, make us to despise the pleasing things of this world and ever to delight in the consolations of Heaven, through Christ Our Lord. R. *Amen.*

O God of tender mercies, pour forth Thy light over the hearts of Thy faithful people, and graciously listening to the glorious prayers of blessed Elizabeth, make us to think little of worldly prosperity and to be ever gladdened by heavenly consolation, through Our Lord Jesus Christ, Who liveth and reigneth with God the Father and the Holy Spirit, world without end. R. *Amen.*

St. Elizabeth of Hungary, Patroness of the Third Order of St. Francis: Born in 1207 of a noble family, at age four Elizabeth was brought to Wartburg castle to be raised as the betrothed of Ludwig, the future landgrave. At age 14, deeply in love, Elizabeth married Ludwig. She bore four children and also practiced great charity to the poor, building two hospitals—one next to the castle. After six years of marriage, Ludwig died of the plague while on a crusade. Elizabeth was heartbroken, and was also forced to leave the castle. She made provision for her children and then became a Franciscan tertiary, and devoted herself to prayer and care of the sick and poor. Elizabeth died in her 24th year, in 1231.

LITANY OF
SAINT FRANCIS OF ASSISI

(For private use only.)

Lord, have mercy on us.
  Christ, have mercy on us.
Lord, have mercy on us. Christ, hear us.
  Christ, graciously hear us.
God the Father of Heaven,
  Have mercy on us.
God the Son, Redeemer of the world,
  Have mercy on us.
God the Holy Spirit,
  Have mercy on us.
Holy Trinity, One God,
  Have mercy on us.

Holy Mary, conceived without sin, *pray for us.*
Holy Mary, special patroness of the three Orders of
  Saint Francis, *pray for us.*
Saint Francis, seraphic patriarch, *etc.*
Saint Francis, most prudent father,
Saint Francis, despiser of the world,
Saint Francis, model of penance,
Saint Francis, conqueror of vices,
Saint Francis, imitator of the Saviour,
Saint Francis, bearer of the marks of Christ,
Saint Francis, sealed with the character of Jesus,
Saint Francis, example of purity,
Saint Francis, image of humility,
Saint Francis, abounding in grace,
Saint Francis, reformer of the erring,
Saint Francis, healer of the sick,
Saint Francis, pillar of the Church,
Saint Francis, defender of the Faith,

Saint Francis, champion of Christ,
Saint Francis, defender of thy children,
Saint Francis, invulnerable shield,
Saint Francis, confounder of the heretics,
Saint Francis, converter of the pagans,
Saint Francis, supporter of the lame,
Saint Francis, raiser of the dead,
Saint Francis, healer of the lepers,
Saint Francis, our advocate,

Lamb of God, Who takest away the sins of the world,
  Spare us, O Lord.
Lamb of God, Who takest away the sins of the world,
  Graciously hear us, O Lord.
Lamb of God, Who takest away the sins of the world,
  Have mercy on us.

Christ, hear us.
  Christ, graciously hear us.

V. Pray for us, O blessed father Francis,
R. *That we may be made worthy of the promises of
  Christ.*

Let Us Pray

O Lord Jesus Christ, Who, when the world was
growing cold, in order to renew in our hearts the
flame of love, imprinted the sacred marks of Thy Passion on the body of our blessed father Francis, mercifully grant that by his merits and prayers we may
persevere in bearing the cross and may bring forth
fruits worthy of penance, Thou Who livest and reignest, world without end. R. *Amen.*

*St. Francis of Assisi, The Seraphic Father and Founder of the
Three Franciscan Orders:* St. Francis was born around 1181 at
Assisi in Umbria, Italy, son of a rich merchant. After a vision of
Christ, St. Francis embraced poverty and the care of the sick and
poor. In the church of San Damiano, St. Francis heard these words
coming from the crucifix: "Go and repair My house, which you

see is falling down." When his father publicly disinherited him as a madman, St. Francis devoted himself entirely to the virtue of poverty (personified as "Lady Poverty"), to preaching, to care of the sick and poor—especially lepers, and to establishing the Friars Minor, the Poor Clares, and the Franciscan lay Tertiaries (Third Order). Among his supernatural gifts was the stigmata. In 1223 St. Francis built the first Christmas crèche, a custom which has continued to our own day. St. Francis died in 1226 and was canonized in 1228. He is one of the most famous, most influential, and most beloved saints in the history of the Church.

LITANY OF
SAINT CLARE

(For private use only.)

Lord, have mercy on us.
Christ, have mercy on us.
Lord, have mercy on us. Christ, hear us.
Christ, graciously hear us.
God the Father of Heaven,
Have mercy on us.
God the Son, Redeemer of the world,
Have mercy on us.
God the Holy Ghost,
Have mercy on us.
Holy Trinity, One God,
Have mercy on us.

Holy Mary,
Pray for us.
Holy Mother Clare,
Pray for us.
Holy Mother Clare, renowned in deed and name, *etc.*
Holy Mother Clare, brighter than the light,
Holy Mother Clare, great in merits,
Holy Mother Clare, free from the stain of sin,
Holy Mother Clare, bright light illumining
    the world,
Holy Mother Clare, new luminary,
Holy Mother Clare, star of the heavens,
Holy Mother Clare, renowned virgin,
Holy Mother Clare, saintly virgin,
Holy Mother Clare, prudent virgin,
Holy Mother Clare, shining splendor
    of Heaven,
Holy Mother Clare, friend of the Cross,

Holy Mother Clare, mourning dove,
Holy Mother Clare, spouse of God,
Holy Mother Clare, disciple of Christ,
Holy Mother Clare, city of the Saviour,
Holy Mother Clare, vessel of purity,
Holy Mother Clare, pattern of obedience,
Holy Mother Clare, model of patience,
Holy Mother Clare, marvel of abstinence,
Holy Mother Clare, prodigy of sanctity,
Holy Mother Clare, mother of poverty,
Holy Mother Clare, flower of virginity,
Holy Mother Clare, palm of fecundity,
Holy Mother Clare, fountain of charity,
Holy Mother Clare, endowed with every virtue,
Holy Mother Clare, guardian of consecrated virgins,
Holy Mother Clare, little plant of the Friars Minor,
Holy Mother Clare, sweetest mistress,
Holy Mother Clare, despising vanities,
Holy Mother Clare, triumphing over the demons,
Holy Mother Clare, most devoted to the Blessed
  Sacrament,
Holy Mother Clare, emulating our holy father Saint
  Francis,
Holy Mother Clare, craving the food of the word of
  God,

Lamb of God, Who takest away the sins of the world,
  Spare us, O Lord.
Lamb of God, Who takest away the sins of the world,
  Graciously hear us, O Lord.
Lamb of God, Who takest away the sins of the world,
  Have mercy on us, O Lord.

Christ, hear us.
  Christ, graciously hear us.

V. Pray for us, O blessed mother Clare,
R. *That we may be made worthy of the promises of
  Christ.*

Let Us Pray

We beseech Thee, O Lord, that Thy servants who are renewing the votive commemoration of Thy holy virgin, our mother Clare, may by her intercession become partakers of the heavenly joys, and co-heirs with Thine only-begotten Son, Thou Who livest and reignest, world without end. R. *Amen.*

O God, Who wast pleased that our holy mother Saint Clare, by the splendor of her virtues, should become a guiding light to innumerable virgins, grant through her intercession and merits that those virgins may always walk in this light here on earth and may be found worthy to enjoy the perpetual serenity of Thy Face in Heaven, through Jesus Christ Our Lord. R. *Amen.*

St. Clare, Foundress of the Poor Clares: Born in Assisi of a noble family in 1194, St. Clare refused to marry at age twelve, and at age eighteen ran away from her family on Palm Sunday night of the year 1212 to take the vows of religion and receive the Franciscan habit from St. Francis of Assisi. She was joined by her sister Agnes, who also ran away from home and who was miraculously preserved from being dragged back home by 12 armed men sent by her father. Later, both daughters were joined by another sister and by their mother. St. Clare and her followers lived solely on alms; like St. Francis, they loved the virtue of poverty. St. Clare suffered from illness for 27 years. She also performed many miracles. When the soldiers of Emperor Frederick II's army on the attack were scaling the convent walls, St. Clare, though ill, had herself carried out to the gate. There she had the Blessed Sacrament set up in sight of the enemy. She pleaded with Our Lord to spare her "children," the nuns. Our Lord answered her, "I will have them always in My care." The marauders suddenly fled. St. Clare is often pictured with a monstrance to commemorate this miraculous deliverance. She died in 1253.

LITANY OF
SAINT ANTHONY OF PADUA
Litany One
(For private use only.)

Lord, have mercy on us.
  Christ, have mercy on us.
Lord, have mercy on us. Christ, hear us.
  Christ, graciously hear us.
God the Father of Heaven,
  Have mercy on us.
God the Son, Redeemer of the world,
  Have mercy on us.
God the Holy Spirit,
  Have mercy on us.
Holy Trinity, One God,
  Have mercy on us.

Holy Mary, *pray for us.*
Saint Anthony of Padua, *pray for us.*
Saint Anthony, glory of the Friars Minor, *etc.*
Saint Anthony, ark of the Testament,
Saint Anthony, sanctuary of heavenly wisdom,
Saint Anthony, destroyer of worldly vanity,
Saint Anthony, conqueror of impurity,
Saint Anthony, example of humility,
Saint Anthony, lover of the Cross,
Saint Anthony, martyr of desire,
Saint Anthony, generator of charity,
Saint Anthony, zealous for justice,
Saint Anthony, terror of infidels,
Saint Anthony, model of perfection,
Saint Anthony, consoler of the afflicted,
Saint Anthony, restorer of lost things,
Saint Anthony, defender of innocence,
Saint Anthony, liberator of prisoners,

219

Saint Anthony, guide of pilgrims,
Saint Anthony, restorer of health,
Saint Anthony, performer of miracles,
Saint Anthony, restorer of speech to the mute,
Saint Anthony, restorer of hearing to the deaf,
Saint Anthony, restorer of sight to the blind,
Saint Anthony, disperser of devils,
Saint Anthony, reviver of the dead,
Saint Anthony, tamer of tyrants,

From the snares of the devil, *Saint Anthony, deliver
    us.*
From thunder, lightning and storms,
    Saint Anthony, deliver us.
From all evil of body and soul,
    Saint Anthony, deliver us.
Through thine intercession,
    Saint Anthony, protect us.
Throughout the course of life,
    Saint Anthony, protect us.

Lamb of God, Who takest away the sins of the world,
    Spare us, O Lord.
Lamb of God, Who takest away the sins of the world,
    Graciously hear us, O Lord.
Lamb of God, Who takest away the sins of the world,
    Have mercy on us.

V. Saint Anthony, pray for us,
R. *That we may be made worthy of the promises of
    Christ.*

Let Us Pray

O my God, may the pious commemoration of Saint
Anthony, Thy confessor and doctor, give joy to Thy
Church, that she may ever be strengthened with Thy
spiritual assistance, and merit to attain everlasting
joy. Through Christ Our Lord. R. *Amen.*

St. Anthony of Padua, Wonder-Worker, Patron of Lost Objects, Doctor of the Church, Hammer of Heretics, etc.: Born in Lisbon, Portugal in 1195, St. Anthony became a Franciscan priest and then preached with enormous success all over Italy. He was followed by great crowds and he converted innumerable people. A saint of angelic purity, he was one of the greatest miracle-workers in the history of the Church. St. Anthony is also known as "Hammer of Heretics" for his warfare against various forms of Manichaeanism. St. Anthony died in 1231 and was canonized 11 months later.

LITANY OF
SAINT ANTHONY OF PADUA
Litany Two
(For private use only.)

Lord, have mercy on us.
Christ, have mercy on us.
Lord, have mercy on us. Christ, hear us.
Christ, graciously hear us.
God the Father of Heaven,
Have mercy on us.
God the Son, Redeemer of the world,
Have mercy on us.
God the Holy Spirit,
Have mercy on us.
Holy Trinity, One God,
Have mercy on us.

Holy Mary,
Pray for us.
Holy Father, Saint Francis,
Pray for us.
Saint Anthony of Padua, *etc.*
Saint Anthony, glory of the Franciscan Order,
Saint Anthony, martyr in desiring to die
   for Christ,
Saint Anthony, pillar of the Church,
Saint Anthony, worthy priest of God,
Saint Anthony, apostolic preacher,
Saint Anthony, teacher of truth,
Saint Anthony, terror of evil spirits,
Saint Anthony, comforter of the afflicted,
Saint Anthony, helper in necessities,
Saint Anthony, deliverer of captives,
Saint Anthony, guide of the erring,

Saint Anthony, restorer of lost things,
Saint Anthony, chosen intercessor,
Saint Anthony, continuous worker of miracles,

Be merciful unto us, *spare us, O Lord.*
Be merciful unto us, *hear us, O Lord.*

From all evil,
   O Lord, deliver us.
From all sin,
   O Lord, deliver us.
From all dangers of body and soul, *etc.*
From the snares of the devil,
From pestilence, famine and war,
From eternal death,
Through the merits of Saint Anthony,
Through his zeal for the conversion of sinners,
Through his desire for the crown of
   martyrdom,
Through his fatigues and labors,
Through his preaching and teaching,
Through his tears and penance,
Through his patience and humility,
Through his glorious death,
Through the number of his wonderful deeds,
In the day of judgment,

We sinners *beseech Thee, hear us.*

That Thou mayest bring us to true penance,
   We beseech Thee, hear us.
That Thou mayest grant us patience in our trials,
   We beseech Thee, hear us.
That Thou mayest assist us in our needs, *etc.*
That Thou mayest grant us our petitions,
That Thou mayest kindle the fire of Thy love in us,
That Thou mayest favor us with the protection and
   intercession of Saint Anthony,
Son of God,

Lamb of God, Who takest away the sins of the world,
  Spare us, O Lord.
Lamb of God, Who takest away the sins of the world,
  Graciously hear us, O Lord.
Lamb of God, Who takest away the sins of the world,
  Have mercy on us.

Christ, hear us.
  Christ, graciously hear us.

V. Pray for us, O blessed Anthony,
R. *That we may become worthy of the promises of
  Christ.*

Let Us Pray

Almighty and eternal God, Thou didst glorify Thy
faithful confessor and doctor Saint Anthony with the
gift of working miracles. Graciously grant that what
we seek with confidence through his merits, we may
surely receive through his prayers. Through Christ
Our Lord. R. *Amen.*

LITANY OF
SAINT GERTRUDE THE GREAT

Antiphon: Lord Jesus! In union with that love which drew Thee down upon earth and caused Thee to fulfill the work of our Redemption,
   I offer Thee this prayer.

Lord, have mercy.
   Lord, have mercy.
Christ, have mercy.
   Christ, have mercy.
Lord, have mercy.
   Lord, have mercy.
Christ, hear us.
   Christ, graciously hear us.

God the Father of Heaven,
   Have mercy on us.
God the Son, Redeemer of the world,
   Have mercy on us.
God the Holy Ghost,
   Have mercy on us.
Holy Trinity, One God,
   Have mercy on us.

Holy, Mary, *pray for us.*
All ye holy choirs of angels, *pray for us.*
All ye saints and elect of God, *etc.*
Saint Gertrude,
Thou chaste virgin,
Thou beloved daughter of the Heavenly Father,
Thou chosen bride of Jesus Christ,
Thou temple of the Holy Ghost,
Thou joy of the Holy Trinity,

Thou fragrant flower in the hand of Jesus Christ,
Thou ever-blooming spring flower,
Thou rose without thorns,
Thou chaste dove without the stain of sin,
Thou earthly seraph,
Thou living sanctuary,
Thou strong protection of all who venerate thee,

Jesus Christ, Spouse of Saint Gertrude, *have mercy on us.*
Through her humility, *have mercy on us.*
Through her charity, *etc.*
Through her untiring patience,
Through the ardent love she bore Thee,
Through the delight with which Thou didst dwell in her heart,
Through the love which Thou hast for her,
Through the love with which Thou hast chosen her from eternity,
Through the love with which Thou didst so sweetly attract her to Thyself,
Through the love with which Thou so delightfully didst unite her to Thyself,
Through the love with which Thou so complacently dwelt in her heart,
Through the love with which Thou didst end her life with a happy death,
Through the love with which Thou hast conferred on her eternal life,
Through the love with which Thou lovest and rejoicest all the blessed,
Jesus Christ,

Lamb of God, Who takest away the sins of the world, *Spare us, O Lord.*
Lamb of God, Who takest away the sins of the world, *Graciously hear us, O Lord.*
Lamb of God, Who takest away the sins of the world, *Have mercy on us.*

V. Pray for us, O holy virgin Saint Gertrude,

R. *That we may be made worthy of the promises of Christ.*

Let Us Pray

O Lord Jesus, by the love Thou didst bear to the virginal heart of Saint Gertrude and by which Thou hast promised that no sinner who would honor and love her should die a sudden and unprovided death, grant me, I beseech Thee, this grace, and let me so love Thee and repent of my sins that with faith and confidence I may expect a happy death. R. *Amen.*

O God, Who in the heart of the holy virgin Gertrude didst provide for Thyself a pleasing abode, through her merits do Thou cleanse from our hearts every stain of sin and grant that we may enjoy fellowship with her for evermore, through Our Lord Jesus Christ, Thy Son, Who liveth and reigneth with Thee and the Holy Ghost, one God, world without end. R. *Amen.*

St. Gertrude the Great, Virgin: Born in 1256 in Germany, St. Gertrude was raised, from age 5, by the Benedictine nuns at Helfta, and eventually she joined the Order herself. In her 26th year, Our Lord began to visit her in visions, which are described in her book of *Revelations.* St. Gertrude was a great apostle of devotion to the Sacred Heart of Jesus, and she received many mystical favors from Our Lord; she is one of the Church's greatest mystical writers. St. Gertrude died in 1301 or 1302.

LITANY OF
ST. RITA OF CASCIA
Litany One
(For private use only.)

Lord, have mercy on us.
Christ, have mercy on us.
Lord, have mercy on us. Christ, hear us.
Christ, graciously hear us.
God the Father of Heaven,
Have mercy on us.
God the Son, Redeemer of the world,
Have mercy on us.
God the Holy Ghost,
Have mercy on us.
Holy Trinity, One God,
Have mercy on us.

Immaculate Mary, Mother of God, *pray for us.*
Holy Mary, Mother of purest love, *pray for us.*
Holy Mary, pierced with a sword of grief, *etc.*
Holy Mary, comforter of the afflicted,
Holy Mary, Queen of all saints,
Holy Mary, Protectress of St. Rita,
O Saint Rita, our advocate and protectress,
O Saint Rita, predestined by the Lord,
O Saint Rita, gift of Heaven,
O Saint Rita, foretold by an angel,
O Saint Rita, remarkable in childhood,
O Saint Rita, enamored of solitude,
O Saint Rita, example of obedience,
O Saint Rita, united to the Divine will,
O Saint Rita, of untiring patience,
O Saint Rita, model of gentleness,
O Saint Rita, type of the Christian mother,
O Saint Rita, mirror of Christian spouses,

O Saint Rita, miracle of fortitude,

O Saint Rita, heroic in sacrifice,

O Saint Rita, generous in forgiving,

O Saint Rita, tender benefactress of thine enemies,

O Saint Rita, martyr in penitence,

O Saint Rita, abased through humility,

O Saint Rita, embracing voluntary poverty,

O Saint Rita, exemplary as a widow,

O Saint Rita, beloved of Jesus,

O Saint Rita, permitted to converse with thy Divine Spouse,

O Saint Rita, prompt at the Divine call,

O Saint Rita, mirror of conventual life,

O Saint Rita, mystical rose of every virtue,

O Saint Rita, sweet honey of the comb,

O Saint Rita, bouquet of fragrant myrrh,

O Saint Rita, wedded to the Passion of Christ,

O Saint Rita, pierced with a thorn,

O Saint Rita, deep sea of contrition,

O Saint Rita, in ecstasies before the Blessed Sacrament,

O Saint Rita, consumed with Divine love,

O Saint Rita, bidden to the Bridegroom's throne,

O Saint Rita, received in Heaven with joy,

O Saint Rita, arrayed in unspeakable glory,

O Saint Rita, incorrupt in thy chaste body,

O Saint Rita, Advocate of the Impossible,

O Saint Rita, Advocate of Desperate Cases,

O Saint Rita, light of Holy Church,

O Saint Rita, cure for the unfaithful,

O Saint Rita, balm for every sorrow,

O Saint Rita, balsam for every ill,

O Saint Rita, persevering in prayer,

O Saint Rita, confident in thy prayer,

O Saint Rita, who can obtain everything from thy dying Jesus,

O Saint Rita, who knows the way to His Sacred Heart,

O Saint Rita, our powerful advocate,

Lamb of God, who takest away the sins of the world,
   Spare us, O Lord.
Lamb of God, who takest away the sins of the world,
   Graciously hear us, O Lord.
Lamb of God, who takest away the sins of the world,
   Have mercy on us.

Thou hast signed Thy servant Rita
   With the signs of Thy Love and Passion.

Pray for us, Saint Rita,
   *That we may be made worthy of the promises of
   Christ.*

Let Us Pray

O God, who in Thine infinite tenderness hast
vouchsafed to regard the prayer of thy servant Blessed
Rita and dost grant to her supplication that which is
impossible to human forethought, skill and efforts, in
reward of her compassionate love and firm reliance
upon Thy promises, have pity upon our adversity and
succor us in our calamities, that the unbeliever may
know that Thou art the recompense of the humble, the
defense of the helpless, and the strength of those who
trust in Thee, through Jesus Christ our Lord. R.
Amen.

St. Rita of Cascia, Advocate of the Impossible: St. Rita (c.
1381-1457), who was born in Spoleto, Italy, wanted to become a
nun, but was given in marriage to a man who treated her cruelly.
When he was murdered by enemies, Rita's two sons resolved on
avenging their father's murder, but through Rita's prayers they
gave up their plan; both sons died within a year, reconciled to God.
Rita then became an Augustinian nun. She reached great sanctity,
received the stigmata of a thorn in her forehead, and became
known for miracles both during her life and after her death.

LITANY OF
SAINT RITA OF CASCIA
Litany Two
(For private use only.)

Lord, have mercy on us.
Christ, have mercy on us.
Lord, have mercy on us. Christ, hear us.
Christ, graciously hear us.
God the Father Almighty,
Have mercy on us.
God the Son, Redeemer of the world, Who hast said,
"Ask, and you shall receive; seek, and you shall
find; knock, and it shall be opened unto you,"
Have mercy on us.
God the Holy Ghost, Spirit of Wisdom,
Understanding, Counsel and Knowledge,
Have mercy on us.
Holy Trinity, One God, infinite in power,
Have mercy on us.

Holy Mary, who dost never refuse a petition,
Pray for us.
Immaculate Virgin, Queen of Heaven and earth,
Pray for us.
Our Lady of the Sacred Heart, *etc.*
Holy angels, spirits of humility,
Holy principalities, protectors of religious
communities,
Holy virtues, angels of fortitude,
Holy cherubim, angels of light,
Saint Rita, Advocate of the
Impossible,
St. Rita, consecrated to God,
St. Rita, lover of Jesus Crucified,
St. Rita, bride of the suffering Saviour,

St. Rita, filled with compassion for the sufferings of
    Christ,

St. Rita, crowned by an angel with a crown of thorns,

St. Rita, who didst bear the wound of this mysterious
    crown on thy forehead,

St. Rita, who didst firmly trust in the loving mercy of
    Jesus,

St. Rita, who didst importune the dying Saviour with
    ardent supplications,

St. Rita, who didst never doubt a gracious answer to
    thy prayer,

That we may renounce all self-love, *pray for us, Saint
    Rita.*

That we may confidently trust in the promises of
    Jesus, *pray for us, Saint Rita.*

That the enemies of our salvation may be put to
    confusion, *etc.*

That we may ever perfectly fulfill the will of God,

That our inclinations to evil may be destroyed,

That the Faith in all its purity may be spread over our
    land,

That a holy zeal may fill our hearts,

That we may infuse a holy love for chastity into all
    who come in contact with us,

That in all our actions and omissions we may
    endeavor to promote a tender charity,

That we may be delivered from all avarice, vainglory
    and rash judgment,

That great saints may arise in our land who will edify
    the people and dispel the darkness of unbelief,

That we may be delivered from all interior enemies,

Lamb of God, Who takest away the sins of the world,
    Spare us, O Lord.

Lamb of God, Who takest away the sins of the world,
    Graciously hear us, O Lord.

Lamb of God, Who takest away the sins of the world,
    Have mercy on us.

V. Pray for us, Saint Rita,

R. *That we may be made worthy of the promises of Christ.*

Let Us Pray

O God, Who in Thine infinite tenderness dost deign to hearken to the prayer of St. Rita, and to grant to her supplication that which seems impossible to human foresight, skill and efforts, in reward for her compassionate love and firm reliance upon Thy promises, have pity upon our adversity and succor us in our calamities, that the unbeliever may know that Thou art the recompenser of the humble, the defense of the helpless and the strength of those who trust in Thee, through Jesus Christ Our Lord. R. *Amen.*

O God, Who to St. Rita didst vouchsafe the great grace to love her enemies in very truth, and both in her heart and on her brow to bear the stigmata of Thy Passion, have regard, we beseech Thee, to her merits and her prayers, and grant that we may in such wise show mercy to our enemies, and so meditate on the pains of Thy Passion as to make our own the blessedness promised to those who are meek and to those who mourn, Who livest and reignest world without end. R. *Amen.*

O glorious Saint Rita, who didst miraculously participate in the sorrowful Passion of Our Lord Jesus Christ, obtain for me the grace to suffer with resignation the troubles of this life and protect me in all my needs. R. *Amen.*

LITANY OF SAINT ANGELA MERICI

(For private use only.)

Lord, have mercy on us.
Christ, have mercy on us.
Christ, hear us.
Christ, graciously hear us.
God the Father of Heaven,
Have mercy on us.
God the Son, Redeemer of the world,
Have mercy on us.
God the Holy Spirit,
Have mercy on us.
Holy Trinity, One God,
Have mercy on us.

Holy Mary, Mother of God, and faithful guardian of
our mother Saint Angela, *pray for us.*
Saint Angela Merici, *pray for us.*
St. Angela, favored with the choicest gifts of God
from thine infancy, *etc.*
St. Angela, who didst give thyself to the practice of all
the virtues from thy tenderest years,
St. Angela, who didst always preserve a spotless
purity,
St. Angela, who by thy love for holy purity, didst
merit to receive thy name,
St. Angela, who from childhood found thy delight in
solitude,
St. Angela, who led an angelic life in the house of thy
parents,
St. Angela, who didst daily bear on thy body the
mortification of Jesus,
St. Angela, whose gift it was to reconcile the bitterest
enemies,

St. Angela, who at thirteen became a tertiary of St.
Francis and ever remained faithful,

St. Angela, gifted with the graces of prayer and
contemplation,

St. Angela, who visited the Holy Land, and there
followed the bloody footprints of Jesus,

St. Angela, who triumphed over the illusions of the
devil,

St. Angela, who wast not afflicted at the loss of thy
sight in visiting the holy places,

St. Angela, whose sight was miraculously restored in
the Island of Candia,

St. Angela, whom the love of God had wounded and
whom this same love cured,

St. Angela, model of perfect self-denial and true
humility,

St. Angela, who, like Jacob, wast permitted to see the
mysterious ladder,

St. Angela, chosen by God to be the mother of many
holy virgins,

St. Angela, foundress of the illustrious Order of the
Ursulines,

St. Angela, to whom God promised that this Order
should always subsist,

St. Angela, who, filled with joy, didst give up thy soul
in the embrace of the Lord,

St. Angela, whose body remained incorruptible after
death,

St. Angela, patroness of Christian
mothers,

St. Angela, protectress of young girls,

St. Angela, our mother and advocate,

Lamb of God, Who takest away the sins of the world,
Spare us, O Lord.

Lamb of God, Who takest away the sins of the world,
Hear us, O Lord.

Lamb of God, Who takest away the sins of the world,
Have mercy on us.

V. Pray for us, O glorious mother Saint Angela,
R. *That we may be made worthy of the promises of Christ.*

Let Us Pray

O God, Who by means of our blessed mother Saint Angela didst cause a new Order of holy virgins to flourish in Thy Church, grant, through her intercession, that we may imitate her angelic virtues, and forsaking all earthly things, may be found worthy of eternal bliss, through Jesus Christ Our Lord. R. *Amen.*

St. Angela Merici, Foundress of the Ursulines: St. Angela was born around the year 1470 in Lombardy, Italy. At age 13 she became a Franciscan tertiary and lived a life of great austerity. She and 27 companions formed the Ursulines, the Church's first teaching order of women, to teach young girls. St. Angela died in 1540, at age 70.

LITANY OF SAINT TERESA OF AVILA
The Glory of Spain
(For private use only.)

Lord, have mercy on us.
  Christ, have mercy on us.
Lord, have mercy on us. Christ, hear us.
  Christ, graciously hear us.
God the Father of Heaven,
  Have mercy on us.
God the Son, Redeemer of the world,
  Have mercy on us.
God the Holy Ghost, the Sanctifier,
  Have mercy on us.
Holy Trinity, One God,
  Have mercy on us.

Holy Mary, Mother of God, *pray for us.*
Holy Mary, Our Lady of Mount Carmel, *pray for us.*
Saint Teresa of Avila, *etc.*
St. Teresa, whose heart was transverberated by the love of God,
St. Teresa, most humble servant of God,
St. Teresa, most zealous for the glory of God,
St. Teresa, woman truly strong in mind,
St. Teresa, truly detached from all created objects,
St. Teresa, great light of the Catholic Church,
St. Teresa, reformer and glory of the Carmelite Order,
St. Teresa, queen of mystical theology,
St. Teresa, lustrous name of Avila and Spain,
St. Teresa, who didst forever glorify the name of Teresa,
St. Teresa, wishing to suffer or to die,
St. Teresa, exclaiming, "O Lord, how sweet and pleasing are Thy ways!"

St. Teresa, desiring so much the salvation of souls,
St. Teresa, tasting and seeing how sweet is the Lord, even in this vale of miseries,
St. Teresa, exclaiming, "O death, who can fear thee who art the way to true life!"
St. Teresa, true lover of the Cross of Christ,
St. Teresa, who didst live to love, who died to love, and who wilt love eternally,

Lamb of God, Who takest away the sins of the world, *Spare us, O Lord.*
Lamb of God, Who takest away the sins of the world, *Hear us, O Lord.*
Lamb of God, Who takest away the sins of the world, *Have mercy on us.*

V. Pray for us, O holy Saint Teresa,
R. *That we may be made worthy of the promises of Christ.*

Let Us Pray

O God, Who didst replenish the heart of Thy blessed servant St. Teresa with the treasures of Thy divine love, grant that, like her, we may love Thee and suffer all things for Thee and in union with Thee, that we may gain souls for Thee, and that we may secure the salvation of our own soul. This we beg through the merits of our Saviour and the intercession of Thy glorious virgin Teresa. R. *Amen.*

St. Teresa of Avila, Foundress, Mystic, and Doctor of the Church: Born in 1515 at Avila, Spain, St. Teresa (of Jesus) is one of the greatest women the world has ever known. She entered the Carmelite convent at age 21, and with the help of St. John of the Cross and St. Peter of Alcantara she reformed most of the Carmelite convents in Spain and founded 16 new ones. She attained the highest degree of mystical life and wrote several classics of spiritual literature: *The Life* of Teresa of Jesus (her autobiography), *The Way of Perfection,* and *The Interior Castle.* St. Teresa of Avila died in 1582. She was the first woman to be declared a Doctor of the Church.

LITANY OF
SAINT JOHN OF THE CROSS
(For private use only.)

Lord, have mercy on us.
  Christ, have mercy on us.
Lord, have mercy on us. Christ, hear us.
  Christ, graciously hear us.
God, the Father of Heaven,
  Have mercy on us.
God the Son, Redeemer of the world,
  Have mercy on us.
God the Holy Ghost,
  Have mercy on us.
Holy Trinity, One God,
  Have mercy on us.

Holy Mary, Mother of God, Queen and
  Beauty of Carmel, *pray for us.*
Saint John of the Cross, *pray for us.*
St. John, our glorious father, *etc.*
Beloved child of Mary, the Queen of Carmel,
Fragrant flower of the garden of Carmel,
Admirable possessor of the spirit of Elias,
Foundation stone of the Carmelite reform,
Spiritual son, and beloved father of St. Teresa,
Most vigilant in the practice of virtue,
Treasure of charity,
Abyss of humility,
Most perfect in obedience,
Invincible in patience,
Constant lover of poverty,
Dove of simplicity,
Thirsting for mortification,
Prodigy of holiness,

Mystical Doctor,
Model of contemplation,
Zealous preacher of the Word of God,
Worker of miracles,
Bringing joy and peace to souls,
Terror of devils,
Model of penance,
Faithful guardian of Christ's vineyard,
Ornament and glory of Carmel,

Lamb of God, Who takest away the sins of the world,
Spare us, O Lord.
Lamb of God, Who takest away the sins of the world,
Graciously hear us, O Lord.
Lamb of God, Who takest away the sins of the world,
Have mercy on us.

V. Holy father Saint John of the Cross, pray for us,
R. *That we may be made worthy of the promises of Christ.*

Let Us Pray

O God, Who didst instill into the heart of Saint John of the Cross, Thy confessor and our father, a perfect spirit of self-abnegation and a surpassing love of Thy Cross, grant that assiduously following in his footsteps, we may attain to eternal glory. Through Christ Our Lord. R. *Amen.*

St. John of the Cross, Reformer of Carmel and Doctor of the Church: St. John of the Cross was born in Old Castile, Spain, in 1542. He became a Carmelite in 1563, was ordained a priest, and then met St. Teresa of Avila, who persuaded him to help her with the Carmelite Reform. John and four companions became the first Discalced (shoeless) Carmelite monks. St. John of the Cross established several houses of Discalced Carmelites. For five years he was the spiritual director of the nuns at St. Teresa's convent. He suffered much from dissension between the Calced and Discalced Carmelites, and from dissension among Discalced Carmelites themselves. St. John of the Cross underwent much persecution, and during his last years was treated cruelly, but he bore imprisonment and his other sufferings with silent joy. He died ill and forsaken in exile at a monastery in Andalusia, southern Spain, in 1591. St. John of the Cross is one of the Church's greatest mystics. He is known as the "Mystical Doctor" and has given the Church some of her greatest mystical writings: *The Ascent of Mount Carmel, The Dark Night of the Soul, The Spiritual Canticle,* and *Living Flame of Love.*

LITANY OF
SAINT IGNATIUS LOYOLA
(For private use only.)

Lord, have mercy on us.
Christ, have mercy on us.
Lord, have mercy on us. Christ, hear us.
Christ, graciously hear us.
God the Father of Heaven,
Have mercy on us.
God the Son, Redeemer of the world,
Have mercy on us.
God the Holy Ghost,
Have mercy on us.

Queen of the Society of Jesus, *pray for us.*
St. Joseph, heavenly patron of the Society of Jesus,
pray for us.
St. Ignatius, most devoted to the Blessed Trinity, *etc.*
St. Ignatius, devoted son to our eternal Father,
St. Ignatius, oracle of the Holy Spirit,
St. Ignatius, lover of Our Lord,
St. Ignatius, loyal knight of Our Lady,
St. Ignatius, founder of the Society of Jesus,
St. Ignatius, standard bearer of the King of kings,
St. Ignatius, whose only ambition was to promote the
   Kingdom of Christ and the greater glory of God,
St. Ignatius, burning with zeal for the conversion of
   the heathen,
St. Ignatius, eagerly longing to rescue the Holy Land
   from the infidel,
St. Ignatius, intrepid foe of heresy and of the enemies
   of Christ's Church,
St. Ignatius, valiant and faithful champion of the
   Vicar of Christ,

St. Ignatius, "insignis" companion of Jesus,

St. Ignatius, our most loving father,

St. Ignatius, glorious example to thy sons,

St. Ignatius, like Our Lord in thy humility,

St. Ignatius, like Our Lord in thy modesty,

St. Ignatius, like Our Lord in thy obscurity,

St. Ignatius, like Our Lord in constant labors,

St. Ignatius, like Our Lord in sympathy for the weak,

St. Ignatius, like Our Lord in thy courage,

St. Ignatius, consumed with a great desire for humiliation with Our Lord,

St. Ignatius, constant in the practice of corporal penance,

St. Ignatius, staunch defender of poverty as the firm wall of religion,

St. Ignatius, lover of angelic purity and innocence,

St. Ignatius, skilled master in the school of holy obedience,

St. Ignatius, living always in God's presence,

St. Ignatius, model of interior peace,

St. Ignatius, inspired writer of the *Spiritual Exercises,*

St. Ignatius, patron of all retreats and retreat houses,

(St. Ignatius, author of our constitutions and rules,)

St. Ignatius, victorious over the powers of darkness,

St. Ignatius, holy father of many saints and martyrs,

St. Ignatius, model of fervor to all priests,

St. Ignatius, burning with seraphic love at the Holy Sacrifice of the Mass,

(St. Ignatius, comfort to all our superiors,)

(St. Ignatius, encouragement to all our scholastics,)

(St. Ignatius, devoted father to our novices,)

(St. Ignatius, source of sweetness to our brothers,)

St. Ignatius, glorious intercessor in Heaven for thy society on earth,

(That we may become true sons of our Holy Father,) *we beseech Thee, Lord, to hear us.*

(That we may grow in the true spirit of the Society of Jesus,) *we beseech Thee, Lord, to hear us.*

That we may become impressed with the priceless value of our vocation, *etc.*

That we may ever seek that high perfection to which our vocation urges us,

That we may increase in knowledge and love and imitation of Thee,

That we may excel in perfect obedience,

That we may become men of prayer,

That we may drink deeply from that fountain of truly divine wisdom, the *Spiritual Exercises,*

That in our mental prayer we may ever be faithful to the teaching of St. Ignatius,

That our hearts may be detached from every creature and fixed solely and immovably upon the blessed will of God,

That worldliness may have no part in our lives,

That in our religious life we may be men crucified to the world, and to whom the world is crucified,

That we may have the grace to understand and defeat all the wiles and snares of Satan,

That like St. Ignatius we may order our life and our work with supernatural prudence,

That we may always be Thy energetic and enthusiastic companions,

(That we may be true and dependable and useful sons to our mother, the Society,)

That the purity of our lives ever be a living proof of our devotion to the Mother of God,

That we may be holy and unspotted in God's sight in charity,

That we may embrace the world in our apostolic zeal for the salvation of souls,

That we may have the gift of attracting all hearts to Thy love and service,

Lamb of God, Who takest away the sins of the world, *Spare us, O Lord.*

Lamb of God, Who takest away the sins of the world, *Graciously hear us, O Lord.*

Lamb of God, Who takest away the sins of the world,
   Have mercy on us, O Lord.

V. Pray for us, Saint Ignatius,
R. *That we may be made worthy of the promises of*
   Christ.

Let Us Pray

O God, Who in Thy most merciful Providence didst
call Thy faithful servant, Ignatius of Loyola (our
father), to a life of the most exalted sanctity in the
very close imitation of Thy Divine Son, grant, we
beseech Thee, that through his powerful intercession,
we may persevere in following in the footsteps of this
Thy servant until we breathe forth our souls to Thee
as faithful followers of Christ Our King. R. *Amen.*

St. Ignatius Loyola, Founder of the Jesuits: St. Ignatius
(1491-1556) was the youngest of 13 children. While recuperating
from a battle wound at age 30, he read a life of Christ and lives of
the saints, which influenced him to devote himself thenceforth entirely to Christ. He founded the Society of Jesus (the Jesuits),
which soon founded schools and seminaries all over Europe. St. Ignatius' *Spiritual Exercises* is one of the great classics of spiritual
literature.

The invocations in parentheses are for use by members of the
Society of Jesus.

LITANY OF
SAINT FRANCIS XAVIER

(For private use only.)

Lord, have mercy.
Lord, have mercy.
Christ, have mercy.
Christ, have mercy.
Lord, have mercy.
Lord, have mercy.
Christ, hear us.
Christ, graciously hear us.
God the Father of Heaven,
Have mercy on us.
God the Son, Redeemer of the world,
Have mercy on us.
God the Holy Ghost,
Have mercy on us.
Holy Trinity, One God,
Have mercy on us.

Holy Mary, Virgin Mother of God,
Pray for us.
Saint Ignatius, founder of the Society of Jesus,
Pray for us.
Saint Francis Xavier, the glory and second pillar of
that holy Institute, *etc.*
Apostle of the Indies and Japan,
Legate of the Holy Apostolic See,
Preacher of the truth and doctor of the nations,
Vessel of election, to carry the Name of Jesus Christ
to the kings of the earth,
Shining light to those who sat in the shadow of death,
Full of burning zeal for the glory of God,
Unwearied propagator of the Christian Faith,

246

Most watchful shepherd of souls,
Most constant meditator on divine things,
Most faithful follower of Jesus Christ,
Most ardent lover of evangelical poverty,
Most perfect observer of religious obedience,
Thou who didst burn with the fire of Divine Love,
Who didst generously despise all earthly things,
Most able guide in the way of perfection,
Model of apostolic men,
Model of all virtues,
Light of infidels and master of the faithful,
Angel in life and manners,
Patriarch in affection for and care of God's people,
Prophet mighty in word and works,
Whom all nations and the Church have with one voice
    associated with the glorious choir of Apostles,
Who wast adorned with the crown of virgins,
Who didst aspire to the palm of martyrs,
Confessor in virtue and profession of life,
In whom we reverence, through the Divine Goodness,
    the merits of all saints,
Whom the winds and the sea obeyed,
Who didst take by assault the cities that had revolted
    from Jesus Christ,
Who wast the terror of the armies of infidels,
Scourge of demons and destroyer of idols,
Powerful defense against shipwreck,
Father of the poor and refuge of the miserable,
Sight to the blind and strength to the lame,
Protector in time of war, famine, and plague,
Wonderful worker of miracles,
Who wast endued with the gift of tongues,
Who wast endued with the wondrous power of raising
    the dead,
Resounding trumpet of the Holy Ghost,
Light and glory of the East,
Through the cross, which thou didst so often raise
    among the Gentiles,

Saint Francis Xavier, *we beseech thee, hear us.*

Through the Faith, which thou didst so marvelously propagate, *we beseech thee, hear us.*

Through thy miracles and prophecies, *etc.*

Through the perils and shipwrecks which thou didst endure,

Through the pains and labors, in the midst of which thou didst so ardently exclaim, "Still more! Still more!"

Through thy heavenly raptures, in the midst of which thou didst so fervently exclaim, "Enough, enough, Lord, enough!"

Through the glory and happiness which now thou dost enjoy in Heaven,

Friend of the heavenly Bridegroom,
   Intercede for us.
Blessed Francis Xavier, beloved of God and men,
   Intercede for us.

Lamb of God, Who takest away the sins of the world,
   Spare us, O Lord.
Lamb of God, Who takest away the sins of the world,
   Graciously hear us, O Lord.
Lamb of God, Who takest away the sins of the world,
   Have mercy on us.

Christ, hear us.
   Christ, graciously hear us.

V. Pray for us, Saint Francis Xavier,
R. *That we may be made worthy of the promises of Christ.*

Let Us Pray

O God, Who by the preaching and miracles of blessed Francis wast pleased to add to Thy Church the nations of the Indies, mercifully grant that we who venerate his glorious merits may imitate his virtues, through Our Lord Jesus Christ Thy Son, Who with Thee and the Holy Ghost liveth and reigneth, one God, world without end. R. *Amen.*

St. Francis Xavier, Patron of Foreign Missions: Born in 1506 in a castle in Spain, of noble parents, St. Francis Xavier was one of St. Ignatius' original seven followers and proved to be perhaps the greatest individual missionary to the heathen since St. Paul. In 10 years he did the work of a thousand individual missionaries, and he performed countless miracles. St. Francis Xavier converted hundreds of thousands, especially in India and Japan, and the impact of his work lasted for centuries. He is known as the "Apostle of the Indies" and the "Apostle of Japan." St. Francis Xavier died in 1552 when he was about to enter China.

LITANY OF
SAINT PHILIP NERI
(For private use only.)

Lord, have mercy.
  Lord, have mercy.
Christ, have mercy.
  Christ, have mercy.
Lord, have mercy.
  Lord, have mercy.
Christ, hear us.
  Christ, graciously hear us.
God the Father of Heaven,
  Have mercy on us.
God the Son, Redeemer of the world,
  Have mercy on us.
God the Holy Spirit,
  Have mercy on us.
Holy Trinity, One God,
  Have mercy on us.

Holy Mary, *pray for us.*
Holy Mother of God, *pray for us.*
Holy Virgin of virgins, *etc.*
Saint Philip,
Vessel of the Holy Spirit,
Child of Mary,
Apostle of Rome,
Counsellor of popes,
Voice of prophecy,
Man of primitive times,
Winning saint,
Hidden hero,
Sweetest of fathers,
Flower of purity,

Martyr of charity,
Heart of fire,
Discerner of spirits,
Choicest of priests,
Mirror of the divine life,
Pattern of humility,
Example of simplicity,
Light of holy joy,
Image of childhood,
Picture of old age,
Director of souls,
Gentle guide of youth,
Patron of thine own,
Thou who observed chastity in thy youth,
Who sought Rome by divine guidance,
Who hid so long in the catacombs,
Who received the Holy Spirit into thy heart,
Who experienced such wonderful ecstasies,
Who so lovingly served the little ones,
Who washed the feet of pilgrims,
Who ardently thirsted after martyrdom,
Who distributed the daily word of God,
Who turned so many hearts to God,
Who conversed so sweetly with Mary,
Who raised the dead,
Who set up thy houses in all lands,

Lamb of God, Who takest away the sins of the world,
    Spare us, O Lord.
Lamb of God, Who takest away the sins of the world,
    Graciously hear us, O Lord.
Lamb of God, Who takest away the sins of the world,
    Have mercy on us.

Christ, hear us.
    Christ, graciously hear us.

V. Remember thy congregation.
R. *Which thou hast possessed from the beginning.*

Let Us Pray

O God, Who hast exalted blessed Philip, thy confessor, in the glory of Thy saints, grant that, as we rejoice in his commemoration, so may we profit by the example of his virtues, through Christ Our Lord. R. *Amen.*

St. Philip Neri, Apostle of Rome and Founder of the Congregation of the Oratory: St. Philip was born in Florence, Italy in 1515. At age 18 he spent two years living by himself in prayer and penance in Rome. After reading of the great missionary work St. Francis Xavier was doing in India, St. Philip wanted to pursue the same path, but through a vision he received a message from St. John the Evangelist: "Rome is to be your Indies." St. Philip also received a mystical experience of divine love which enlarged his heart so that it literally broke two of his ribs. Philip was ordained and spent the rest of his life converting and sanctifying souls in the city of Rome, which had become lukewarm and corrupt; he became famous as a confessor. St. Philip founded the Congregation of the Oratory, a community of priests who do not take the vows of religion. Through his own holiness, and also through his cheerfulness and his gifts of miracles (he raised a boy from the dead) and of reading hearts, St. Philip Neri transformed the city of Rome in his own lifetime and thereby exerted an incalculable influence on the Universal Church. He died in 1595.

LITANY OF
SAINT ALOYSIUS GONZAGA
(For private use only.)

Lord, have mercy on us.
Christ, have mercy on us.
Lord, have mercy on us. Christ, hear us.
Christ, graciously hear us.
God the Father of Heaven,
Have mercy on us.
God the Son, Redeemer of the world,
Have mercy on us.
God the Holy Spirit,
Have mercy on us.
Holy Trinity, One God,
Have mercy on us.

Holy Mary, *pray for us.*
Holy Mother of God, *pray for us.*
Holy Virgin of virgins, *etc.*
Saint Aloysius Gonzaga,
Beloved child of Christ,
The delight of the Blessed Virgin,
Most chaste youth,
Angelic youth,
Most humble youth,
Model of young students,
Despiser of riches,
Enemy of vanities,
Scorner of honors,
Honor of princes,
Jewel of the nobility,
Flower of innocence,
Ornament of the religious state,
Mirror of mortification,

Mirror of perfect obedience,
Lover of angelical poverty,
Most affectionately devout,
Most zealous observer of rules,
Most desirous of the salvation of souls,
Perpetual adorer of the Holy Eucharist,
Particular client of Saint Ignatius,

Be merciful,
  Spare us, O Lord.
Be merciful,
  Hear us, O Lord.

From the concupiscence of the eyes,
  O Lord, deliver us.
From the concupiscence of the flesh,
  O Lord, deliver us.
From the pride of life, *etc.*
Through the merits and intercession of Saint
  Aloysius,
Through his angelical purity,
Through his sanctity and glory,

Lamb of God, Who takest away the sins of the world,
  Spare us, O Lord.
Lamb of God, Who takest away the sins of the world,
  Graciously hear us, O Lord.
Lamb of God, Who takest away the sins of the world,
  Have mercy on us.

Christ, hear us.
  Christ, graciously hear us.

V. Pray for us, Saint Aloysius,
R. *That we may be made worthy of the promises of
  Christ.*

Let Us Pray

O God, distributor of heavenly gifts, Who united in
the angelic youth, Aloysius, wonderful innocence of

life to an equal severity of penance, grant, through his merits and prayers, that we who have not followed the example of his innocence may imitate his practice of penance, through Our Lord Jesus Christ. R. *Amen.*

St. Aloysius Gonzaga, Patron of Christian Youth: Born in 1568 in Lombardy, Italy, St. Aloysius, as a member of the noble Gonzaga family, was destined for a life in the military, at court, and in government. But at age 17, he abdicated and renounced everything to become a Jesuit. He was admirable for his great penance and austerities, both before and after entering the Society of Jesus. St. Aloysius died in 1591, at age 23, before reaching ordination to the priesthood. Many miracles followed immediately upon his death, and the Church has declared him "Patron of Christian Youth."

LITANY OF
SAINT JOHN BERCHMANS

(For private use only.)

Lord, have mercy on us.
Christ, have mercy on us.
Lord, have mercy on us.
Christ, graciously hear us.

Holy Mary, *pray for us.*
Saint John Berchmans, whom the Lord preserved from evil, *pray for us.*
St. John Berchmans, who did all things well, *etc.*
St. John Berchmans, faithful in little things,
St. John Berchmans, devoted server at Holy Mass,
St. John Berchmans, obedient to thy parents,
St. John Berchmans, submissive to thy teachers,
St. John Berchmans, model for thy companions,
St. John Berchmans, who from earliest childhood chose the Blessed Virgin as guardian of thy chastity,
St. John Berchmans, who so tenderly called Mary thy Mother,
St. John Berchmans, zealous promoter of devotion to Mary,
St. John Berchmans, mirror of the religious life,
St. John Berchmans, lover of the Blessed Sacrament,
St. John Berchmans, lover of the missions,
St. John Berchmans, lover of mortification,
St. John Berchmans, faithful to thy holy Rule,
St. John Berchmans, faithful imitator of St. Aloysius,
St. John Berchmans, ornament of the Society of Jesus,
St. John Berchmans, model of students,
St. John Berchmans, patron of youth,

Lamb of God, Who takest away the sins of the world,
Spare us, O Lord.
Lamb of God, Who takest away the sins of the world,
Graciously hear us, O Lord.
Lamb of God, Who takest away the sins of the world,
Have mercy on us.

Christ, hear us.
Christ, graciously hear us.

V. Pray for us, Saint John Berchmans,
R. *That we may be worthy of the promises of Christ.*

Let Us Pray

Grant, we beseech Thee, O Lord God, that we Thy servants may follow, in Thy service, the example of innocence and fidelity by which the angelic St. John Berchmans consecrated to Thee the flower of his youth, through Christ Our Lord. R. *Amen.*

St. John Berchmans, Patron of Altar Boys: St. John Berchmans was born in 1599 in Diest, Brabant, in Flanders. As a youth, he declared, "If I do not become a saint when I am young, I shall never become one." In 1616 he became a Jesuit novice. As a Jesuit, he practiced perfection in little things; he said, "My penance is to live the common life," and he let himself be ruled "like a baby a day old," as he himself wrote. He served Mass with such total devotion that he sometimes distracted the celebrant. He walked to Rome to study at the Roman College; at the college his talent, enthusiasm and application to study had rarely been equalled and never surpassed. His biographer says that there was always a smile playing about his mouth. In 1621 St. John Berchmans fell ill from prolonged study, from the strain of preparation for a public disputation, and from the summer heat. After four days he was asked if he had anything on his conscience; he answered, "Nothing at all." Two days later he died peacefully. Numerous miracles followed his death. St. John Berchmans is one of the three illustrious young saints of the Society of Jesus, the other two being St. Aloysius Gonzaga and St. Stanislaus Kostka.

LITANY OF
SAINT MARTIN DE PORRES
(For private use only.)

Lord, have mercy on us.
  Christ, have mercy on us.
Lord, have mercy on us. Christ, hear us.
  Christ, graciously hear us.
God the Father of Heaven,
  Have mercy on us.
God the Son, Redeemer of the world,
  Have mercy on us.
God the Holy Ghost,
  Have mercy on us.
Holy Trinity, One God,
  Have mercy on us.

Holy Mary, Queen of the Most Holy Rosary,
  Pray for us.
St. Martin, ever in the presence of God,
  Pray for us.
St. Martin, faithful servant of Christ, *etc.*
St. Martin, lover of the Holy Eucharist,
St. Martin, devoted to our Blessed Mother,
St. Martin, spiritual patron of Americans,
St. Martin, raised from the depths to a heavenly
  mansion,
St. Martin, honored son of Saint Dominic,
St. Martin, lover of the Most Holy Rosary,
St. Martin, apostle of mercy,
St. Martin, winged minister of charity,
St. Martin, miraculously conveyed to far-distant
  lands,
St. Martin, freed from the barriers of time and space,
St. Martin, seeking the conversion of sinners,

St. Martin, protector of the tempted and repentant,
St. Martin, helper of souls in doubt and darkness,
St. Martin, compassionate to the sorrowful and afflicted,
St. Martin, consoler of the discouraged and unfortunate,
St. Martin, peacemaker in all discords,
St. Martin, touched by all suffering,
St. Martin, comforter of the sick and dying,
St. Martin, angel to hospitals and prisons,
St. Martin, worker of miraculous cures,
St. Martin, guardian of the homeless child,
St. Martin, humbly hiding God-given powers,
St. Martin, devoted to holy poverty,
St. Martin, model of obedience,
St. Martin, lover of heroic penance,
St. Martin, strong in self-denial,
St. Martin, performing menial tasks with holy ardor,
St. Martin, gifted with prophecy,
St. Martin, symbol of interracial brotherhood,

Lamb of God, Who takest away the sins of the world,
Spare us, O Lord.
Lamb of God, Who takest away the sins of the world,
Graciously hear us, O Lord.
Lamb of God, Who takest away the sins of the world,
Have mercy on us.

V. Pray for us, Saint Martin,
R. *That we may be made worthy of the promises of Christ.*

Let Us Pray

O God, the exalter of the humble, Who didst make Saint Martin, Thy confessor, to enter the heavenly Kingdom, grant through his merits and intercession that we may so follow the example of his humility on earth as to deserve to be exalted with him in Heaven, through Christ Our Lord. R. *Amen.*

St. Martin de Porres, Helper in Hopeless Cases: A mulatto born illegitimately in Lima, Peru in 1579, St. Martin de Porres lived his life as a Dominican lay brother, known for his holiness, miracles, bilocation, cures—including cures of sick animals, speaking to and being understood by animals, and for his care for the poor, especially for African slaves. He was a close friend of St. Rose of Lima. St. Martin de Porres died in 1639.

LITANY OF
SAINT FRANCIS DE SALES
(For private use only.)

Lord, have mercy on us.
Christ, have mercy on us.
Lord, have mercy on us. Christ, hear us.
Christ, graciously hear us.
God the Father of Heaven,
Have mercy on us.
God the Son, Redeemer of the world,
Have mercy on us.
God the Holy Ghost,
Have mercy on us.
Holy Trinity, One God,
Have mercy on us.

Saint Francis, admirable bishop, *pray for us.*
Saint Francis, beloved of God, *pray for us.*
Saint Francis, imitator of Jesus Christ, *etc.*
Saint Francis, filled with the gifts of the Lord,
Saint Francis, favorite of the Mother of God,
Saint Francis, most devout to the saints,
Saint Francis, burning with love for the Cross of
    Christ,
Saint Francis, most closely united to the divine will,
Saint Francis, vessel of election,
Saint Francis, light of the Church,
Saint Francis, perfect model of religious,
Saint Francis, source of wisdom,
Saint Francis, defender of the Catholic Faith,
Saint Francis, good shepherd of thy people,
Saint Francis, incomparable preacher,
Saint Francis, scourge of heresy,
Saint Francis, salt of the earth,

Saint Francis, model of justice,
Saint Francis, mirror of humility,
Saint Francis, despiser of the world,
Saint Francis, lover of poverty,
Saint Francis, type of sweetness,
Saint Francis, conqueror of carnal passions,
Saint Francis, terror of devils,
Saint Francis, merciful prop to penitents,
Saint Francis, refuge of sinners,
Saint Francis, providence of the poor,
Saint Francis, consoler of the afflicted,
Saint Francis, example of perfection,
Saint Francis, ark of holiness,
Saint Francis, imitator of the purity of the angels,
Saint Francis, cherub of wisdom,
Saint Francis, seraph of love,
Saint Francis, our holy patriarch,
Saint Francis, our sweet light,
Saint Francis, our mighty protector,
Saint Francis, our guide in the ways of God,
Saint Francis, our refuge,
Saint Francis, emulator of the angels,
Saint Francis, imitator of the Apostles,
Saint Francis, sharer in the glory of the martyrs,
Saint Francis, glory of holy confessors,
Saint Francis, teacher and director of virgins,
Saint Francis, glorious fellow citizen of all the saints,

Lamb of God, Who takest away the sins of the world,
Spare us, O Lord.
Lamb of God, Who takest away the sins of the world,
Graciously hear us, O Lord.
Lamb of God, Who takest away the sins of the world,
Have mercy on us.

V. Pray for us, O blessed Francis de Sales,
R. *That we may be made worthy of the promises of Christ.*

Let Us Pray *

O God, by Whose gracious will the blessed Francis, Thy confessor and bishop, became all things unto all men for the saving of their souls, mercifully grant that being filled with the sweetness of Thy love, we may, through the guidance of his counsels and the aid of his merits, attain unto the joys of life everlasting. R. *Amen.*

*This prayer was composed by Pope Alexander VII and given in his own handwriting, together with the brief of beatification of Saint Francis de Sales, to the Bishop of Puy on December 28th, 1661, in the presence of Father de Chaugy. *(This information was obtained from the unpublished letters of Father de Chaugy).*

St. Francis de Sales, Bishop of Geneva and Doctor of the Church: Born in 1567 in the family castle in Savoy, France, St. Francis became a doctor of civil and ecclesiastical law, but then gave up law to become a priest. He was also consecrated a bishop. He converted many, and reconverted thousands from Calvinism. Known for his great learning and gentleness, he wrote two great spiritual classics: *Introduction to the Devout Life* and *Treatise on the Love of God.* With St. Jane Frances de Chantal he founded the Order of Visitation nuns. St. Francis de Sales died in 1622.

LITANY OF
SAINT VINCENT DE PAUL
(For private use only.)

Lord, have mercy.
  Christ, have mercy.
Lord, have mercy. Christ, hear us.
  Christ, graciously hear us.

V. The just shall spring up like the lily,
R. *And flourish forever before the Lord. Alleluia.*

Holy Mary, Mother of God,
  Pray for us.
Holy Mary, comforter of the afflicted,
  Pray for us.
Saint Vincent de Paul, *etc.*
St. Vincent, who at the tenderest age didst display a
  wisdom most mature,
St. Vincent, who from thy childhood wast full of pity
  and compassion,
St. Vincent, who like David, from a simple shepherd
  becamest a ruler and pastor of the people of God,
St. Vincent, who in thy captivity by Turkish pirates
  didst preserve perfect freedom,
St. Vincent the just man, who didst live by faith,
St. Vincent, always supported on the firm anchor of a
  Christian hope,
St. Vincent, always inflamed with the fire of perfect
  charity,
St. Vincent, truly simple, upright, and fearing God,
St. Vincent, true disciple of Jesus Christ, always meek
  and humble of heart,
St. Vincent, perfectly mortified in heart
  and mind,

St. Vincent, ever animated with the spirit of Our
Lord,

St. Vincent, generous maintainer of the
glory of God,

St. Vincent, ever inwardly burning and ever
outwardly transported with zeal for souls,

St. Vincent, who in Christian poverty didst find the
precious pearl and the rich treasure of the Gospel,

St. Vincent, like to the angels in thy purity,

St. Vincent, faithful in obedience and victorious in
word and deed,

St. Vincent, who didst fly the slightest appearance of
evil,

St. Vincent, who in all thine actions didst aspire to the
practice of perfect virtue,

St. Vincent, who didst remain like a rock amidst the
stormy sea of this world,

St. Vincent, invincible amidst the arrows
of adversity,

St. Vincent, as patient in suffering as thou wast
indulgent in forgiving,

St. Vincent, ever docile and obedient son of the Holy
See,

St. Vincent, who hadst exceeding horror of the novel
ways and subtle words of heretics,

St. Vincent, destined by a special Providence to
announce the Gospel to the poor,

St. Vincent, father and model of
ecclesiastics,

St. Vincent, prudent founder of the Congregation of
the Mission,

St. Vincent, wise institutor of the Congregation of the
Sisters of Charity,

St. Vincent, tender in compassionating and prompt in
relieving the necessities of the poor,

St. Vincent, equally fervent in the practice of prayer
and in ministry of the word,

St. Vincent, admirable in imitation of the life and
virtues of Jesus,

St. Vincent, who didst persevere to the end in
shunning evil and doing good,
St. Vincent, who as in life so in death wast most
precious in the sight of God,
St. Vincent, glory of France and pride
of Paris,
St. Vincent, patron of all charitable
associations,

Lamb of God, Who takest away the sins of the world,
Spare us, O Lord.
Lamb of God, Who takest away the sins of the world,
Graciously hear us, O Lord.
Lamb of God, Who takest away the sins of the world,
Have mercy on us.

V. The Lord hath led the just man through right ways,
R. *And showed unto him the Kingdom of God.*

Let Us Pray

O God, Who by an effect of Thine infinite goodness, hast renewed in our days, in the apostolic
character and humility of Thy blessed servant Vincent, the spirit of Thy well-beloved Son—to preach
the Gospel to the poor, relieve the afflicted, console
the miserable, and add new luster to the ecclesiastical
order—grant, we beseech Thee, through his powerful
intercession, that we also, delivered from the great
misery of sin, may labor to please Thee by the practice of the same humility, through Jesus Christ Our
Lord, Who liveth with Thee and the Holy Ghost, ever
one God, world without end. R. *Amen.*

O God, Who for the preaching of the Gospel to the
poor, and for promoting the honor of the priesthood,
didst endue blessed Vincent with the zeal of an apostle, grant, we humbly pray Thee, that we who venerate his holy life may profit by the examples of virtue
he has left us. R. *Amen.*

St. Vincent de Paul, Founder of the Congregation of the Mission and Co-Founder of the Daughters of Charity: St. Vincent de Paul was born in 1580 in France. He was ordained in 1600, and in 1605 was captured by Turkish pirates who took him as a slave to Africa. He escaped and returned to France, where he founded the Congregation of the Mission (the Lazarists, or the Vincentians) to do all kinds of charitable and priestly work, including ransoming Christian slaves in Africa. He was responsible for saving the lives of vast numbers of people during the wars in Lorraine, France; for this he is known as the Father of his Country. Yet St. Vincent considered spiritual starvation as far worse than any bodily affliction. With St. Louise de Marillac, he also founded the Daughters of Charity who cared for the sick, poor, aged, insane, galley slaves, and soldiers on the battlefield. St. Vincent de Paul died in 1660.

LITANY OF
SAINT ALPHONSUS LIGUORI

(For private use only.)

Lord, have mercy on us.
Christ, have mercy on us.
Lord, have mercy on us. Christ, hear us.
Christ, graciously hear us.
God the Father of Heaven,
Have mercy on us.
God the Son, Redeemer of the world,
Have mercy on us.
God the Holy Ghost,
Have mercy on us.
Holy Trinity, One God,
Have mercy on us.

Holy Mary, Virgin Immaculate, *pray for us.*
Saint Alphonsus Maria de Ligouri, *pray for us.*
St. Alphonsus, model of piety from tenderest youth,
    etc.
St. Alphonsus, scourge of heresies,
St. Alphonsus, defender of the Catholic Faith,
St. Alphonsus, always occupied in evangelizing the
    poor,
St. Alphonsus, tender comforter of the afflicted,
St. Alphonsus, instructed in the divine art of
    converting sinners,
St. Alphonsus, enlightened guide in the path of
    perfection,
St. Alphonsus, who became all things to all men to
    gain all for Jesus Christ,
St. Alphonsus, new ornament of the religious state,
St. Alphonsus, bold champion of ecclesiastical
    discipline,

St. Alphonsus, model of submission and devotion to the Sovereign Pontiff,

St. Alphonsus, who didst watch unceasingly over the flock committed to thee,

St. Alphonsus, full of solicitude for the common good of the Church,

St. Alphonsus, glory of the priesthood and of the episcopate,

St. Alphonsus, shining mirror of all virtues,

St. Alphonsus, full of tenderest love for the Infant Jesus,

St. Alphonsus, inflamed with divine love whilst offering the Holy Sacrifice of the Mass,

St. Alphonsus, fervent adorer of Jesus Christ in the Holy Eucharist,

St. Alphonsus, penetrated with lively compassion while meditating on the sufferings of our Divine Saviour,

St. Alphonsus, specially devoted to the Blessed Virgin Mary,

St. Alphonsus, favored by apparitions of the Mother of God,

St. Alphonsus, leading an angelic life,

St. Alphonsus, a true patriarch in thy paternal solicitude for the people of God,

St. Alphonsus, endowed with the gifts of prophecy and miracles,

St. Alphonsus, an apostle by the extent and fruit of thy labors,

St. Alphonsus, a martyr by thy austerities,

St. Alphonsus, a confessor by thy writings full of the Spirit of God,

St. Alphonsus, a virgin by thy purity of soul and body,

St. Alphonsus, a model of missionaries,

St. Alphonsus, founder of the Order of the Most Holy Redeemer,

St. Alphonsus, our tender father and powerful protector,

Lamb of God, Who takest away the sins of the world,
Spare us, O Lord.
Lamb of God, Who takest away the sins of the world,
Graciously hear us, O Lord.
Lamb of God, Who takest away the sins of the world,
Have mercy on us.

Christ, hear us.
Christ, graciously hear us.

V. Pray for us, Saint Alphonsus,
R. *That we may be made worthy of the promises of
Christ.*

Let Us Pray

O God, Who through the blessed Alphonsus Maria,
Thy confessor and bishop, inflamed with zeal for
souls, hast enriched Thy Church with a new progeny,
we beseech Thee that, taught by his saving counsels
and strengthened by his example, we may happily
come to Thee, through Christ Our Lord. R. *Amen.*

*St. Alphonsus Mary de Liguori, Founder of the Redemptorists,
Bishop of St. Agatha, and Doctor of the Church:* St. Alphonsus was
born in 1696 to a noble Neopolitan family. He became a very suc-
cessful lawyer but abandoned law to become a priest, and later a
bishop. He founded the Congregation of the Most Holy Redeemer,
the Redemptorists, which has become famous for giving "missions" to enkindle and rejuvenate souls with true religious fervor.
St. Alphonsus' great work entitled *Moral Theology* is still studied,
and he wrote numerous devotional books, the most famous being
The Glories of Mary. St. Alphonsus died in 1787, within two
months of his 91st birthday.

LITANY OF
SAINT GERARD MAJELLA
(For private use only.)

Lord, have mercy on us.
Christ, have mercy on us.
Lord, have mercy on us. Christ, hear us.
Christ, graciously hear us.
God the Father of Heaven,
Have mercy on us.
God the Son, Redeemer of the world,
Have mercy on us.
God the Holy Ghost,
Have mercy on us.
Holy Trinity, One God,
Have mercy on us.

Holy Mary, Mother of Perpetual Help,
Pray for us.
Saint Joseph, foster-father of Christ,
Pray for us.
Saint Alphonsus, founder of the Congregation of the
Most Holy Redeemer, *etc.*
Saint Gerard Majella,
St. Gerard, enriched with extraordinary graces from
early youth,
St. Gerard, perfect model of a faithful servant,
St. Gerard, bright pattern of the working classes,
St. Gerard, great lover of prayer and work,
St. Gerard, seraph of love toward the Blessed
Sacrament,
St. Gerard, living image of the crucified Saviour,
St. Gerard, zealous client of the Immaculate Virgin
Mary,
St. Gerard, bright mirror of innocence and penance,

St. Gerard, admirable model of heroic obedience,

St. Gerard, silent victim of ignominious calumny,

St. Gerard, great before God by thy deep humility,

St. Gerard, truly wise by thy childlike simplicity,

St. Gerard, supernaturally enlightened in divine mysteries,

St. Gerard, solely desirous of pleasing God,

St. Gerard, zealous promoter of the conversion of sinners,

St. Gerard, wise counselor in the choice of vocation,

St. Gerard, enlightened guide in the direction of souls,

St. Gerard, loving friend of the poor and afflicted,

St. Gerard, safe refuge in sickness and sorrow,

St. Gerard, wonderful protector of unbaptized children,

St. Gerard, compassionate intercessor in every necessity,

St. Gerard, honor and glory of the Redemptorist Order,

Lamb of God, Who takest away the sins of the world, *Spare us, O Lord.*

Lamb of God, Who takest away the sins of the world, *Graciously hear us, O Lord.*

Lamb of God, Who takest away the sins of the world, *Have mercy on us.*

V. Pray for us, Saint Gerard,

R. *That we may be made worthy of the promises of Christ.*

Let Us Pray

O God, Who wast pleased to draw blessed Gerard to Thyself from his youth, and to render him conformable to the image of Thy crucified Son, grant, we beseech Thee, that following his example, we may be transformed into the selfsame image, through the same Christ Our Lord. R. *Amen.*

St. Gerard Majella, Patron of Women in Childbirth: Born in 1726 in southern Italy, St. Gerard joined the Redemptorist Order in 1749 as a lay brother, and was professed by the Order's founder, St. Alphonsus Liguori. St. Gerard converted many sinners. He was favored by God with infused knowledge, ecstasies, prophecy, bilocation and miracles, and became famous during his own lifetime. He died in 1755.

LITANY OF
SAINT JOHN VIANNEY,
THE CURÉ OF ARS

(For private use only.)

Lord, have mercy on us.
Lord, have mercy on us.
Christ, have mercy on us.
Christ, have mercy on us.
Lord, have mercy on us.
Lord, have mercy on us.
Christ, hear us.
Christ, graciously hear us.
God the Father of Heaven,
Have mercy on us.
God the Son, Redeemer of the world,
Have mercy on us.
God the Holy Ghost,
Have mercy on us.
Holy Trinity, One God,
Have mercy on us.

Holy Mary, Mother of God, *pray for us.*
Saint John-Mary Vianney, *pray for us.*
St. John Vianney, endowed with grace
    from thine infancy, *etc.*
St. John Vianney, model of
    filial piety,
St. John Vianney, devoted servant of the
    Immaculate Heart of Mary,
St. John Vianney, spotless lily of purity,
St. John Vianney, faithful imitator of the
    sufferings of Christ,
St. John Vianney, abyss of humility,
St. John Vianney, seraph of prayer,

St. John Vianney, faithful adorer of the Most Blessed Sacrament,

St. John Vianney, ardent lover of holy poverty,

St. John Vianney, true son of St. Francis of Assisi,

St. John Vianney, exemplary Franciscan tertiary,

St. John Vianney, tender friend of the poor,

St. John Vianney, penetrated with the fear of God's judgment,

St. John Vianney, fortified by divine visions,

St. John Vianney, who was tormented by the evil spirit,

St. John Vianney, perfect model of sacerdotal virtue,

St. John Vianney, firm and prudent pastor,

St. John Vianney, inflamed with zeal,

St. John Vianney, faithful attendant on the sick,

St. John Vianney, indefatigable catechist,

St. John Vianney, who didst preach in words of fire,

St. John Vianney, wise director of souls,

St. John Vianney, specially gifted with the spirit of counsel,

St. John Vianney, enlightened by light from Heaven,

St. John Vianney, formidable to Satan,

St. John Vianney, compassionate with every misery,

St. John Vianney, providence of the orphans,

St. John Vianney, favored with the gift of miracles,

St. John Vianney, who didst reconcile so many sinners to God,

St. John Vianney, who didst confirm so many of the just in the way of virtue,

St. John Vianney, who didst taste the sweetness of death,

St. John Vianney, who dost now rejoice in the glory of Heaven,

St. John Vianney, who givest joy to those who invoke thee,

St. John Vianney, heavenly patron of parish priests,

St. John Vianney, model and patron of directors of souls,

Lamb of God, Who takest away the sins of the world,
Spare us, O Lord.
Lamb of God, Who takest away the sins of the world,
Hear us, O Lord.
Lamb of God, Who takest away the sins of the world,
Have mercy on us.

Christ, hear us.
Christ, graciously hear us.

V. Pray for us, blessed Jean-Marie Vianney,
R. *That we may be made worthy of the promises of Christ.*

Let Us Pray

Almighty and merciful God, Who didst bestow upon blessed John Mary Vianney wonderful pastoral zeal and a great fervor for prayer and penance, grant, we beseech Thee, that by his example and intercession we may be able to gain the souls of our brethren for Christ, and with them attain to everlasting glory, through the same Lord Jesus Christ Thy Son, Who liveth and reigneth with Thee and the Holy Ghost, one God, world without end. R. *Amen.*

St. John Vianney, The Curé of Ars, Patron of Parish Priests: Born in 1786, St. Jean-Marie Baptiste Vianney became a priest and was assigned to the parish in Ars, France, where he heard confessions for 13-17 hours daily. People from far and wide flocked to Ars, and St. John Vianney converted thousands in his lifetime. He had the gift of reading hearts. For five years he lived on one meal per day of boiled potatoes. The devil physically assailed him off and on over a period of 30 years. St. John Vianney died in 1859.

LITANY OF
SAINT PHILOMENA
(For private use only.)

Lord, have mercy on us.
   Christ, have mercy on us.
Lord, have mercy on us. Christ, hear us.
   Christ, graciously hear us.
God the Father of Heaven,
   Have mercy on us.
God the Son, Redeemer of the world,
   Have mercy on us.
God the Holy Spirit,
   Have mercy on us.
Holy Trinity, One God,
   Have mercy on us.

Holy Mary, Queen of Virgins,
   Pray for us.
Saint Philomena,
   Pray for us.
Saint Philomena, filled with abundant graces
   from the cradle, *etc.*
Saint Philomena, model of virgins,
Saint Philomena, temple of the most perfect
   humility,
Saint Philomena, victim of the love of Christ,
Saint Philomena, example of strength and
   perseverance,
Saint Philomena, invincible athlete
   of chastity,
Saint Philomena, mirror of most
   heroic virtues,
Saint Philomena, firm and intrepid
   before torments,

Saint Philomena, scourged like thy Divine Spouse,

Saint Philomena, pierced by a shower of arrows,

Saint Philomena, consoled in chains by the Mother of God,

Saint Philomena, miraculously cured in prison,

Saint Philomena, sustained by angels in the midst of tortures,

Saint Philomena, who preferred humiliation and death to the splendor of a throne,

Saint Philomena, who converted the witnesses of thy martyrdom,

Saint Philomena, who wore out the fury of thy executioners,

Saint Philomena, patroness of the innocent,

Saint Philomena, patroness of youth,

Saint Philomena, refuge of the unfortunate,

Saint Philomena, health of the sick and infirm,

Saint Philomena, new light of the Church Militant,

Saint Philomena, who confounds the impiety of our age,

Saint Philomena, who reanimates the faith and courage of the faithful,

Saint Philomena, whose name is glorious in Heaven and terrible in Hell,

Saint Philomena, illustrious by the most splendid miracles,

Saint Philomena, powerful with God,

Saint Philomena, who reigns in glory,

Lamb of God, Who takest away the sins of the world, *Spare us, O Lord.*

Lamb of God, Who takest away the sins of the world, *Graciously hear us, O Lord.*

Lamb of God, Who takest away the sins of the world, *Have mercy on us.*

V. Pray for us, Saint Philomena,

R. *That we may be made worthy of the promises of Christ.*

Let Us Pray

We beg Thee, O Lord, to grant us the pardon of our sins by the intercession of Saint Philomena, virgin and martyr, who was always pleasing in Thy sight by her eminent chastity and by the profession of every virtue. R. *Amen.*

This litany is attributed to Saint John Vianney, the Curé of Ars.

St. Philomena, Martyr: The existence of St. Philomena, an early Roman martyr, came to light when the bones of a young girl, a vial of blood, and an inscription reading "Peace be with you, Philomena" were discovered in St. Priscilla's catacomb in Rome. In 1805 the remains were moved to the church of Mugnano del Cardinale near Nola, Italy. Miracles were reported at her tomb, and devotion to her became widespread; her most famous devotee was St. John Vianney, the Curé of Ars. St. Philomena's cult was authorized in 1837 by Pope Gregory XVI, but her name was dropped from the Roman calendar in 1961, along with several other names, because of a lack of authentic historical information. However, St. Philomena may still be honored privately.

LITANY OF
SAINT THERESE
OF THE CHILD JESUS
Litany One
(For private use only.)

Lord, have mercy on us.
Christ, have mercy on us.
Lord, have mercy on us. Christ, hear us.
Christ, graciously hear us.
God the Father of Heaven,
Have mercy on us.
God the Son, Redeemer of the world,
Have mercy on us.
God the Holy Spirit,
Have mercy on us.
Holy Trinity, One God,
Have mercy on us.

Holy Mary, Mother of God, *pray for us.*
Our Lady of Victory, *pray for us.*
Our Lady of Mount Carmel, *etc.*
Saint Therese of the Child Jesus,
Saint Therese of the Holy Face,
Saint Therese, spouse of Jesus,
Saint Therese, child of Mary,
Saint Therese, devoted to Saint Joseph,
Saint Therese, angel of innocence,
Saint Therese, model child,
Saint Therese, pattern of religious,
Saint Therese, flower of Carmel,
Saint Therese, zealous to save souls,
Saint Therese, converter of hardened hearts,
Saint Therese, healer of the diseased,
Saint Therese, filled with love for the Blessed
  Sacrament,

Saint Therese, filled with angelic fervor,

Saint Therese, filled with loyalty to the Holy Father,

Saint Therese, filled with a tender love for the Church,

Saint Therese, filled with extraordinary love for God and neighbor,

Saint Therese, wounded with a heavenly flame,

Saint Therese, victim of divine love,

Saint Therese, patient in sufferings,

Saint Therese, eager for humiliations,

Saint Therese, consumed with love of God,

Saint Therese, rapt in ecstasy,

Saint Therese, dedicated to pray for priests,

Saint Therese, who refused God nothing,

Saint Therese, who desired always to be as a little child,

Saint Therese, who taught the way of spiritual childhood,

Saint Therese, who gave perfect example of trust in God,

Saint Therese, whom Jesus filled with a desire for suffering,

Saint Therese, who found perfection in little things,

Saint Therese, who sought bitterness in this life,

Saint Therese, who told us to call thee "little Therese,"

Saint Therese, who gained countless souls for Christ,

Saint Therese, who promised after thy death a shower of roses,

Saint Therese, who foretold: "I will spend my Heaven doing good upon earth,"

Saint Therese, Patroness of the Missions,

Lamb of God, Who takest away the sins of the world, *Spare us, O Lord.*

Lamb of God, Who takest away the sins of the world, *Graciously hear us, O Lord.*

Lamb of God, Who takest away the sins of the world, *Have mercy on us.*

V. Pray for us, Saint Therese,
R. *That we may be made worthy of the promises of Christ.*

Let Us Pray

Hear our prayer, O Lord, we beseech Thee, as we venerate Saint Therese, Thy virgin and martyr of love and longing to make Thee loved, and grant us, through her intercession, the gift of childlike simplicity and the spirit of complete dedication to Thy divine service, Thou who livest and reignest world without end. R. *Amen.*

St. Therese of the Child Jesus, The "Little Flower": Born in 1873 in France of middle-class parents, the youngest of nine children, St. Therese entered the Carmelite convent in Lisieux at age 15 and lived a hidden life of great love of God through the practice of her "Little Way." She died in 1897 at age 24 after writing her autobiography, *The Story of a Soul,* one of the most widely read spiritual books of all time. With St. Francis Xavier, she is Patron of the Missions. St. Pius X called St. Therese "the greatest saint of modern times."

LITANY OF SAINT THERESE
OF THE CHILD JESUS
Litany Two
(For private use only.)

Lord, have mercy on us.
Christ, have mercy on us.
Lord, have mercy on us. Christ, hear us.
Christ, graciously hear us.
God the Father of Heaven,
Have mercy on us.
God the Son, Redeemer of the world,
Have mercy on us.
God the Holy Spirit,
Have mercy on us.
Holy Trinity, One God,
Have mercy on us.

Holy Mary, *pray for us,*
Our Lady of Victory, *pray for us,*
Saint Therese, servant of God, *etc.*
Saint Therese, victim of the merciful love of God,
Saint Therese, spouse of Jesus,
Saint Therese, gift of Heaven,
Saint Therese, remarkable in childhood,
Saint Therese, an example of obedience,
Saint Therese, lover of the will of God,
Saint Therese, lover of peace,
Saint Therese, lover of patience,
Saint Therese, lover of gentleness,
Saint Therese, heroic in sacrifice,
Saint Therese, generous in forgiving,
Saint Therese, benefactress of the needy,
Saint Therese, lover of Jesus,
Saint Therese, devoted to the Holy Face,
Saint Therese, consumed with divine love of God,

Saint Therese, advocate of extreme cases,
Saint Therese, persevering in prayer,
Saint Therese, a powerful advocate with God,
Saint Therese, showering roses,
Saint Therese, doing good upon earth,
Saint Therese, answering all prayers,
Saint Therese, lover of holy chastity,
Saint Therese, lover of voluntary poverty,
Saint Therese, lover of obedience,
Saint Therese, burning with zeal for God's glory,
Saint Therese, inflamed with the Spirit of Love,
Saint Therese, child of benediction,
Saint Therese, perfect in simplicity,
Saint Therese, so remarkable for trust in God,
Saint Therese, gifted with unusual intelligence,
Saint Therese, never invoked without some answer,
Saint Therese, teaching us the sure way,
Saint Therese, victim of Divine Love,

Lamb of God, Who takest away the sins of the world,
    Spare us, O Lord.
Lamb of God, Who takest away the sins of the world,
    Graciously hear us, O Lord.
Lamb of God, Who takest away the sins of the world,
    Have mercy on us.

V. Saint Therese, the Little Flower of Jesus,
R. *Pray for us.*

Let Us Pray

O God, Who inflamed with Thy Spirit of Love the soul of Thy servant Therese of the Child Jesus, grant that we may also love Thee and may make Thee much loved. R. *Amen.*

LITANY OF
SAINT PIUS X

(For private use only.)

Lord, have mercy on us.
Christ, have mercy on us.
Lord, have mercy on us. Christ, hear us.
Christ, graciously hear us.
God the Father of Heaven,
Have mercy on us.
God the Son, Redeemer of the world,
Have mercy on us.
God the Holy Spirit,
Have mercy on us.
Holy Trinity, One God,
Have mercy on us.

Holy Mary, Mother of God,
Pray for us.
Saint Joseph, Patron of the Universal Church,
Pray for us.
Saint Pius X, model for priests, *etc.*
Saint Pius X, wise bishop,
Saint Pius X, humble cardinal and patriarch,
Saint Pius X, pope of peace,
Saint Pius X, zealous teacher,
Saint Pius X, devoted to the poor,
Saint Pius X, consoler of the sick,
Saint Pius X, lover of poverty,
Saint Pius X, humble of heart,
Saint Pius X, faithful to duty,
Saint Pius X, heroic in the practice
    of all virtues,
Saint Pius X, filled with the spirit
    of self-sacrifice,

Saint Pius X, who aimed to restore all things in Christ,
Saint Pius X, who brought little children to the Table
of the Lord,
Saint Pius X, who counseled daily and frequent
Communion for all,
Saint Pius X, who urged us to know and to love the
sacred liturgy,
Saint Pius X, who sought everywhere the diffusion of
Christian teaching,
Saint Pius X, who reformed the music
of the Church,
Saint Pius X, who taught us the value
of Catholic Action,
Saint Pius X, who consecrated the faithful to the lay
apostolate,
Saint Pius X, who wished to be known as a poor
pastor of souls,
Saint Pius X, who answers the prayers of those who
cry to thee,

Lamb of God, Who takest away the sins of the world,
Spare us, O Lord.
Lamb of God, Who takest away the sins of the world,
Graciously hear us, O Lord.
Lamb of God, Who takest away the sins of the world,
Have mercy on us.

V. Pray for us, Saint Pius X,
R. *That we may be made worthy of the promises of
Christ.*

Let Us Pray

O God, who filled the soul of Saint Pius X with a
burning charity and called him to be the Vicar of
Christ, grant that through his intercession we may
follow in the footsteps of Jesus, Our Divine Master;
and may our prayers to this saintly Pope be fruitful for
life both here and hereafter, through the same Christ
Our Lord. R. *Amen.*

Pope St. Pius X: Born Giuseppi Sarto to poor Italian parents in 1835, this saint was the second of 10 children. He became a priest, a bishop, and in 1903, Supreme Pontiff of the Universal Church. Pope St. Pius X is especially known for his measures against the Modernist heresy, for encouraging frequent Holy Communion, and for lowering the age for First Holy Communion from 12 to 7. He died in 1914 and is the first pope to be canonized since Pope St. Pius V was canonized in 1712.

LITANIES FOR PARTICULAR NEEDS AND INTENTIONS

"Be nothing solicitous; but in everything, by prayer and supplication, with thanksgiving, let your petitions be made known to God."

—Philippians 4:6

LITANY OF THE
MERCY OF GOD

(For private use only.)

Lord, have mercy on us.
  Christ, have mercy on us.
Lord, have mercy on us. Christ, hear us.
  Christ, graciously hear us.
God the Father of Heaven,
  Have mercy on us.
God the Son, Redeemer of the world,
  Have mercy on us.
God the Holy Spirit,
  Have mercy on us.
Holy Trinity, One God,
  Have mercy on us.

Mercy of God, supreme attribute of the Creator,
  We trust in Thee.
Mercy of God, greatest perfection of the Redeemer,
  We trust in Thee.
Mercy of God, unfathomable love of the Sanctifier,
  etc.
Mercy of God, inconceivable mystery of the Holy
  Trinity,
Mercy of God, expression of the greatest power of the
  Most High,
Mercy of God, revealed in the creation of the
  heavenly spirits,
Mercy of God, summoning us to existence out of
  nothingness,
Mercy of God, embracing the whole universe,
Mercy of God, bestowing upon us immortal life,
Mercy of God, shielding us from merited
  punishments,

Mercy of God, raising us from the misery of sin,

Mercy of God, justifying us in the Word Incarnate,

Mercy of God, flowing from the wounds of Christ,

Mercy of God, gushing from the Most Sacred
Heart of Jesus,

Mercy of God, giving to us the Most Blessed Virgin
Mary as Mother of Mercy,

Mercy of God, shown in the revelation of the
divine mysteries,

Mercy of God, manifested in the institution of the
universal Church,

Mercy of God, contained in the institution of the
Holy Sacraments,

Mercy of God, bestowed upon mankind in the
Sacraments of Baptism and Penance,

Mercy of God, granted in the Sacraments of the
Altar and the Priesthood,

Mercy of God, shown in calling us to the
Holy Faith,

Mercy of God, revealed in the conversion
of sinners,

Mercy of God, manifested in the sanctification
of the just,

Mercy of God, fulfilled in the perfecting of the
saintly,

Mercy of God, font of health for the sick and the
suffering,

Mercy of God, solace of anguished hearts,

Mercy of God, hope of souls afflicted
with despair,

Mercy of God, always and everywhere
accompanying all people,

Mercy of God, anticipating us with graces,

Mercy of God, peace of the dying,

Mercy of God, refreshment and relief of the
souls in Purgatory,

Mercy of God, heavenly delight of the blessed,

Mercy of God, crown of all the saints,

Mercy of God, inexhaustible source of miracles,

Lamb of God, Who didst show us Thy greatest mercy in redeeming the world on the cross,
Spare us, O Lord.
Lamb of God, Who dost mercifully offer Thyself for us in every Holy Mass,
Graciously hear us, O Lord.
Lamb of God, Who takest away the sins of the world through Thine inexhaustible Mercy,
Have mercy on us.

Lord, have mercy on us.
Christ, have mercy on us.
Lord, have mercy on us.

V. The tender mercies of the Lord are over all His works.
R. *The mercies of the Lord I will sing forever.*

Let Us Pray

O God, Whose Mercy is infinite and Whose treasures of pity are inexhaustible, graciously look down upon us and increase in us Thy Mercy so that we may never, even in the greatest trials, give way to despair, but may always trustfully conform ourselves to Thy Holy Will, which is Mercy itself. Through Our Lord Jesus Christ, the King of Mercy, Who with Thee and the Holy Spirit doth show us Mercy forever and ever.
R. *Amen.*

LITANY FOR A HAPPY DEATH

(For private use only.)

Lord, have mercy on us.
Christ, have mercy on us.
Lord, have mercy on us. Christ, hear us.
Christ, graciously hear us.
God the Father of Heaven,
Have mercy on us.
God the Son, Redeemer of the world,
Have mercy on us.
God the Holy Spirit,
Have mercy on us.
Holy Trinity, One God,
Have mercy on us.

Holy Mary, *pray for us.*
All ye holy angels and archangels, *pray for us.*
Holy Abraham, *etc.*
Saint John the Baptist,
Saint Joseph,
All ye holy patriarchs and prophets,
Saint Peter,
Saint Paul,
Saint Andrew,
Saint John,
Saint Jude,
All ye holy apostles and evangelists,
All ye holy disciples of Our Lord,
All ye holy innocents,
Saint Stephen,
Saint Lawrence,
All ye holy martyrs,
Saint Sylvester,
Saint Gregory,

Saint Augustine,
Saint Basil,
Saint Ambrose,
Saint Francis de Sales,
Saint Vincent de Paul,
Saint Aloysius,
Saint Stanislaus,
All ye holy bishops and confessors,
Saint Benedict,
Saint Dominic,
Saint Francis of Assisi,
Saint Ignatius,
Saint Philip Neri,
Saint Camillus de Lellis,
Saint John of God,
All ye holy monks, hermits, and founders
    of religious orders,
Saint Mary Magdalen,
Saint Lucy,
Saint Scholastica,
Saint Teresa,
Saint Catherine,
Saint Clare,
Saint Ursula,
Saint Angela Merici,
Saint Jane Frances de Chantal,
Saint Barbara,
All ye holy virgins and widows,

All ye saints of God, *intercede for us.*

Be merciful unto us, *Spare us, O Lord.*
Be merciful unto us, *Hear us, O Lord.*

From Thy anger, *O Lord, deliver us.*
From the peril of death, *O Lord, deliver us.*
From an evil death, *etc.*
From the pains of Hell,
From all evil,

From the power of the devil,
By Thy Nativity,
By Thy Cross and Passion,
By Thy death and burial,
By Thy glorious Resurrection,
By the grace of the Holy Spirit, the Comforter,
In the Day of Judgment,

We sinners beseech Thee, *hear us.*

That Thou wouldst spare us, *we beseech Thee,*
    hear us.
That Thou wouldst vouchsafe to bring us unto true
    repentance, *we beseech Thee, hear us.*
That Thou wouldst vouchsafe to grant eternal rest to
    all the faithful departed, *we beseech Thee, hear us.*

Lamb of God, Who takest away the sins of the world,
    Have mercy on us.
Lamb of God, forgive us our sins;
    Grant that we may die in Thy love and Thy grace.
Lamb of God, by Thy Precious Blood,
    We beseech Thee to hear us and to lead us to life
    everlasting.

Lord, have mercy on us.
    Christ, have mercy on us.
Lord, have mercy on us.

Let Us Pray

We beseech Thy clemency, O Lord, that Thou
wouldst vouchsafe so to strengthen Thy servants in
Thy grace that, at the hour of death, the enemy may
not prevail over us, and that we may deserve to pass
with Thy angels into everlasting life. R. *Amen.*

O Jesus, Who during Thy prayer to the Father in
the garden wert so filled with sorrow and anguish that
there came forth from Thee a bloody sweat; *have*
mercy on us.

Have mercy on us, O Lord; *have mercy on us.*

O Jesus, Who wast betrayed by the kiss of a traitor into the hands of the wicked, seized and bound like a thief, and forsaken by Thy disciples; *have mercy on us.*

Have mercy on us, O Lord, *have mercy on us.*

O Jesus, Who by the unjust council of the Jews wast sentenced to death, led like a malefactor before Pilate, scorned and derided by impious Herod; *have mercy on us.*

Have mercy on us, O Lord, *have mercy on us.*

O Jesus, Who wast stripped of Thy garments and most cruelly scourged at the pillar; *have mercy on us.*

Have mercy on us, O Lord, *have mercy on us.*

O Jesus, Who wast crowned with thorns, buffeted, struck with a reed, blindfolded, clothed with a purple garment, in many ways derided, and overwhelmed with reproaches; *have mercy on us.*

Have mercy on us, O Lord, *have mercy on us.*

O Jesus, Who wast less esteemed than the murderer Barabbas, rejected by the Jews, and unjustly condemned to the death of the cross; *have mercy on us.*

Have mercy on us, O Lord, *have mercy on us.*

O Jesus, Who wast loaded with a cross, and led to the place of execution as a lamb to the slaughter; *have mercy on us.*

Have mercy on us, O Lord, *have mercy on us.*

O Jesus, Who wast numbered among thieves, blasphemed and derided, made to drink of gall and vinegar, and crucified in dreadful torment from the sixth to the ninth hour; *have mercy on us.*

Have mercy on us, O Lord, *have mercy on us.*

O Jesus, Who didst expire on the Cross, Who wast pierced with a lance in the presence of Thy holy Mother, and from Whose side poured forth Blood and water; *have mercy on us.*

Have mercy on us, O Lord, *have mercy on us.*

O Jesus, Who wast taken down from the Cross, and bathed in the tears of Thy most sorrowing Virgin Mother; *have mercy on us.*

Have mercy on us, O Lord, *have mercy on us.*

O Jesus, Who wast covered with bruises, marked with the Five Wounds, embalmed with spices, and laid in the sepulcher; *have mercy on us.*

Have mercy on us, O Lord, *have mercy on us.*

V. He has truly borne our sorrows,
R. *And He has carried our griefs.*

Let Us Pray

O God, Who for the redemption of the world deigned to be born, to be circumcised, to be rejected by the Jews, and betrayed by Judas with a kiss; to be bound with fetters, and led like an innocent lamb to the slaughter; to be ignominiously brought before Annas, Caiphas, Pilate, and Herod; to be accused by false witnesses, to be scourged, buffeted, and reviled; to be spat upon, to be crowned with thorns, and struck with a reed; to be blindfolded, to be stripped of Thy garments, to be nailed to a cross and raised thereon; to be numbered among thieves, to be made to drink of gall and vinegar, and to be pierced with a lance: By these Thy most holy sufferings, O Lord, which we Thy servants commemorate, and by Thy most holy Cross and death, deliver us from the pains of Hell, and conduct us, as Thou didst conduct the penitent thief, into Thy paradise, Thou Who livest and reignest, world without end. R. *Amen.*

LITANY FOR THE
SOULS IN PURGATORY

(For private use only.)

Lord, have mercy on us.
Christ, have mercy on us.
Lord, have mercy on us. Christ, hear us.
Christ, graciously hear us.
God the Father of Heaven,
Have mercy on the souls of the faithful departed.
God the Son, Redeemer of the world,
Have mercy on the souls of the faithful departed.
God the Holy Spirit,
Have mercy on the souls of the faithful departed.
Holy Trinity, One God,
Have mercy on the souls of the faithful departed.

Holy Mary,
Pray for the souls of the faithful departed.
Holy Mother of God,
Pray for the souls of the faithful departed.
Saint Michael, *etc.*
Saint Gabriel,
All ye holy angels and archangels,
Saint John the Baptist,
Saint Joseph,
All ye holy patriarchs and prophets,
Saint Peter,
Saint Paul,
Saint John,
All ye holy apostles and evangelists,
Saint Stephen,
Saint Lawrence,
All ye holy martyrs,
Saint Gregory,

Saint Ambrose,
All ye holy bishops and confessors,
Saint Mary Magdalen,
Saint Catherine,
All ye holy virgins and widows,

All ye saints of God,
 *Make intercession for the souls of the faithful
 departed.*

Be merciful,
 Spare them, O Lord.
Be merciful,
 Hear them, O Lord.

From all evil,
 O Lord, deliver them.
From Thy wrath,
 O Lord, deliver them.
From the flame of fire, *etc.*
From the region of the shadow of death,
Through Thine Immaculate Conception,
Through Thy Nativity,
Through Thy Most Holy Name,
Through the multitude of Thy tender mercies,
Through Thy most bitter Passion,
Through Thy most Sacred Wounds,
Through Thy most Precious Blood,
Through Thine ignominious death, by which
 Thou hast destroyed our death,

We sinners,
 We beseech Thee, hear us.
O Thou Who didst absolve the sinner woman and
 hear the prayer of the good thief,
 We beseech Thee, hear us.
That thou wouldst release our deceased parents,
 relations and benefactors from the bonds of their
 sins and the punishment for them, *etc.*

That Thou wouldst hasten the day of visiting Thy
faithful detained in the receptacles of sorrow,
and wouldst transport them to the city of
eternal peace,

That Thou wouldst shorten the time of expiation
for their sins and graciously admit them into
the holy sanctuary, into which no unclean
thing can enter,

That through the prayers and alms of
Thy Church, and especially by the inestimable
Sacrifice of Thy Holy Altar, Thou wouldst
receive them into the tabernacle of rest
and crown their longing hopes with everlasting
fruition,

Son of God,

Lamb of God, Who takest away the sins of the world,
Grant them eternal rest.

Lamb of God, Who takest away the sins of the world,
Grant them eternal rest.

Lamb of God, Who takest away the sins of the world,
Grant them eternal rest.

Christ, hear us.
Christ, graciously hear us.
Lord, have mercy on us.
Christ, have mercy on us.
Lord, have mercy on us.

Our Father, *etc.*
V. And lead us not into temptation,
R. *But deliver us from all evil. Amen.*

V. From the gates of Hell,
R. *Deliver their souls, O Lord.*
V. May they rest in peace.
R. *Amen.*
V. O Lord, hear my prayer,
R. *And let my cry come unto Thee.*

Let Us Pray

O God, Creator and Redeemer of all the faithful, grant to the souls of Thy departed servants the remission of all their sins, that through our pious supplications they may obtain the pardon which they have always desired. Through Jesus Christ Our Lord. R. *Amen.*

O God, the Giver of pardon and the Lover of the salvation of men, we beg Thy clemency on behalf of our brethren, kinsfolk and benefactors who have departed this life, that by the intercession of the Blessed Virgin Mary and of all the saints, Thou wouldst receive them into the joys of Thine everlasting kingdom. Through Christ Our Lord. R. *Amen.*

O God, to Whom it belongs always to have mercy and to spare, be favorably propitious to the souls of Thy servants and grant them the remission of all their sins, that being delivered from the bonds of this mortal life, they may be admitted to life everlasting. Through Jesus Christ Our Lord. R. *Amen.*

SHORT LITANY FOR
THE SOULS IN PURGATORY

(For private use only.)

The just shall be in everlasting remembrance;
He shall not fear the evil hearing.

V. Absolve, O Lord, the souls of the faithful departed
from every bond of sin,
R. *And by the help of Thy grace may they be enabled to
escape the avenging judgment, and to enjoy the
happiness of eternal life.*

Because in Thy mercy are deposited the souls that
departed in an inferior degree of grace,
Lord, have mercy.
Because their present suffering is greatest in the
knowledge of the pain that their separation from
Thee is causing Thee,
Lord, have mercy.
Because of their present inability to add to Thy
accidental glory, *etc.*
Not for our consolation, O Lord; not for their release
from purgative pain, O God; but for Thy joy and
the greater accidental honor of Thy throne, O
Christ the King,

For the souls of our departed friends, relations and
benefactors, *grant light and peace, O Lord.*
For those of our family who have fallen asleep in Thy
bosom, O Jesus, *grant light and peace, O Lord.*
For those who have gone to prepare our place, *etc.*
(For those who were our brothers [or sisters] in
Religion,)
For priests who were our spiritual directors,

For men or women who were our teachers in school,
For those who were our employers (or employees),
For those who were our associates in daily toil,
For any soul whom we ever offended,
For our enemies now departed,
For those souls who have none to pray for them,
For those forgotten by their friends and kin,
For those now suffering the most,
For those who have acquired the most merit,
For the souls next to be released from Purgatory,
For those who, while on earth, were most devoted to
   God the Holy Ghost, to Jesus in the Most Blessed
   Sacrament, to the holy Mother of God,
For all deceased popes and prelates,
For all deceased priests, seminarians and religious,
For all our brethren in the Faith everywhere,
For all our separated brethren who deeply loved
   Thee, and would have come into Thy household
   had they known the truth,
For those souls who need, or in life asked, our
   prayers,
For those, closer to Thee than we are, whose prayers
   we need,

That those may be happy with Thee forever, who on
   earth were true exemplars of the Catholic Faith,
   grant them eternal rest, O Lord.
That those may be admitted to Thine unveiled
   Presence, who as far as we know never committed
   mortal sin, *grant them eternal rest, O Lord.*
That those may be housed in glory, who lived always
   in recollection and prayer, *etc.*
That those may be given the celestial joy of beholding
   Thee, who lived lives of mortification and
   self-denial and penance,
That those may be flooded with Thy love, who denied
   themselves even Thy favors of indulgence and who
   made the heroic act for the souls who had gone
   before them,

That those may be drawn up to the Beatific Vision,
who never put obstacles in the way of sanctifying
grace and who ever drew closer in mystical union
with Thee,

V. Eternal rest give unto them, O Lord,
R. *And let perpetual light shine upon them.*

Let Us Pray

Be mindful, O Lord, of Thy servants and
handmaids, *N.* and *N.,* who are gone before us with
the sign of faith and repose in the sleep of grace. To
these, O Lord, and to all who rest in Christ, grant, we
beseech Thee, a place of refreshment, light and peace,
through the same Christ Our Lord. R. *Amen.*

LITANY
FOR PRIESTS

God the Father,
Son,
And Holy Spirit,
   We beseech Thee, hear us.

Jesus, our High Priest,
Sacrifice,
And Teacher,
   We beseech Thee, hear us.

Bless our Holy Father,
Our bishops,
And priests,
   We beseech Thee, hear us.

Give them the strength of
   Thy grace,
And the love of Thy Heart,
And the spirit of sacrifice of Thine
   own divine life,
   We beseech Thee, hear us.

Make them firm in faith,
Holy in conduct,
And faithful in Thy service,
   We beseech Thee, hear us.

Fill them with the zeal of the Apostles,
With the courage of the martyrs,
With the spirit of the confessors,
   We beseech Thee, hear us.

Grant that they may convert the sinners,
Correct the erring,
Teach the ignorant,
  We beseech Thee, hear us.

Strengthen them with joy in their labors,
With patience in their sufferings,
With endurance in their struggles,
  We beseech Thee, hear us.

Preserve them in love for the little ones,
In zeal for the education of youth,
In loyalty to people and country,
  We beseech Thee, hear us.

Bless their words in the pulpit,
Their instructions in school,
Their admonitions in the confessional and at the
  sickbed,
  We beseech Thee, hear us.

Preserve them from the temptations of the wicked
  enemy,
From the hostile plots of unscrupulous men,
From all occasions of sin,
  We beseech Thee, hear us.

Make us one with them in faith,
Loyal in divine service,
And holy in life,
  We beseech Thee, hear us.

Give us holy bishops,
Holy priests,
Holy missionaries,
  We beseech Thee, hear us.

LITANY OF HUMILITY

(For private use only.)

O Jesus, meek and humble of heart,
   Hear me.

From the desire of being esteemed,
   Deliver me, O Jesus.
From the desire of being loved,
   Deliver me, O Jesus.
From the desire of being extolled, *etc.*
From the desire of being honored,
From the desire of being praised,
From the desire of being preferred to others,
From the desire of being consulted,
From the desire of being approved,
From the fear of being humiliated,
From the fear of being despised,
From the fear of suffering rebukes,
From the fear of being calumniated,
From the fear of being forgotten,
From the fear of being ridiculed,
From the fear of being wronged,
From the fear of being suspected,

That others may be loved more than I,
   Jesus, grant me the grace to desire it.
That others may be esteemed more than I,
   Jesus, grant me the grace to desire it.
That, in the opinion of the world,
   others may increase and I may decrease, *etc.*
That others may be chosen and I set aside,
That others may be praised and I go unnoticed,
That others may be preferred to me
   in everything,

That others may become holier than I,
  provided that I may become as holy as I should,

Here, in this all-embracing prayer, His Eminence Cardinal Merry del Val lays bare in a developmental, step-by-step fashion the embodiment of the totality of his conquest of self and of his entire spiritual life, revealing the secret sanctuary wherein he found the Source of Peace. He was accustomed to recite this litany after the celebration of Mass.

LITANY FOR INTERIOR PEACE
(For private use only.)

V. Jesus, meek and humble of heart,
R. *Make my heart like unto Thine.*

From the desire of being esteemed,
   Deliver me, Jesus.
From the desire of being loved,
   Deliver me, Jesus.
From the desire to be sought, *etc.*
From the desire to be mourned,
From the desire of praise,
From the desire of preference,
From the desire of influence,
From the desire of approval,
From the desire of authority,
From the fear of humiliations,
From the fear of being despised,
From the fear of repulse,
From the fear of calumny,
From the fear of oblivion,
From the fear of ridicule,
From the fear of injury,
From the fear of suspicion,

That others may be loved more than myself,
   Jesus, grant this desire.

That others may be more highly esteemed,
   Jesus, grant this desire.

That others may grow and increase in honor, and I
   decrease,
   Jesus, grant that I may desire it.

Jesus, mercy.
Our Lady, help us.

Let Us Pray

Pour forth Thy grace into our hearts, we beseech Thee, O Lord, that we who refrain from sin by self-denial, may be afflicted in time rather than condemned to eternal punishment, through Our Lord and Saviour Jesus Christ. R. *Amen.*

LITANY TO THE LAMB OF GOD
IN TIME OF WAR
(For private use only.)

V. The Lord give you peace;
R. *Peace and good will.*

O Lord Jesus Christ, Who didst say to Thy Apostles, "Peace I leave with you, My peace I give unto you," look not upon my sins, but upon the faith of Thy Church, and vouchsafe to her that peace and unity which is agreeable to Thy will, Who livest and reignest, God forever and ever. R. *Amen.*

Lord, have mercy.
  Christ, have mercy.
Lord, have mercy. Jesus hear us.
  Jesus, graciously hear us.

By the hymn of the angels at Thy birth,
  Grant us peace.
By Thy salutation to the Apostles,
  Grant us peace.
By Thy voice to the waves of Galilee, *etc.*
By Thy blessing to the sinner,
By Thy prayers for unity among Thy disciples,
By the love that was to mark Thy followers,
By the great peace offering of the Cross,
By Thy parting promise, "My peace I leave you,"

From the ambition of empire,
  Deliver us, O Lord.
From the greed for territory,
  Deliver us, O Lord.
From the blindness that is injustice, *etc.*

From the selfishness that is theft,
From the liberty which is license,
From the love of money which is idolatry,
From the hate that is murder,
From the hardness that will not pardon,
From the pride that will not ask pardon,

By the helpless cry of orphans,
We beseech Thee, hear us.
By the anguished tears of widows,
We beseech Thee, hear us.
By the groans of the dying, *etc.*
By the dead in unblessed graves,
That Thou wouldst make all nations to dwell as one,
That the hearts of rulers may be as wax in Thy hands,
That having learned in affliction, we may turn to
    Thee,
That wars may cease from the earth,
By Thy title, "Prince of Peace,"
Lord God of Armies,

Lamb of God, Who takest away the sins of the world,
    Grant us peace.
Lamb of God, Who takest away the sins of the world,
    Grant us peace.
Lamb of God, who takest away the sins of the world,
    Grant us peace.

V. I am the Salvation of the people, saith the Lord;
R. *In whatever tribulation they shall cry to Me, I will
    hear them.*

Let Us Pray

Jesus, meek and humble of heart, teach us, who
have sinned against Heaven and before Thee, the saving grace of a true humility, that we and all the peoples of this world may acknowledge and bewail that
spirit of materialism and self-seeking and lust for
power and vengeance which has plunged the family of
nations into war, until in Thy just wrath the world

suffers that punishment which, by turning from Thee, it has brought upon itself. In humility and penance, may we lessen the guilt and hasten true peace, without victory, save the victory of union with Thee. R. *Amen.*

Most Sacred Heart of Jesus,
   Have mercy on us.
Most Sacred Heart of Jesus,
   Have mercy on us.
Most Sacred Heart of Jesus,
   Have mercy on us.

Give peace, O Lord, in our days,
   For there is none other that fighteth for us, but only Thou, Our God.

V. Let there be peace in Thy strength, O Lord,
R. *And plenty in Thy strong places.*

Let Us Pray

O God, from Whom proceed all holy desires, all right counsels and all just works, grant unto us Thy servants that peace which the world cannot give, that our hearts may be devoted to Thy service, and that being delivered from the fear of our enemies, we may pass our time in peace under Thy protection, through Christ Our Lord. R. *Amen.*

Immaculate Queen of Peace,
   Pray for us.

The body of this litany to the Lamb of God was written about 1915 by or under the auspices of Pope Benedict XV (1914-1922) during World War I.

LITANY
FOR SUNDAY
(For private use only.)

Lord, have mercy on us.
Christ, have mercy on us.
Christ, hear us.
Christ, graciously hear us.
God the Father of Heaven,
Have mercy on us.
God the Son, Redeemer of the world,
Have mercy on us.
God the Holy Ghost,
Have mercy on us.
Holy Trinity, One God,
Have mercy on us.

V. This is the day which the Lord hath made.
R. *Let us rejoice, and be glad therein.*

Jesus, Who on this day of the week didst arise from
the dead, *have mercy on us.*
Jesus, Who on the same day didst put on a life
immortal, *have mercy on us.*
Jesus, Who on the same day didst appear to Mary
Magdalen and to the Apostles, *etc.*
Jesus, Who on the same day didst open the eyes of the
two disciples going to Emmaus,
Jesus, Who on the same day didst comfort Thine
Apostles, and give them peace,
Jesus, Who on the same day didst confirm Thine
Apostles in the faith of the Resurrection by
showing them Thy hands and Thy feet,
Jesus, Who on the same day didst breathe on the
Apostles and give them the Holy Ghost,

Jesus, Who on the same day didst open their
    understanding to know the Scriptures,
Jesus, Who on the same day didst give them power to
    remit sins,
Jesus, Who on the same day didst send the Apostles
    on their mission, and didst command them to go
    and teach all nations,
Jesus, Who on a Sunday didst condescend to the
    weakness of St. Thomas, and by the evidence of
    Thy sacred Wounds didst heal his unbelief,
Jesus, Who on a Sunday didst send down the Holy
    Ghost upon the Apostles, and thus prepare them for
    laying the foundation of Thy Church,
Jesus, Who on the same day didst move Thy Apostle
    Peter to preach the first Christian sermon to the
    Jews, to the conversion of three thousand,

Be merciful, O Jesus, and spare us.
    Be merciful, O Jesus, and hear us.

From the abuse of this day which we are commanded
    to keep holy, *preserve us, O Lord.*
From sloth and indevotion, *preserve us, O Lord.*
From neglect of prayer, and of Thy Sacred Word, *etc.*
From all occasions of misspending this day,
From whatever is an offense to God, or a scandal to
    the weak,

We sinners
    Beseech Thee to hear us.

That we may have Thy grace to sanctify this day as
    Thou hast commanded,
    We beseech Thee, hear us.
That we may this day labor to arise to a new life,
    We beseech Thee, hear us.
That we may this day examine into the state of our
    souls, and resolve to amend whatever is displeasing
    to Thee, *etc.*

That we may this day be so strengthened in our faith
as to bend our whole endeavors upon seeking those
eternal goods which faith has taught us to obtain,

That Thy Holy Spirit would this day take possession
of our hearts, and so confirm us in every duty that
no earthly considerations may be able to prevail
against us to the transgression of Thy law,

That we may this day join with the Church
Triumphant in praising, adoring and praying to
Thee, and preparing our souls to celebrate with
them an eternal Sabbath,

That we may not give this day to earth or to self-love,
but may offer it to Thee, Who art our only
everlasting Good,

Son of God, Who hast forever hallowed this day,

Lamb of God, Who takest away the sins of the world,
Spare us, O Lord.

Lamb of God, Who takest away the sins of the world,
Hear us, O Lord.

Lamb of God, Who takest away the sins of the world,
Have mercy on us.

Christ, hear us.
Christ, graciously hear us.

Let Us Pray

O God, the Protector of all who hope in Thee and
without Whom nothing can have either strength or
holiness, multiply Thy mercy, we beseech Thee, upon
us, that Thou being our Ruler and our Guide, we may
so pass through the goods of this life as not to lose
those which are eternal. Through Jesus Christ Our
Lord. R. *Amen.*

LITANY FOR THE
CHURCH IN OUR TIME

(For private use only.)

Lord, have mercy on us.
  Christ, have mercy on us.
Lord, have mercy on us. Christ, Divine Founder of
  the Church,
  Hear us.
Christ, Who warned of false prophets,
  Graciously hear us.
God the Father of Heaven,
  Have mercy on us.
God the Son, Redeemer of the world,
  Have mercy on us.
God the Holy Spirit,
  Have mercy on us.
Holy Trinity, One God,
  Have mercy on us.

Holy Mary, Mother of the Church,
  Pray for us.
Saint Joseph, Patron of the Universal Church,
  Pray for us.
Saint Michael, defender in the day of battle, *etc.*
Saint Peter, the Rock upon which Christ built His
  Church,
Saint Paul, protector of the faithful remnant,
Saint Francis of Assisi, rebuilder of the Church,
Saint Anthony, Hammer of Heretics,
Saint Pius V, champion of the Tridentine Mass,
Saint Pius X, foe of Modernism,

All ye holy angels and archangels,
  Pray that we may resist the snares of the devil.

Saint Catherine of Siena,
Pray that Christ's Vicar may oppose the spirit of the world.

Saint John Fisher,
Pray that bishops may have the courage to combat heresy and irreverence.

Saint Francis Xavier,
Pray that zeal for souls may be rekindled in the clergy.

Saint Charles Borromeo,
Pray that seminaries may be protected from false teachings.

Saint Vincent de Paul,
Pray that seminarians may return to a life of prayer and meditation.

Saint Therese of the Child Jesus,
Pray that religious may rediscover their vocation of love and sacrifice.

Saint Thomas More,
Pray that the laity may not succumb to the Great Apostasy.

Saint Francis de Sales,
Pray that the Catholic press may again become a vehicle of truth.

Saint John Bosco,
Pray that our children may be protected from immoral and heretical instruction.

Saint Pascal Baylon,
Pray that profound reverence for the Most Blessed Sacrament may be restored.

Saint Dominic,
Pray that we may ever treasure the Holy Rosary.

Lamb of God, Who takest away the sins of the world,
Spare us, O Lord.

Lamb of God, Who takest away the sins of the world,
Graciously hear us, O Lord.

Lamb of God, Who takest away the sins of the world,
Have mercy on us.

Christ, hear us.
  Christ, graciously hear us.

V. Pray for us, O Holy Mother of God,
R. *That we may be made worthy of the promises of Christ.*

Let Us Pray

Jesus our God, in these dark hours when Thy Mystical Body is undergoing its own crucifixion, and when it would almost seem to be abandoned by God the Father, have mercy, we beg of Thee, on Thy suffering Church. Send down upon us the Divine Consoler, to enlighten our minds and strengthen our wills.

Thou, O Second Person of the Most Blessed Trinity, Who canst neither deceive nor be deceived, Who hast promised to be with Thy Church until the End of Time, grant us a mighty faith, that we may not falter; help us to do Thy Holy Will at all times, especially during these hours of grief and uncertainty. May Thy Most Sacred Heart and the Immaculate and Sorrowful Heart of Thy Holy Mother be our sure refuge in time and in eternity. R. *Amen.*

OTHER RESPONSORY PRAYERS— PETITIONS, PRAISES, PRAYERS, PROMISES

"Let the word of Christ dwell in you abundantly, in all wisdom: teaching and admonishing one another in psalms, hymns, and spiritual canticles, singing in grace in your hearts to God."

—Colossians *3:16*

THIRTY-THREE PETITIONS IN HONOR OF THE SACRED HUMANITY OF OUR LORD JESUS CHRIST

(For private use only.)

O good Jesus, Word of the Eternal Father,
   Convert me.
O good Jesus, Son of Mary,
   Make me her child.
O good Jesus, My Master,
   Teach me.
O good Jesus, Prince of peace,
   Give me peace.
O good Jesus, my Refuge,
   Receive me.
O good Jesus, my Pastor,
   Feed my soul.
O good Jesus, Model of patience,
   Comfort me.
O good Jesus, meek and humble of heart,
   Make my heart like unto Thine.
O good Jesus, my Redeemer,
   Save me.
O good Jesus, my God and my All,
   Possess me.
O good Jesus, the true Way,
   Direct me.
O good Jesus, Eternal Truth,
   Instruct me.
O good Jesus, Life of the blessed,
   Make me live in Thee.
O good Jesus, my Support,
   Strengthen me.
O good Jesus, my Justice,
   Justify me.

O good Jesus, my Mediator,
Reconcile me to Thy Father.
O good Jesus, Physician of my soul,
Heal me.
O good Jesus, my Judge,
Absolve me.
O good Jesus, my King,
Govern me.
O good Jesus, my Sanctification,
Sanctify me.
O good Jesus, Abyss of goodness,
Pardon me.
O good Jesus, Living Bread from Heaven,
Satiate me.
O good Jesus, the Father of the prodigal,
Receive me.
O good Jesus, Joy of my soul,
Refresh me.
O good Jesus, my Helper,
Assist me.
O good Jesus, Magnet of love,
Attract me.
O good Jesus, my Protector,
Defend me.
O good Jesus, my Hope,
Sustain me.
O good Jesus, Object of my love,
Make me love Thee.
O good Jesus, Fountain of life,
Cleanse me.
O good Jesus, my Propitiation,
Purify me.
O good Jesus, my Last End,
Let me obtain Thee.
O good Jesus, my Glory,
Glorify me. Amen.

V. Jesus, hear my prayer.
R. *Jesus, graciously hear me.*

Let Us Pray

O Lord Jesus Christ, Who hast said, "Ask and you shall receive, seek and you shall find, knock and it shall be opened unto you," mercifully attend to our supplications, and grant us the gift of Thy divine charity, that we may ever love Thee with our whole hearts, and may never cease from praising Thee, Who livest and reignest world without end. R. *Amen*.

INVOCATIONS TO THE
HEART OF JESUS
With an Act of Oblation
(For private use only.)

Heart of Jesus in the Eucharist,
  I adore Thee.
Sweet Companion of our exile,
  I adore Thee.
Eucharistic Heart of Jesus, *etc.*
Heart solitary, Heart humiliated,
Heart abandoned, Heart forgotten,
Heart despised, Heart outraged,
Heart ignored by men,
Heart, Lover of our hearts,
Heart pleading for love,
Heart patient in waiting for us,
Heart eager to hear our prayers,
Heart desiring that we should pray to Thee,
Heart, Source of fresh graces,
Heart silent, desiring to speak to souls,
Heart, sweet Refuge of the hidden life,
Heart, Teacher of the secrets of union with God,
Heart of Him Who sleeps, yet ever watches,

Eucharistic Heart of Jesus, *have mercy on us.*

Jesus Victim, I wish to comfort Thee; I unite myself to Thee; I offer myself in union with Thee. I count myself as nothing before Thee; I desire to forget myself in order to think of Thee, to be forgotten and despised for love of Thee, not to be understood, not to be loved, except by Thee. I will hold my peace that I may listen to Thee; I will forsake myself that I may lose myself in Thee.

326

Grant that I may quench Thy thirst for my salvation, Thy burning thirst for my sanctification, and that, being purified, I may bestow on Thee a pure and true love. I would no longer weary Thine expectations; take me, I give myself to Thee. I entrust to Thee all my actions—my mind that Thou mayest enlighten it, my heart that Thou mayest direct it, my will that Thou mayest establish it, my misery that Thou mayest relieve it, my soul and my body that Thou mayest feed them.

Eucharistic Heart of my Jesus, Whose Blood is the life of my soul, may it be no longer I who live, but Thou alone Who livest in me. R. *Amen.*

THE DIVINE PRAISES

(For public or private use.)

Blessed be God.
Blessed be God.
Blessed be His Holy Name.
Blessed be His Holy Name.
Blessed be Jesus Christ, true God and true man.
Blessed be Jesus Christ, true God and true man.
Blessed be the name of Jesus.
Blessed be the name of Jesus.
Blessed be His most Sacred Heart.
Blessed be His most Sacred Heart.
Blessed be His most Precious Blood.
Blessed be His most Precious Blood.
Blessed be Jesus in the Most Holy Sacrament
of the Altar.
*Blessed be Jesus in the Most Holy Sacrament
of the Altar.*
Blessed be the Holy Spirit, the Paraclete.
Blessed be the Holy Spirit, the Paraclete.
Blessed be the great Mother of God, Mary most holy.
Blessed be the great Mother of God, Mary most holy.
Blessed be her holy and Immaculate Conception.
Blessed be her holy and Immaculate Conception.
Blessed be her glorious Assumption.
Blessed be her glorious Assumption.
Blessed be the name of Mary, Virgin and Mother.
Blessed be the name of Mary, Virgin and Mother.
Blessed be Saint Joseph, her most chaste spouse.
Blessed be Saint Joseph, her most chaste spouse.
Blessed be God in His angels and in His saints.
Blessed be God in His angels and in His saints.

PRAYER TO THE HOLY FACE
OF JESUS

(For private use only.)

Holy Face of Jesus,
  Be my joy.
Holy Face of Jesus,
  Be my strength.
Holy Face of Jesus,
  Be my health.
Holy Face of Jesus,
  Be my courage.
Holy Face of Jesus,
  Be my wisdom.
Holy Face of Jesus, Image of the Father,
  Provide for me.
Holy Face of Jesus, Mirror of Thy Priestly Heart,
  Be my zeal.
Holy Face of Jesus, Gift of the Spirit,
  Show me Thy love.
Holy Face of Jesus, saddened by sorrow,
  Grant my requests through Thy merits. Amen.

This prayer was composed by Rev. Emery Pethro of Detroit, Michigan, U.S.A.

PROMISES OF
CONSOLATION TO CHRIST
(For private use only.)

We promise for the future that
We will console Thee, O Lord.
For the forgetfulness and ingratitude of men,
We will console Thee, O Lord.
For the way Thou art neglected in Thy holy
tabernacle, *etc.*
For the crimes of sinners,
For the sacrileges which profane Thy
Sacrament of Love,
For the irreverence displayed in
Thy presence,
For the coldness on the part of
Thy children,
For their contempt of Thy
loving invitations,
For the faithlessness of those who
call themselves Thy friends,
For the bad example we have given,
For the abuse of Thy grace,
For our long delay in loving Thee,
For our past sins,
For our own unfaithfulness,
For our indifference in Thy service,
For keeping Thee waiting at the door of our hearts,
For Thy sighs and tears,
We will console Thee, O Lord.

SALUTATIONS TO MARY

(For private use only.)

Hail Mary! *Daughter of God the Father.*
Hail Mary! *Mother of God the Son.*
Hail Mary! *Spouse of God the Holy Ghost.*
Hail Mary! *Temple of the Most Blessed Trinity.*
Hail Mary! *Pure Lily of the*
    Effulgent Trinity, God.
Hail Mary! *Celestial Rose of the ineffable*
    Love of God.
Hail Mary! *Virgin pure and humble, of whom the*
    King of Heaven willed to be born and with thy milk
    to be nourished.
Hail Mary! *Virgin of virgins.*
Hail Mary! *Queen of Martyrs, whose soul*
    a sword transfixed.
Hail Mary! *Lady most blessed, unto whom all power in*
    Heaven and earth is given.
Hail Mary! *My Queen and my Mother! My life, my*
    sweetness and my hope.
Hail Mary! *Mother most amiable.*
Hail Mary! *Mother most admirable.*
Hail Mary! *Mother of Divine Love.*
Hail Mary, Immaculate! *Conceived without sin!*

Hail Mary, Full of Grace, The Lord is with thee!
    Blessed art thou among women and blessed is the
    Fruit of thy womb, Jesus!

Blessed be thy spouse, *Saint Joseph.*
Blessed be thy father, *Saint Joachim.*
Blessed be thy mother, *Saint Anne.*
Blessed be thy guardian, *Saint John.*
Blessed be thy holy angel, *Saint Gabriel.*

Glory be to God the Father, *Who chose thee.*
Glory be to God the Son, *Who loved thee.*
Glory be to God the Holy Spirit, *Who espoused thee.*

O Glorious Virgin Mary,
  May all men love and praise thee.
Holy Mary, Mother of God, Pray for us and bless us,
  Now and at death, in the Name of Jesus,
  thy Divine Son.

This litany was composed by Saint John Eudes (1601-1680).

INVOCATIONS TO
OUR LADY OF LOURDES
(For private use only.)

I

Lord, we adore Thee!
  Lord, we believe in Thee!
Lord, we hope in Thee!
  Lord, we love Thee!
O Jesus, Thou art the Christ, the Son
  of the living God!
  *O Jesus, Thou art the Bread which
  came down from Heaven!*
O Jesus, Thy Flesh is Food indeed!
  O Jesus, Thy Blood is Drink indeed!
Lord, if Thou wilt, Thou canst
  make me whole!
  Lord, Thy will be done!

O Mary, health of the sick,
  Pray for us!
O Mary, conceived without sin,
  Pray for us who have recourse to thee!
Queen of Peace,
  Pray for us!
Our Lady of Lourdes,
  Bless the Pope, the Vicar of Jesus Christ!
Our Lady of Lourdes,
  Bless our country!
Our Lady of Lourdes,
  Give us holy priests!
Saint Bernadette,
  Pray for us!

Lord, we adore Thee!
Lord, we bless Thee!
All peoples of the world,
Praise the Lord!

Glory be to the Father, and to the Son, and to the
Holy Ghost,
*As it was in the beginning, is now, and ever shall be,
world without end. Amen.*

II

Blessed be He Who comes in the name
of the Lord!
Thou art the Christ, the Son of the living God!
Thou art my Lord and my God!
Lord, we believe, do but increase our faith!
Lord, increase our love!
Lord, if Thou wilt, Thou canst make me whole!
Lord, that I may see!
Lord, that I may hear!
Lord, that I may walk!
Lord, Thy will be done!
Sacred Heart of Jesus,
Have mercy on us!
O Mary, Mother of Jesus Christ,
Pray for us!
Comforter of the afflicted,
Pray for us!
O Mary,
Show thyself our Mother!
Queen taken up into Heaven,
Pray for us!
Queen of missions,
Convert all infidels!
Queen of martyrs,
Strengthen the persecuted!
Saint Bernadette,
Pray for us!

Lord, we praise Thee!
Lord, we bless Thee!
All peoples of the world,
Praise the Lord!

Glory be to the Father, and to the Son, and to the
Holy Ghost,
*As it was in the beginning, is now, and ever shall be,
world without end. Amen.*

III

Lord, we believe,
Do but increase our faith!
Jesus in the Holy Eucharist,
Strengthen the unity of Thy Church!
Jesus in the Holy Eucharist,
Spread fraternal love in Thy Church!
Jesus in the Holy Eucharist,
Increase the holiness of Thy Church!
O Jesus, Living Bread,
Be our Food!
O Jesus, Light of the world,
Enlighten our minds!
O Jesus, all-powerful,
Sustain our weakness!
O Jesus,
Grant that we all may love one another!

Lord, Thou art the resurrection and the life!
Lord, if Thou wilt, Thou canst make me whole!
Jesus, Son of David, *Have mercy on us!*

Mary most kind,
Pray for us!
Queen of Peace,
Pray for us!
Our Lady of Lourdes,
Bless the Pope, Vicar of Jesus Christ!

Our Lady of Lourdes,
Bless our country!
Our Lady of Lourdes,
Give us holy priests!
Saint Bernadette,
Pray for us!

Lord, we bless Thee!
Lord, we adore Thee!
All peoples of the world,
Praise the Lord!

Glory be to the Father, and to the Son, and to the
Holy Ghost,
*As it was in the beginning, is now, and ever shall be,
world without end. Amen.*

IV

Hosanna!
Hosanna to the Son of David!
Sacred Heart of Jesus,
Have mercy on us!
Jesus, Author of Life,
Have mercy on us!

Lord, save us, we perish!
Lord, he whom Thou dost love is sick!
Lord, that I may see!
Lord, that I may hear!
Lord, that I may walk!
Lord, if Thou wilt, Thou canst make me whole!
Lord, speak but the word and my soul shall be healed!
Lord, Thy will be done!

Queen of the most Holy Rosary,
Pray for us!
Queen of Heaven and earth,
Pray for us!

Queen of the Missions, *convert all infidels!*
Queen of Martyrs, *give strength to the persecuted!*
Queen of Peace, *pray for us!*
Saint Bernadette, *pray for us!*

Lord, we bless Thee!
   Lord, we adore Thee!
All peoples of the world,
   Praise the Lord!
Hosanna!
   Hosanna!
Hosanna to the Son of David!
   Hosanna in Excelsis!

Glory be to the Father, and to the Son, and to the
   Holy Ghost,
   As it was in the beginning, is now, and ever shall be,
   world without end. Amen.

Let Us Pray

O ever Immaculate Virgin, Mother of Mercy, Health of the Sick, Comforter of the Afflicted, thou knowest my wants, my troubles, my sufferings; deign to cast upon me a look of mercy. By appearing in the grotto of Lourdes thou wert pleased to make it a privileged sanctuary from where thou dost dispense thy favors, and already many sufferers have obtained the cure of their infirmities, both spiritual and corporal. I come, therefore, with the most unbounded confidence, to implore thy maternal intercession. Obtain, O loving Mother, the granting of my requests. Through gratitude for thy favors, I will endeavor to imitate thy virtues, that I may one day share in thy glory. R. *Amen.*

V. O Mary, conceived without sin,
R. *Pray for us who have recourse to thee.*

INVOCATIONS TO
OUR LADY OF BANNEUX,
THE VIRGIN OF THE POOR

(For private use only.)

Blessed Virgin of the Poor,
  Lead us to Jesus, Source of grace.
Blessed Virgin of the Poor,
  Save all nations.
Blessed Virgin of the Poor,
  Relieve the sick.
Blessed Virgin of the Poor,
  Alleviate suffering.
Blessed Virgin of the Poor,
  Pray for each one of us.
Blessed Virgin of the Poor,
  We believe in thee.
Blessed Virgin of the Poor,
  Believe in us.
Blessed Virgin of the Poor,
  We will pray hard.
Blessed Virgin of the Poor,
  Bless us.
Blessed Virgin of the Poor, Mother of the Saviour,
  Mother of God,
  We thank thee.

Let Us Pray

Our Lady of Banneux, Mother of Our Saviour,
Mother of God, Virgin of the Poor, since thou hast
promised to believe in us if we believe in thee, I put
all my trust in thee.

Deign to listen to the prayers that thou hast asked
be addressed to thee; have pity on all our spiritual and
temporal miseries. Restore to sinners the treasure of

Faith, and give to the poor their daily bread.

Deign to relieve suffering, to heal the sick and to pray for us, so that thus through thy intercession, the reign of Christ the King may extend over all nations. R. *Amen*.

THE CROWN OF TWELVE STARS
(For private use only.)

V. Let us offer praise and thanksgiving to the Most
   Holy Trinity, Who has shown us the Virgin Mary,
   clothed with the sun, the moon under her feet, and
   on her head a mystic crown of twelve stars.

R. *Forever and ever. Amen.*

V. Let us give praise and thanks to the Eternal
   Father, Who chose her for His daughter.

R. *Amen.*

Our Father, *etc. (silently).*

1

V. Praised be the Eternal Father, Who predestined
   her to be the Mother of His Divine Son.

R. *Amen.*

(Together:) God hail thee, Mary, full of grace, the
   Lord is with thee; blessed art thou among women,
   and blessed is the Fruit of thy womb, Jesus. Holy
   Mary, Mother of God, pray for us sinners now and
   at the hour of our death. Amen.

2

V. Praised be the Eternal Father, Who preserved her
   from all stain of sin in her conception.

R. *Amen.*

God hail thee, Mary, *etc.*

3

V. Praised be the Eternal Father, Who adorned her at
   her birth with His most excellent gifts.

R. *Amen.*

God hail thee, Mary, *etc.*

4

V. Praised be the Eternal Father, Who gave her Saint
Joseph to be her companion and most pure spouse.
R. *Amen.*

God hail thee, Mary, *etc.*
Glory be to the Father, *etc.*

V. Let us give praise and thanks to the Divine Son,
Who chose her for His Mother.
R. *Amen.*

Our Father, *etc.*

5

V. Praised be the Divine Son, Who became incarnate
in her womb and there abode for nine months.
R. *Amen.*

God hail thee, Mary, *etc.*

6

V. Praised be the Divine Son, Who was born of her
and was nourished at her breast.
R. *Amen.*

God hail thee, Mary, *etc.*

7

V. Praised be the Divine Son, Who in His childhood
willed to be taught by her.
R. *Amen.*

God hail thee, Mary, *etc.*

8

V. Praised be the Divine Son, Who revealed to her the
mystery of the Redemption of the world.
R. *Amen.*

God hail thee, Mary, *etc.*
Glory be to the Father, *etc.*

V. Let us give praise and thanks to the Holy Spirit,
Who took her for His spouse.
R. *Amen.*

Our Father, *etc.*

9

V. Praised be the Holy Spirit, Who revealed first to
her His Name of Holy Spirit.
R. *Amen.*

God hail thee, Mary, *etc.*

10

V. Praised be the Holy Spirit, by Whose operation she
was at once Virgin and Mother.
R. *Amen.*

God hail thee, Mary, *etc.*

11

V. Praised be the Holy Spirit, by Whose power she
was the living temple of the ever-blessed Trinity.
R. *Amen.*

God hail thee, Mary, *etc.*

12

V. Praised be the Holy Spirit, by Whom
she was exalted in Heaven above every
living creature.
R. *Amen.*

God hail thee, Mary, *etc.*
Glory be to the Father, *etc.*

Antiphon: Let us praise Mary, who hath done so
much for our good, and let us say to her: God hail
thee, Mary, Mother of Clemency, Comfortress of the
Afflicted, Redemptress of Captives. Thou art the
glory of Jerusalem, thou art the joy of Israel, thou art
the honor of our people.

V. Remember thy congregation, O Mary.
R. *Which belongs to thee from the beginning.*

Let Us Pray

O God, Who by means of the Most Glorious
Mother of Thy Divine Son, didst enrich the Church
with a new religious family for the redemption of the
faithful of Christ from pagan oppression, grant, we
beseech Thee, that we may be freed from our sins and
from the bondage of the devil by the merits and intercession of her whom we devoutly venerate as the
foundress of so great a work. R. *Amen.*

Hail, Holy Queen, *etc. (to be said for the Holy Catholic Church, for the propagation of the Faith, for peace
among Christian peoples and the extirpation of heresy).*

The congregation referred to in this prayer is the Order of Our
Lady of Ransom (the Mercedarians), now called the Order of Our
Lady of Mercy. The Order of Our Lady of Ransom was founded by
St. Peter Nolasco (c. 1189-1258) to ransom Christian slaves from
the Moors. In addition to the usual three vows, the Mercedarians
took a fourth vow: to give themselves up, if necessary, in exchange
for a slave.

SALUTATIONS TO THE
HEARTS OF JESUS AND MARY
(For private use only.)

Hail, Heart most holy!
Hail, Heart most gentle!
Hail, Heart most humble!
Hail, Heart most pure!
Hail, Heart most devout!
Hail, Heart most wise!
Hail, Heart most patient!
Hail, Heart most obedient!
Hail, Heart most vigilant!
Hail, Heart most faithful!
Hail, Heart most blessed!
Hail, Heart most merciful!
Hail, most loving Hearts of Jesus and Mary!
We revere Thee!
We glorify Thee!
We give Thee thanks!
We love Thee with all our heart,
    with all our soul, and with all our strength.
We offer Thee our heart.
We give it to Thee.
We consecrate it to Thee.
We immolate it to Thee.
Receive it and possess it wholly.
Purify it.
Enlighten it.
Sanctify it.
That Thou mayest live and reign in it
    now, always, and forever and ever.

R. *Amen.*

This prayer was composed by St. John Eudes in 1643.

AFFECTIONATE SALUTATIONS
TO MARY
(For private use only.)

I greet thee, Mary,
  Daughter of God the Father.
I greet thee, Mary,
  Mother of the Son of God.
I greet thee, Mary,
  Spouse of the Holy Spirit.
I greet thee, Mary,
  Temple of the Blessed Trinity.
I greet thee, Mary,
  White Lily of the resplendent Trinity.
I greet thee, Mary,
  Fragrant Rose of the heavenly court.
I greet thee, Mary,
  *Virgin full of meekness and humility, of whom the
  King of Heaven willed to be born and nourished by
  thy milk.*
I greet thee, Mary,
  Virgin of virgins.
I greet thee, Mary,
  *Queen of martyrs, whose soul was pierced by the
  sword of sorrows.*
I greet thee, Mary,
  *Lady and Mistress, to whom all power has been
  given in Heaven and on earth.*
I greet thee, Mary,
  *Queen of my heart, my sweetness, my life and all my
  hope.*
I greet thee, Mary,
  Mother most amiable.
I greet thee, Mary,
  Mother most admirable.

I greet thee, Mary,
   Mother of beautiful love.
I greet thee, Mary,
   Conceived without sin.
I greet thee, Mary,
   Full of grace, the Lord is with thee, blessed art thou among women, and blessed be the Fruit of thy womb.

Blessed be thy spouse,
   Saint Joseph.
Blessed be thy father,
   Saint Joachim.
Blessed be thy mother,
   Saint Anne.
Blessed be thy angel,
   Saint Gabriel.
Blessed be the Eternal Father,
   Who has chosen thee.
Blessed be thy Son,
   Who has loved thee.
Blessed be the Holy Ghost,
   Who has espoused thee.
May all those who love thee bless thee.
   O Blessed Virgin, bless us all in the name of thy dear Son. Amen.

The "Affectionate Salutations to Mary" were promoted in this version by the Servant of God, Father Paul of Moll (1824-1896). The venerable Father Paul assured one of his friends that those who devoutly venerate Mary with these affectionate salutations may rely on her powerful protection and blessing. Once while giving a copy of these Salutations to a girl from Eecloo, Father Paul said to her, "These Salutations are so beautiful! Say them every morning. From on high, in Heaven, the Blessed Virgin will then give you her blessing. Yes, yes, would to God that you could see her! The Blessed Virgin blesses you then; I know it quite well." He said further that it is impossible not to be heard favorably when we recite these Salutations to Mary for the conversion of sinners.

INVOCATIONS TO THE
IMMACULATE HEART OF MARY
(For private use only.)

Heart of Mary, *pray for us,*
Heart of Mary, like unto the Heart of Jesus,
   pray for us,
Heart of Mary, united to the Heart of Jesus, *etc.*
Heart of Mary, Instrument of the Holy Spirit,
Heart of Mary, Sanctuary of the Divinity,
Heart of Mary, Tabernacle of God Incarnate,
Heart of Mary, always exempt from sin,
Heart of Mary, always full of grace,
Heart of Mary, blessed among all hearts,
Heart of Mary, Illustrious Throne of Glory,
Heart of Mary, Abyss and Prodigy of humility,
Heart of Mary, Glorious Holocaust of Divine Love,
Heart of Mary, nailed to the cross of Jesus,
Heart of Mary, Comfort of the Afflicted,
Heart of Mary, Refuge of Sinners,
Heart of Mary, Hope of the Agonizing,
Heart of Mary, Seat of Mercy.

V. Pray for us, O holy Mother of God,
R. *That we may be made worthy of the promises of
   Christ.*

Let Us Pray

Almighty and eternal God, Who prepared a worthy
dwelling place for the Holy Spirit in the Heart of the
Blessed Virgin Mary, vouchsafe, we beseech Thee, to
grant unto us who devoutly keep this commemoration
in honor of the same most pure Heart, the grace to
order our lives according to Thine own Heart.
Through Christ Our Lord. R. *Amen.*

THE
ANIMA CHRISTI
OF ST. ELIZABETH ANN SETON
(For private use only.)

Soul of Jesus,
  Sanctify me.
Blood of Jesus,
  Wash me.
Passion of Jesus,
  Comfort me.
Wounds of Jesus,
  Hide me.
Heart of Jesus,
  Receive me.
Spirit of Jesus,
  Enliven me.
Goodness of Jesus,
  Pardon me.
Beauty of Jesus,
  Draw me.
Humility of Jesus,
  Humble me.
Peace of Jesus,
  Pacify me.
Love of Jesus,
  Inflame me.
Kingdom of Jesus,
  Come to me.
Grace of Jesus,
  Replenish me.
Mercy of Jesus,
  Pity me.
Sanctity of Jesus,
  Sanctify me.

Purity of Jesus,
  Purify me.
Cross of Jesus,
  Support me.
Nails of Jesus,
  Hold me.
Mouth of Jesus,
  Bless me in life, in death, in time and eternity.
Mouth of Jesus,
  Defend me in the hour of death.
Mouth of Jesus,
  Call me to come to Thee.
Mouth of Jesus,
  Receive me with Thy saints in glory evermore.

Let Us Pray

Unite me to Thyself, O adorable Victim. Life-giving heavenly Bread, feed me, sanctify me, reign in me, transform me to Thyself, live in me; let me live in Thee; let me adore Thee in Thy life-giving Sacrament as my God, listen to Thee as to my Master, obey Thee as my King, imitate Thee as my Model, follow Thee as my Shepherd, love Thee as my Father, seek Thee as my Physician who wilt heal all the maladies of my soul. Be indeed my Way, Truth and Life; sustain me, O heavenly Manna, through the desert of this world, till I shall behold Thee unveiled in Thy glory.
R. *Amen.*

This *Anima Christi* was composed by Saint Elizabeth Ann Seton on the Feast of Corpus Christi, 1816.

MEMORIAL PRAYER
FOR THE SUFFERING SOULS
IN PURGATORY
(For private use only.)

Almighty God, Father of goodness and love, have
    mercy on the poor suffering souls, and grant Thine
    aid:

To my dear parents and ancestors;
    Jesus, Mary, Joseph! My Jesus, mercy.
To my brothers and sisters and other near relatives;
    Jesus, Mary, Joseph! My Jesus, mercy.
To my benefactors, spiritual and temporal; *etc.*
To my former friends and subjects;
To all for whom love or duty bids me pray;
To those who have suffered disadvantage or harm
    through me;
To those who have offended me;
To all those who are especially beloved by Thee;
To those whose release is at hand;
To those who desire most to be united with Thee;
To those who endure the greatest suffering;
To those whose release is most remote;
To those who are least remembered;
To those who are most deserving on account of their
    services to the Church;
To the rich, who now are the most destitute;
To the mighty, who now are as lowly servants;
To the blind, who now see their folly;
To the frivolous, who spent their time in idleness;
To the poor, who did not seek the treasures of
    Heaven;
To the tepid, who devoted little time to prayer;
To the indolent, who were negligent in performing
    good works;

To those of little faith, who neglected the frequent reception of the Sacraments;

To the habitual sinners, who owe their salvation to a miracle of grace;

To parents who failed to watch over their children;

To superiors who were not solicitous for the salvation of those entrusted to them;

To the souls of those who strove for hardly anything but riches and pleasures;

To the worldly-minded, who failed to use their wealth and talents in the service of God;

To those who witnessed the death of others, but would not think of their own;

To those who did not provide for the great journey beyond, and the days of tribulation;

To those whose judgment is so severe because of the great things entrusted to them;

To the popes, rulers, kings and princes;

To the bishops and their counselors;

To my teachers and spiritual advisors;

To the deceased priests of this diocese;

To all the priests and religious of the whole Catholic Church;

To the defenders of the Holy Faith;

To those who died on the battlefield;

To those who are buried in the sea;

To those who died of stroke or heart attack;

To those who died without the last rites of the Church;

To those who shall die within the next twenty-four hours;

To my own poor soul when I shall have to appear before Thy judgment seat;

V. O Lord, grant eternal rest to all the souls of the faithful departed,

R. *And let perpetual light shine upon them.*

V. May they rest in peace.

R. *Amen.*

At your bookdealer or direct from the Publisher.

At your bookdealer or direct from the Publisher.